THE COMPLETE FÉNELON

PARACLETE GIANTS

ABOUT THIS SERIES:

Each Paraclete Giant presents collected works of one of Christianity's greatest writers — "giants" of the faith. These essential volumes share the pivotal teachings of leading Christian figures throughout history with today's theological students and all people seeking spiritual wisdom.

Forthcoming in this Series...

THE COMPLETE JULIAN
by Father John-Julian, OJN
Spring 2009

THE COMPLETE THÉRÈSE
Edited with translations by Robert J. Edmonson, CJ
Fall 2009

For more information, visit www.paracletepress.com.

PARACLETE
GIANTS

The COMPLETE

Fenelon

Translated and Edited by
Robert J. Edmonson, CJ, & Hal M. Helms

PARACLETE PRESS BREWSTER, MASSACHUSETTS

2013 Second printing
2008 First printing
The Complete Fénelon

Introduction, About this Edition, "Meditations on the Heart of God" and "God of My Heart: Meditations on Feasts and Fasts" copyright © 2008 Robert J. Edmonson

"The Royal Way of the Cross" and "Talking with God" copyright © 2008 The Community of Jesus, Inc.

ISBN 978-1-55725-607-2

Library of Congress Cataloging-in-Publication Data

Fénelon, François de Salignac de La Mothe-, 1651–1715.
  [Selections. English. 2008]
  The complete Fénelon / translated and edited by Robert J. Edmonson and Hal M. Helms.
    p. cm.
  ISBN 978-1-55725-607-2
  1. Spirituality--Catholic Church. 2. Spiritual life--Catholic Church. 3. Fénelon, François de Salignac de La Mothe-, 1651-1715--Correspondence. 4. Meditations. 5. Church year medita-tions. I. Edmonson, Robert J. II. Helms, Hal McElwaine. III. Title.
  BX2182.3.F47213 2008
  282--dc22
                              2008021654

10 9 8 7 6 5 4 3 2

Published by Paraclete Press
Brewster, Massachusetts
www.paracletepress.com

Printed in the United States of America

CONTENTS

PART THREE: *Meditations on the Heart of God*

INTRODUCTION TO
The Complete Fénelon

I n 1651, when François Fénelon was born, an exhausted Europe was recovering from the Thirty Years' War. Britain could not provide a balance of power, embroiled as it was in the civil war that had led to the execution of its king in 1649. So the 1648 Peace of Westphalia had left France as the dominant power in Europe. Within France, a series of revolts against the crown had begun in 1648, and the outcome of the struggle was by no means certain.

France dominated in the arts and letters as well as in politics. The creation of the *Académie Française* (the French Academy) in 1635 had standardized the French language. In 1637 René Descartes had established the principles of modern science and philosophy. Throughout Europe, the French language and French science and culture were held in such high esteem that the use of French was widespread in every court. The scene was set for the golden age of French literature.

It was into this moment of history that François Fénelon was born in southwestern France. Like so many of the ancient minor nobility, Fénelon's parents had a large family—and a long list of creditors. But their fervent loyalty to the crown during the revolts brought them letters of gratitude from the king. So when Fénelon chose to follow his uncle, the bishop of Sarlat, in pursuing a career in the church, his family's solid reputation had paved the way for his entry into higher studies. After being ordained and completing his doctorate in 1677, Fénelon soon began to minister, to preach, and to write.

During Fénelon's childhood, the young Louis XIV firmly suppressed the disaffected nobles, and then contrived to keep the most powerful of them under his thumb by building the lavish palace of Versailles and enticing them to live there. He kept them busy with endless balls and theatrical and musical performances.

With the nobles firmly under his control, Louis turned his attention to another perceived threat to the unity of his realm. The Edict of Nantes (1598) had granted a measure of religious liberty to Protestants.

After the death of Louis' queen in 1683 and his marriage to the devout Catholic Madame de Maintenon in 1684, Louis was not long in revoking the right of Protestants to practice their religion. Many fled the country, and those who stayed were required to convert to the Catholic faith.

Fénelon's talent having been quickly recognized, he was named soon after ordination as superior of a Paris mission to new converts to the Catholic church. By 1684 he was invited to preach in Meaux, whose bishop, Bossuet, was counted among France's finest orators. Soon Fénelon was invited to go on a preaching mission with the renowned prelate.

The revocation of the Edict of Nantes in 1685 created a need for the best Catholic preachers in France. The young Fénelon was named director of the mission to convert the Protestants of Saintonge and Aunis—the center of French Protestantism. There, Fénelon won the hearts of the Protestants with his gentleness and moderation. But Fénelon's restraint did not pass unnoticed among more extreme Catholic factions, who blocked his nomination as bishop of Poitiers.

His mission among the Protestants accomplished, Fénelon returned to Paris where he served as spiritual director to the duke and duchess of Beauvilliers and their family of eight daughters. Out of this experience came Fénelon's first major work. *The Education of Girls* revealed a remarkable presentation of the value of education for young women.

In 1689 the duke of Beauvilliers was named governor over the king's sons and grandsons. Having revealed his abilities as a teacher and preacher, Fénelon was immediately made personal tutor to the king's grandson, the young duke of Burgundy. By the age of thirty-eight Fénelon had achieved a prominent platform for his gentle teachings.

For the benefit of his pupil, Fénelon wrote his *Fables* (moral lessons in the form of fairy tales), his *Dialogs of the Dead* (in which bygone historical figures tell what they learned from life), numerous spiritual writings, and *The Adventures of Telemachus* (a commentary in epic style on how kings ought to reign). For nearly ten years he devoted himself to his charge, patiently turning this wild young man into a model of docility.

As tutor to the heir to the throne, Fénelon gained access to the court of Versailles, where a group of devout Christians welcomed his presence and looked to him for guidance and spiritual direction. His friendship and his correspondence with them continued throughout his life.

Among Fénelon's correspondents was Madame de Maintenon, who had founded a school for girls of impoverished nobility; Fénelon was a frequent visitor and speaker at the school.

The peak of Fénelon's career came in the mid-1690s, when he was elected to the *Académie Française* (1693) and appointed archbishop of Cambrai (1695). Another man would have lived out his life as a political favorite and died in comfortable obscurity. Fénelon, however, chose a different path. Surrounded by the untold wealth enjoyed by the courtiers at Versailles and by many members of the clergy, Fénelon sought a different treasure—a treasure that was to cost him the favor of Madame de Maintenon and the king, and his position at the court.

Before we attempt to understand Fénelon's fall from favor and subsequent banishment from the court, we need to understand the era in which he lived.

The religious wars of the sixteenth century and the Thirty Years' War of the seventeenth century brought about widespread disillusionment with religious institutions. Alongside the religious fanaticism of these two centuries, a great flowering of art, music, literature, and philosophy sprang up, as Renaissance humanism gave way to scientific rationalism.

Francis Bacon (1561–1626) denounced reliance on authority and Aristotelian logic, calling for a new scientific method based on inductive generalization from careful observation and experiment.

Galileo (1564–1642) created the science of mechanics and applied the principles of geometry to the motions of bodies.

Thomas Hobbes (1588–1679) later applied the principles of mechanics to every field of knowledge, emphasizing the law of self-preservation as the basis of human behavior.

But it was René Descartes (1596–1650) who had perhaps the most lasting influence on the French mentality. Refusing to accept any belief, even his own existence, until he could prove it to be necessarily true, he made mathematics the model for all science.

Not merely the province of an intellectual elite, these scientific and philosophical views permeated every level of French society, including the church. Their emphasis on the mind's reasoning left little room for the heart. One who sought to experience God with a deeper heart experience was viewed at best as anachronistic, and at worst as a dangerous threat to the strength of the nation.

There were a few whose experiences with God could not be ignored.

The French priest Saint Vincent de Paul (1581–1660) established charitable works to help society's most underprivileged.

The French nun Saint Margaret Mary Alacoque (1647–90) experienced visions of Christ.

The simple French monk known as Brother Lawrence (1620?–91) determined to practice the presence of God throughout his life.[1]

In 1688 Fénelon met a woman whose teachings were to have a profound effect on his experience of God. Though steeped in the culture and teaching of his day, Fénelon felt a perplexing lack in his life that remained unfulfilled until his encounter with Madame Guyon.

Jeanne Guyon (1648–1717) had begun to introduce into France the doctrine of Quietism, based on the belief that perfection lies in the utter abandonment of oneself to God. At first well received by the clergy and the pope, the doctrine soon aroused severe criticism because the abandonment it calls for can turn into passivity.

The archbishop of Paris was quick to criticize Madame Guyon, and in 1688 she was imprisoned. But she was released the next year through the influence of Madame de Maintenon, and during the next several years she was often present at the court, forming a circle of friends including Fénelon. Eventually, however, Madame de Maintenon began to find Madame Guyon's teaching suspect.

Without the aid of her former protectress, Madame Guyon was imprisoned again in 1695. When she was attacked, she called for a theological conference to examine her work. The commission met at Issy, near Paris in 1695, and at its conclusion, thirty-four articles were drawn up condemning certain errors of the Quietist teaching. These articles were signed by Bossuet, Fénelon, and Madame Guyon herself. This time her incarceration was to last until 1703, when she was released on the condition that she live in exile from Paris.

In 1695, the year of Madame Guyon's second imprisonment, Fénelon was made archbishop of Cambrai. Due to the entangled European politics of the time, his appointment carried not only religious authority, but also several titles of nobility and considerable revenues. And Fénelon was still tutor to the king's grandson. At the age of forty-four, this son of impoverished provincial minor nobility had achieved enormous prestige.

But 1695 marked a turning point in Fénelon's life, for in that year he became involved in a controversy with Bossuet over Madame Guyon's teachings. Having at last found satisfaction for his spiritual hunger, Fénelon felt the need to vindicate his spiritual mentor. Concerned that the truth might be lost in the condemnations of Madame Guyon, in 1697 Fénelon published *Explication des maximes des saints*, in which he set forth the difference between true and false spirituality, using the writings and experiences of many saints as verification. But Bossuet, the celebrated orator who had once aided Fénelon's career, now aimed his acerbic pen at the one who rose to Madame Guyon's defense. Immediately fiercely attacking the book, Bossuet in the years following waged a prolonged and bitter literary battle against Fénelon. Thomas Merton explains what happened:

> Bossuet was a court preacher, a "solid" ecclesiastic, a man of duty, no doubt, and a great influence for good at Versailles. But he also knew the meaning of a career, and was too realistically engaged in the practicalities of that career to be bothered with the vicissitudes of interior conflict, or with the experience of trouble and of light which led Fénelon into the ways of the mystics. Dangerous ways, of course. One can well understand Bossuet's consternation at Fénelon's friendship with Mme Guyon. She was not only bizarre and rash, she was not only a distinctly bad influence

among the devout ladies of Versailles, but some of her propositions were so strange as to seem heretical. This Bossuet could see. But because he saw this, he could see nothing else. He could not see that Fénelon saw it just as well. He could not see that Fénelon was able to distinguish between the error and the exaggeration of Mme Guyon's language, her neurotic excesses, and the core of genuineness in her experience. Nor did he realize that Fénelon had gone far beyond Mme Guyon, and had really understood the Catholic tradition of mysticism that led back through St. Francis de Sales and St. John of the Cross to the Fathers of the Church.[2]

The polemic between Fénelon and Bossuet continued for several years. The two prelates appealed to Rome. After months of delay, at the insistence of Bossuet and the King of France, in 1699 Pope Innocent XII issued a bull condemning twenty-three propositions in Fénelon's book. He is said to have been very reluctant to do this, and to have remarked that "Fénelon erred by loving God too much!"

Fénelon's statements were not always as safe as Bossuet's, and in one book [*Maxims of the Saints*] he set down a few formulas which, closely and technically examined, proved to be erroneous or ill-sounding. (Nothing of Fénelon's was ever found to be heretical.) The fact remains that in the realm of mysticism, Fénelon knew what he was talking about and Bossuet did not. Not only was Fénelon experienced in these matters, he was also the better, the more learned and wiser theologian. If the Church (the Pope himself being extremely reluctant) saw fit to censure some of the propositions in which Fénelon sought to refute quietism and correct its excesses, Rome has nevertheless repeatedly approved of the doctrine itself as it has been lived and taught by the saints. The most recent of these is Therese of Lisieux, whose "little way" is not only very close to Fénelon, but often echoes him practically word for word. There is no more quietism in Fénelon than there is in the "little way" or, for that matter, in St. John of the Cross.[3]

In 1699, the same year Fénelon's spiritual writings were condemned, his *Telemachus* was published without his permission. Written for his royal pupil, the book for which Fénelon is best known in secular history states that kings exist for the benefit of their subjects, and denounces war. Louis XIV found the book to be an arrow aimed directly at his autocratic, war–filled reign. Fénelon was stripped of his position at court and exiled to his diocese.

Another man would have become bitter at such self-serving and cynical treatment. Fénelon's reaction to his condemnation and exile revealed the strength of his character. His defense of Madame Guyon had cost him everything he had worked so hard to achieve, but not a trace of bitterness could be found in him.

> Perhaps, after all, this gives us a clue as to the real "crime" of Fénelon in the eyes of the King and of the Court. He refused to submit to their power and he persisted in identifying himself with a cause that was, in their eyes, despicable chiefly because it was weak. This in turn is reflected in the judgment of later generations upon his spirituality. One could hardly do anything but ridicule a doctrine that seemed to put a premium on helplessness, passivity, and "annihilation." And this was a very convenient way of overlooking the real strength, indeed the *superior* moral strength, of Fénelon.[4]

True to the course he had set for himself, Fénelon submitted meekly to his condemnation and exile, and set about with considerable energy to improve the lot of the peasants of his diocese and deepen the spiritual life of all with whom he came in contact.

Right up till his death in 1715, Fénelon never ceased his correspondence with those at court who had become his spiritual children.

When Louis XIV's son died in 1711 and the young duke of Burgundy became the heir to the throne, the devout circles at court were optimistic. Had the young man ascended the throne and followed Fénelon's advice, who knows? Perhaps the horror of the French Revolution would have been avoided. But this was not to be, for the young man died before Louis XIV, and the king's spoiled and inept great-grandson took the throne as Louis XV.

To this day, French historians do not understand Fénelon. At best, he was the hapless upstart who dared to argue with Bossuet and condemn

Louis XIV. At worst, he was a dangerous subversive who threatened the strength of the French nation.

But throughout Fénelon's lifetime and the centuries that have followed, Christians who have felt drawn toward a life of closer communion with God have found in Fénelon's writings a depth of understanding of their struggles that has been a source of profound encouragement. Fénelon's penetrating letters of advice and counsel to his friends have been translated and widely distributed in a number of languages, and have found a wide audience in English translation.

Fénelon's writings show how deeply he was steeped in the Scriptures: words from biblical passages can be found on nearly every page that Fénelon wrote. So acquainted with the Scriptures was Fénelon's audience, that it was his practice to quote from Scripture without giving the reference—his readers would recognize them instantly. To help today's reader catch the freshness of the original, we have been true to his style and have not given Scripture references directly within the text. Readers who wish to find the Scriptures mentioned in these writings will find extensive notes, keyed to the text, at the end of this volume.

It is our prayer that as you read *The Complete Fénelon* and sit at the feet of this wise counselor and teacher, you will find encouragement and strength on your journey toward the heart of God.

One of the first books that Paraclete Press published was a volume of letters by François Fénelon. The editor of that book, Hal M. Helms (1923–1997), entitled it *The Royal Way of the Cross*. Father Hal, as he was known, was a beloved member of The Community of Jesus and a gifted speaker and writer whose gentle spirit and love for Jesus radiated from his life. Using an excellent nineteenth-century translation by H. Sidney Lear, Helms applied his editorial skills to modernizing and editing the text. That well-received volume contained fifty-two of Fénelon's letters.

Requests from readers for more of Fénelon's letters led to Helms's editing another fifty-one letters originally translated by Lear. This second volume was published in 1997 as *Fénelon: Talking with God*. That same year, we asked another editor and member of our Community, Robert J. Edmonson, CJ, to translate eighty-five of Fénelon's meditations on themes from Scripture. Rather than modernizing earlier translations, because Edmonson is expert in the French language, he went back to the original French, using texts printed in the early 1700s. Those meditations were published in a volume entitled *Fénelon: Meditations on the Heart of God*.

The introduction to that last volume, with its in-depth overview of Fénelon's life and influence, was reedited and used as the foundation for the introduction to this new edition of *The Complete Fénelon*, with additions from Helms's introduction to *The Royal Way of the Cross*.

The Complete Fénelon incorporates our three previous editions of Fénelon, and adds to them. For this new book, Edmonson did additional modernization of parts one and two and reedited part three. Then he translated twenty-one personal meditations by Fénelon on important days and seasons of the church year. The new translation, entitled *God of My Heart: Meditations on Feast and Fasts*, constitutes part four of *The Complete Fénelon*, and is published in English here for the first time.

Occasional footnotes throughout the text have been provided by the editors. More exhaustive endnotes explain the details of theological nuance as well as the source of Scripture quotes and allusions.

We have entitled this new book *The Complete Fénelon*, not because it contains everything penned by this prolific writer, but because it contains a comprehensive selection of his writings for Christians in the form of both letters and meditations. Other writings by Fénelon, such as his fables and his political works, are available in editions from other publishers.

THE SCRIPTURE VERSIONS USED IN THIS EDITION

Part 1, *The Royal Way of the Cross*: Unless otherwise indicated, all Scriptures are from NIV.

Parts 2 and 3, *Talking with God* and *Meditations on the Heart of God*: The versions used for the Scriptures are noted individually.

Part 4, *God of My Heart*: Unless otherwise indicated, all Scriptures are from NRSV.

PART ONE

The Royal Way
of the Cross

INTRODUCTION TO PART ONE
The Royal Way of the Cross

I t is important to remember as one reads these letters and meditations, that they were originally written to individuals, and that they often deal with very specific problems. The same is true, of course, of St. Paul's letters in the New Testament. In both cases, it is necessary to bear this in mind to avoid stressing some point out of the context and spirit of the whole. For example, Fénelon speaks in one of his letters about the need for softening the corrective word to others. To whom was he speaking? To someone, no doubt, whose self-righteousness and anger made such words a weapon and expression of self. On the other hand, he rebukes someone else for over-sensitivity to correction, calling such sensitivity the evidence of self-love. He himself invites correction without sparing, and certainly does not mince words or equivocate in speaking truth to those for whom he was responsible. All this needs to be borne in mind when reading or interpreting any individual passage.

This compilation seeks to set forth a multifaceted view of the "royal way of the Cross," as Fénelon saw and expressed it. He believed that God was in all things in his own life and in the lives of his readers—in things fair and things unfair, things pleasant and things unpleasant. And he invites us to share this way of looking at life.

FÉNELON'S TERMINOLOGY

Fénelon often uses words in a different way from their modern meaning. The following definitions will help the reader grasp Fénelon's meanings:

Disintegration: losing our unity by breaking our lives into separate parts.

Mortification: the subjection and denial of bodily passions and appetites by abstinence.

Mortified: having an attitude or practice of mortification.

Recollection: the tranquility of mind that comes from quiet religious contemplation.

Recollected: being in a state of recollection.

Scruples: an excessive concern to be right in small details, particularly where religious restrictions or denials are concerned. We would probably call it a "legalistic" attitude today. Jesus referred to the Pharisees' scruples when he spoke of washing the outside of the cup, while within was all manner of filth and uncleanness that they were overlooking. That is the kind of thing Fénelon is concerned with in those he is counseling.

Scrupulous: being excessively concerned to be right in small details.

1
SEEING OUR TRUE SPIRITUAL STATE BEFORE GOD

In order to make your prayer more profitable, it would be well from the beginning to picture yourself as a poor, naked, miserable wretch, perishing of hunger, who knows only one man of whom he can ask or hope for help. Or picture yourself as a sick person, covered with sores and ready to die unless some compassionate physician will take him in hand and heal him. These are true pictures of our condition before God. Your soul is barer of heavenly treasure than that poor beggar is of earthly possessions. You need them more urgently, and there is no one but God of whom you can ask or expect them. Again, your soul is infinitely more sin-sick than that distressed, stricken patient, and God alone can heal you. Everything depends on his being moved by your prayers. He is able for all this: but remember that he wills to act only when he is asked earnestly and with real neediness.

When once permeated with this truth, then proceed to read over the subject of your meditation, either in Holy Scripture or in whatever book you may be using. Pause after a verse or two, to follow out such reflections as God may put into your mind. In order to help forward your beginnings, to rouse your mind from its ordinary inattention, you would do well to thank him for his Word, the oracle by which he teaches us his will, and for his willingness to teach us. It would be well to humble yourself and confess that you have not heeded his teaching better or profited by it more, examining wherein you have specially neglected it, or are neglecting it, and how far your life has been in conformity to God's will or in opposition to it.

Lay your shame before God. Reflect on the occasions that cause you to commit these faults and the best means of avoiding or remedying them. Consider what the Lord justly requires of you that you may keep from such falls and repent of the past. Think of how greatly you are bound to obey him, however hard it may seem, how profitable it is to do so, how disgraceful and dangerous it would be to leave it undone.

Remember that we are weakness itself, as daily experience proves, and offer yourself to Jesus Christ. Abhor your slackness and faithlessness and ask him to fill your heart with all that he would see in it. Ask him to strengthen this will, so that you may go on doing better. Trust in his goodness and in his solemn promises never to forsake us in time of need. Lean upon his words, and rest in the hope that he will confirm what he has worked in you so far.

⤳ 2
REAL CONVERSION

We must yield to God when he urges us to let him reign with us.

Did you hesitate or resist so much when the world sought to seduce you through its passions and pleasures? Did you resist evil as forcefully as you resist what is good? When it is a question of going astray, being corrupted, lost, of acting against the inmost consciousness of heart and reason by indulging vanity or sensual pleasure, we are not so afraid of going too far; we choose, we yield unreservedly. But when the question is to believe that we, who did not make ourselves, were made by an all-wise, all-powerful Hand—to acknowledge that we owe all to him from whom we received all, and who made us for himself—then we begin to hesitate, to deliberate, to foster subtle doubts as to the simplest, plainest matters. We are afraid of being credulous, we mistrust our own feelings, we shift our ground. We fear to give too much to him for whom nothing can be too much, though we never gave him anything yet. We are actually ashamed of ceasing to be ungrateful, and of letting the world see that we want to serve him! In a word, we are as timid, shrinking, and shy about what is good, as we were bold and unhesitatingly decided concerning what is evil.

All I would ask of you is simply now to follow the leadings of your inmost heart toward what is good, as you once followed those of your worldly passions toward evil. Whenever you examine the foundation of your religion, you will easily see that there is nothing substantial to be said against it, and that those who oppose it do so only to evade the rules of holy living, rejecting God out of self-seeking. But in all honesty, is it fair to be so broad-minded on behalf of self, and so narrow where God is concerned?

Do not argue. Either listen to your own heart, in which God, so long forgotten, is now speaking lovingly, notwithstanding past unfaithfulness; or consult such friends as you know to be right-minded and sincere. Ask them what they find God's service to be, whether they are sorry that they pledged themselves to it, and whether they think they were too credulous or too bold in their conversion. They, like you, were in the world. Ask whether they regret having forsaken it, and whether the intoxication of Babylon is sweeter than the peace of Zion? No, indeed! Whatever crosses may attend the Christian's life, we need never lose that blessed peace of heart through which we accept every suffering, desiring no happiness that God denies. Can the world give as much? You can tell. Are people of the world always satisfied with everything that comes to them, content without all that they do not have? Do they do everything out of love and with their heart?

What are you afraid of? Of leaving that which will soon leave you?

What are you afraid of? Of following too much goodness, finding a too-loving God; of being drawn by an attraction that is stronger than self or the charms of this poor world?

What are you afraid of? Of becoming too humble, too detached, too pure, too true, too reasonable, too grateful to your Father who is in heaven? I implore you, be afraid of nothing so much as of this false fear—this foolish, worldly wisdom that hesitates between God and self, between vice and virtue, between gratitude and ingratitude, between life and death.

↪ 3
WHAT DOES GOD ASK OF YOU?

God has not forgotten you.

What does he ask of you, but to be happy? Have you not realized that we are happy in loving him? Have you not felt that there is no other real happiness, whatever excitement may be found in sensual pleasures, apart from him? Since you know where to find the Fountain of Life, and have once drunk of it, why would you seek foul, earthly cisterns? When will those days return, those bright, happy days, lighted up by the soft rays of loving mercy?

Do whatever you will, only love God, and let his love, revived in your heart, be your guide. Your ears are not yet closed to the sublime language of truth; your heart is made to feel its charms. "Taste and see" the pleasant bread daily spread for us at our Father's table. With such support, who can fear that anything else will be lacking?

I know what it is to be weak; I am a thousand times weaker than you. It is very profitable to have realized what we are; but to that weakness, which is inseparable from our human nature, do not add an estrangement from the very means of strength. Only hearken inwardly to him and despise boldly that which is despicable.

↪ 4
FEAR OF BEING WRONG

Your spiritual progress is more hindered by your excessive fear of giving way to enjoyment in ordinary, innocent things, than it ever could be by that enjoyment itself. Of course, self-indulgence is always to be avoided, especially when we need self-restraint; but you seriously injure yourself by keeping up a perpetual effort to resist even the smallest involuntary pleasure in the details of a well-regulated life. I would have you steadily resist such a tendency. I do not approve of your efforts to reject the enjoyment inevitably attending upon simple food and needed rest.

Speak honestly about your concerns about your health to your doctor, then leave him to decide and give no heed to your own fancies. But obey quietly; that should be the aim of your courage and steadfastness. Without this, you will not acquire the peace that God's children possess, nor will you deserve it. Bear all annoyances of your present condition, which is full of inconveniences and discomfort, in a penitential spirit; these are the penances God assigns you, and they are far more useful than those you may choose for yourself. There is no spot in the world where you would not find yourself beset with your natural taste for enjoyment. Even the strictest solitude would have its thorns.

The best state to be in is the one in which God's hand holds you: do not look beyond it, and be content to accept his will from one moment to another in the spirit of mortification and renunciation. But this acquiescence must be full of trust in God, who loves you even more for not sparing you. You ought to be scrupulous about your scruples rather than about your enjoyment of innocent, ordinary things.

5
FALSE AND REAL HUMILITY

It is false humility to believe ourselves unworthy of God's goodness and to not dare to look to him with trust. True humility lies in seeing our own unworthiness and giving ourselves up to God, never doubting that he can work out the greatest results for and in us. If God's success depends on finding our foundations already laid, we might well fear that our sins had destroyed our chances. But God needs nothing that is in us. He can never find anything there except what he himself has given us. No, we may go further and say that the absolute nothingness of the creature, bound up as it is with sin in a faithless soul, is the fittest of all subjects for the reception of his grace. He delights to pour it out on such souls, for sinful souls who have never experienced anything but their own weakness cannot claim any of God's gifts as their own possession. It is just as St. Paul says: "God chose the foolish things of the world to shame the wise."[1]

Do not fear then, that your past faithlessness must make you unworthy of God's mercy. Nothing is so worthy of mercy as utter weakness. He came from heaven to earth to seek sinners, not the righteous; to seek that which was lost—as indeed all were lost if it were not for him. The physician seeks the sick, not the healthy. Oh, how God loves those who come boldly to him in their foul, ragged garments, and ask, as of a father, for some garment worthy of him!

You wait to be familiar till God shows a smiling face. But I tell you that if you will open your heart thoroughly to him, you will cease to trouble yourself about the particular appearance of his face. Let him turn a severe and displeased countenance upon you as much as he will, he never loves you more than when he threatens. For he threatens only to test, to humble, to detach souls from themselves.

Do you want the consolation God can give, or do you want God himself? If it is the first, then you do not love God for his own sake, but for yours; and in that case, you deserve nothing from him. But if you seek him alone, you will find him even more truly when he tests you than when he comforts you. When he comforts you, you have cause to fear that you might care more for his gifts than for himself; but when he deals roughly with you and you hold on fast, it is to him alone that you cling. The real time for progress is not when we delight in a conscious sweetness, but when faith is dry and cold—if we do not yield to discouragement.

Leave it all to God. It is not your business to judge how he should deal with you, because he knows far better than you do what is good for you. You deserve a certain amount of trial and dryness. Bear it patiently! God does his part when he pushes you away. Try to do yours too, and that is to love him without waiting for him to assure you of his love for you. Your love is a guarantee of his; your confidence will disarm him, and turn all his severity into tenderness. Even if he were not to grow tender, you ought to give yourself up to his just dealings, and accept his intention of nailing you to the cross in union with his beloved Son, Jesus.

Such is the solid food of pure faith and generous love with which you should sustain your soul. I pray that God may make you strong under your troubles.

Expect all, and all will be given you: God and his peace will be with you!

6
THE DECEITFULNESS
OF SELF-LOVE

Generally speaking, I should fear that reading about extraordinary spiritual matters tends to harm weak imaginations. Self-love easily flatters itself that it has attained the altitudes that it has admired in books. It seems to me that the only course in such a case is to take no notice of such things. I advise you never to dwell voluntarily on extraordinary experiences. This is the real way to discover how much self-conceit has to do with these supposed gifts. Nothing tends so much to wound the vanity of self-conceit and bring illusions to light as a simple direction to set aside the marvelous, and to require a person who aspires to the marvelous to act as though nothing of the sort existed. Without such a test, I do not think the genuineness of a person can be proven thoroughly, and without it, I do not think due caution has been taken against delusion.

The blessed John of the Cross advises souls to look beyond such light, and to abide in the twilight of simple faith. If the gifts are real, such detachment will not hinder them from leaving their marks upon the soul; if not, such uncompromising faith will be a sure guarantee against delusion. Moreover, such a line will not keep a soul back from God's true leadings, for there is no opposition. It can only distress self-conceit, which finds a hidden self-satisfaction in such unusual gifts; and that self-conceit is the very thing that needs pruning.

Even if such gifts are unquestionably real and good, it is most important to learn detachment from them, and live by simple faith. However excellent the gifts may be, detachment from them is better still. "And now I will show you the most excellent way"—the way of faith and love; not clinging either to sight, feeling, or taste—only to obedience to the beloved One. Such a way is simple, real, straightforward, free from the snares of pride.

7
CRITICIZING OTHERS

You need greater liberality as to the faults of others. I grant you that you cannot help seeing them when they are forced upon you, or avoid your inevitable conclusions as to the principles on which some seem to act. Neither can you avert a certain annoyance that such things cause. Suffice it if you try to bear with obvious faults, avoiding judging those that are doubtful, and resist the dislike that estranges you from people.

Perfection finds it easy to bear with the imperfections of others, and to be all things to all people. We ought to learn to put up with the most obvious faults in worthy souls, and to leave them alone until God gives the sign for a gradual weeding; otherwise, we are likely to tear up the good grain with the weeds. God often leaves certain infirmities besetting the most advanced souls, such as seem quite out of character with their excellence, just as in reclaimed ground some leave tokens to show how extensive the work of clearance has been. God leaves such tokens to show from where he has brought them.

All such souls must labor at self-amendment at their own rate, and you must labor to endure their imperfections. Your own experience will teach you that correction is a bitter thing; and since you know this, give heed to soften it to others. It is not your great zeal to correct others for their own sake as much as it is your perfectionism that shuts your heart to them.

8
FALSE NOTIONS
OF SPIRITUAL PROGRESS

Almost all who aim at serving God do so more or less for their own sake. They want to win, not to lose. They want to be comforted, not to suffer. They want to possess, not to be deprived. They want to increase, not to diminish. Yet all the while our whole interior progress consists in losing, sacrificing, decreasing, humbling, and stripping self even of God's own gifts, so as to be more completely his. We are often like an invalid who feels his pulse fifty times in the day, and wants the doctor to be perpetually ordering some fresh treatment, or telling him how much better he is.

Some people treat their spiritual director or pastor in this way. They move round and round in a petty circle of easy virtues, never stepping beyond it heartily and generously, while they expect the director (like the physician) to soothe, comfort, encourage, and foster perfectionism, only ordering little sedative treatments that drop into mere habit and routine. As soon as they are deprived of conscious grace—grace that they can feel inwardly, grace that is like the milk of babes—such people fancy that all is lost. But this is a plain proof that they cling too much to the means and overlook the end, and that self is their main object.

Privations are the food of strong minds: They invigorate the soul, take it out of itself, and offer it as a living sacrifice to God. But weak people are in despair at the first touch of privation. They fancy that all their work is being overthrown just when it is really beginning to be solidly fixed and thoroughly purified. They are willing to let God do what he will with them, *provided always* it be something great and perfect. But they have no notion of being cast down and crushed, or of being offered as a sacrifice to be consumed by the divine flames. They seek to live by pure faith, yet want to retain all their worldly wisdom, to be as children, yet great in their own eyes. But what a spiritual mirage this is!

9
THE RIGHT USE
OF TRIALS

People find it very hard to believe that God heaps crosses on those he loves out of loving-kindness. "Why should he take pleasure in causing us to suffer?" they ask. "Could he not make us good without making us so miserable?" Yes, doubtless God could do so, for to him all things are possible. His all-powerful hands hold the human heart and turn it as he pleases, just as people who command the source of a reservoir turn the stream in whatever direction they desire. But though God could save us without crosses, he has not willed to do so, just as he has willed that people should grow up through the weakness and troubles of child-hood, instead of being born fully developed. He is the Master; we can only be silent and adore his infinite wisdom without understanding it. The one thing we do see plainly is that we cannot become really good except in so far as we become humble, unselfish, in all things turning from self to God.

But as that grace operates, it cannot (except through a miracle of the same grace) be other than painful, and God does not perform continual miracles in the order of grace any more than in the order of nature. It would be as great a miracle to see a person full of self die suddenly to self-consciousness and self-interest as it would be to see a child go to bed a mere child and rise up the next morning thirty years old! God hides his work beneath a series of imperceptible events, both in grace and nature, and in this way he subjects us to the mysteries of faith. Not only does he accomplish his work gradually, but also he does it by the most simple and likely means, so that its success appears natural. Otherwise, all that God does would be like a perpetual miracle, and this would overthrow the life of faith by which he would have us exist.

Such a life of faith is necessary, not only to mold the good, by causing us to sacrifice our own reason amid a world of darkness, but also to blind those whose presumption misleads them. Such people see God's works without comprehending them, and take them to be simply natural. They are without true understanding, since understanding is given only to those who mistrust their own judgment and the proud wisdom of humanity.

So it is to ensure that the operation of grace may remain a mystery of faith that God permits it to be slow and painful. He makes use of human inconstancy and ingratitude, and the disappointments and failures that attend human prosperity, to detach us from the created world and its good things. He opens our eyes by letting us realize our own weakness and evil through countless falls. All this seems to go on in the natural course of events, and this series of apparently natural causes consumes us like a slow fire. We would much rather be consumed at once by the flames of pure love, but so speedy a process would cost us nothing. It is utter selfishness that we desire to attain perfection so cheaply and so quickly.

≈ 10
PROLONGED TRIALS

Why do we rebel against our prolonged trials? Because of self-love; and it is that very self-love that God purposes to destroy. As long as we cling to self, his work is not achieved.

What right have we to complain? We suffer from an excessive attachment to the world—above all to self. God orders a series of events that detach us gradually from the world first, and finally from the self also. The operation is painful, but our corruption makes it needful. If the flesh were healthy, the surgeon would not need to probe it. He uses the knife only in proportion to the depth of the wound and the extent of proud flesh. If we feel his operation too keenly, it is because the disease is active. Is it cruelty that makes the surgeon probe us to the quick? No, far otherwise—it is skill and kindness; he would do the same with his only child.

This is how God treats us. He never willingly puts us to any pain. His fatherly heart does not desire to grieve us, but he cuts to the quick so that he may heal the ulcers of our spiritual being. He must tear from us what we love wrongly, unreasonably, or excessively, the thing that hinders his love. In so doing, he causes us to cry out like a child from whom one takes away a knife with which it could injure or kill itself. We cry loudly in our despair, and murmur against God, just as the petulant child murmurs against its mother. But he lets us cry, and saves us nevertheless!

God afflicts us only for our correction. Even when he seems to overwhelm us, it is for our own good, to spare us the greater evil we would do to ourselves. The things for which we weep would have caused us eternal distress. That which we count as loss was then indeed most lost when we fancied that it belonged to us. God has stored it up safely, to be returned to us in eternity. He deprives us of the things we prize only because he wants to teach us to love them purely, truly, and properly in order to enjoy them forever in his presence, and because he wants to do a hundred times better for us than we can even desire for ourselves.

Nothing can happen in the world except by God's permissive will.[2] He does everything, arranges everything, makes everything to be as it is. He counts the hairs of our head, the leaves of every tree, the sand on the seashore, the drops of water from the mighty ocean. When he made the world, his wisdom weighed and measured every atom. Every moment he renews and sustains the breath of life. He knows the number of our days; he holds the cords of life or death. What seems to us weightiest is as nothing in the eyes of God; a little longer or shorter life becomes an imperceptible difference before him. What does it matter whether this frail vessel, this poor clay, should be thrown aside a little sooner or later? How shortsighted and erring we are!

We are aghast at the death of one in the flower of his age. "What a sad loss!" we cry out. But to whom is the loss? What does the one who dies lose?—a few years of vanity, delusion, and peril. God takes that person away from the evil and saves that one from his own weakness and the world's wickedness. What do they lose who love God?—the danger of earthly happiness, a treacherous delight, a snare that caused them to forget God and their own welfare. But in truth they gain the blessing of detachment through the cross. That same blow by which the one who dies is saved prepares those who are left to work out their salvation in hope. Surely, then, it is true that God is very good, very loving, very full of pity with regard to our real needs, even when he seems to overwhelm us and we are most tempted to call him hard.

The sensitiveness of self-love makes us keenly alive to our own condition. The sick person who cannot sleep thinks the night is endless, yet it is no longer than any other night. In our cowardice, we exaggerate all we suffer. Our pain may be severe, but we make it worse by shrinking under it. The real way to get relief is to give ourselves up heartily to God, to accept suffering because God sends it to purify us and make us worthier of him.

The world smiled upon you, and was as a poison to your soul. Would you wish to go on, right up to the hour of death, in ease and pleasure, in the pride of life and soul-destroying luxury, clinging to the world— which is Christ's enemy, and rejecting the cross—which alone can make you holy? The world will turn away and forget, despise, and ignore you. Are you surprised at that, since the world is worldly, unjust, deceitful, and treacherous? Yet you are not ashamed to love this world, from which God snatches you to deliver you from its bondage and make you free.

You complain of your very deliverance. You are your own enemy when you are so alive to the world's indifference, and you cannot endure what is for your real good when you so keenly regret the loss of what is fatal to you. This is the source of all your grief and pain.

11
ANXIETY ABOUT THE FUTURE

The future is in God's hands, not yours. God will rule it according to your need. But if you seek to forecast it in your own wisdom, you will gain nothing but anxiety and anticipation of inevitable trouble. Try only to make use of each day. Each day brings its own good and evil, and sometimes what seems evil becomes good if we leave it to God and do not forestall him with our impatience.

Be sure that God will grant you whatever time you need to reach him. Perhaps he may not give you as much as you would like for your own plans, or to please yourself under the pretext of seeking spiritual perfection, but you will find that neither time nor opportunity for renunciation of self and self-pleasing will be lacking. All other time is lost, however well spent it may seem. Be assured that you will find all such circumstances adapted to your real needs. In proportion as God upsets your own inclinations he will uphold your weakness. Do not be afraid; leave everything to him.

You will always find freedom in God so long as you do not give way to the false idea that you have lost your freedom.

12
THE STRUGGLE OF SELF-WILL

The Spirit of God never inspires us with self-conceit; and far from creating disturbance, the Spirit always fills the heart with peace. What could be a more certain proof of temptation than to be in a kind of despair, rebelling against everything that God gives you to lead you to himself? Such rebellion is not natural, but God allows temptation to drive us to such an extremity in order that we may more easily recognize that it is temptation.

In the same way, he allows us in the presence of others to fall into certain faults, which are altogether contrary to our excessive sensitivity and discretion, in order to mortify the sensitivity and discretion that we cherish so jealously. He causes the ground under us to give way, in order that we may not find any conscious support, either in ourselves or in anyone else. Further, he allows us to imagine that our neighbor judges us quite other than he really does, in order that our self-conceit may lose any flattering prop in that direction.

The remedy is severe, but it needed nothing less to free us from ourselves and to storm the defensive walls of our pride. We want to die, but to die without any pain and in full health. We want to be tested, but only while looking on with conscious superiority to the trial. It is a saying of the old lawyers with respect to donations: You cannot both give and keep. We must give all or nothing when God asks it. If we do not have courage to give, at least we can let him take.

⇌ 13
SELF-DECEIT

Nothing so feeds self-conceit as believing that you are completely devoted to others and never self-seeking, that you are quite free from self-love and always generously devoted to your neighbors.

But all this devotion that seems to be for others is really for yourself. Your self-love reaches the point of perpetual self-congratulation in the mistaken belief that you are free from self-love itself. All your anxiety is fear that you might not be fully satisfied with yourself, and this is the root of your scruples.

If you thought of nothing but God and his glory, you would be as keen and sensitive to the losses of others as to your own. But it is the self that makes you so keen and sensitive. You want God as well as other people to be always satisfied with you, and you want to be satisfied with yourself in all your dealings with God.

You are not used to being content with a simple good will. Your self-love wants a lively feeling, a reassuring pleasure, some kind of charm or excitement. You are guided too much by imagination, and you suppose that your mind and will are inactive unless you are conscious of their workings. So you depend on a kind of excitement similar to that which the passions or the theater arouse.

Because of your excessive refinement, you fall into the opposite extreme—a real coarseness of imagination. Nothing is more opposed to the life of faith and to true wisdom.

There is no more dangerous opening to delusion than the false ways by which people try to avoid delusion. It is imagination that leads us astray. The certainty we seek through imagination, feeling, and taste is one of the most dangerous sources from which fanaticism springs.

This is the chasm of vanity and corruption that God would have us discover in our own heart: we must look on it with the calm and simplicity that belong to true humility. It is self-love that makes us so inconsolable at seeing our own imperfections. To stand face to face with them, however, not flattering or tolerating them, seeking to correct ourselves without becoming peevish—this is to desire what is good for its own sake and for God's sake, rather than merely treating it as a self-satisfying decoration.

So turn against this useless search of yours for the self-satisfaction you find in doing right.

14
THE DANGERS OF IMAGINATION

Abstain completely from imaginary conversations. Although some may tend to kindle pious feelings, this is a dangerous habit. From such conversations you will unconsciously move on to others, and this will foster your excitement or encourage your love of the world. It is far better to suppress them all. I do not mean that you should stop them forcibly—you might as well try to stop a torrent. It is enough if you do not voluntarily harbor them.

When you perceive that your imagination is beginning to work, be satisfied with turning to God, without directly combating these fancies. Let them drop, occupying yourself in some useful way. If they come at a time of meditation or prayer, such idle thoughts should be treated as distractions. Return, then, quietly to God as soon as you are conscious of them, but do so without anxiety, scruples, or agitation.

If such imaginations trouble you when you are engaged in external work, the work will help you to resist such castle building. It would even be well at first to find some other person to talk to, or to set about to do some difficult task, with a view to breaking the thread of such thoughts and getting rid of the habit.

You must positively suppress this trifling with the imagination. It is a waste of time, a very dangerous occupation, and a temptation voluntarily incurred. Never yield to it voluntarily. Perhaps, owing to habit, your imagination will still beset you with fantasies in spite of yourself, but at all events do not yield to them. Try quietly to get rid of them when you become aware that they are occupying you.

15
THE DANGERS
OF HUMAN PRAISE

Showing sorrow for sin and undergoing other humiliating circumstances are far more profitable than success. You know that your troubles made you find out what you never knew before about yourself, and I am afraid that the authority, the success, and the admiration that have now come your way will make you self-satisfied. Such self-satisfaction will mar the best-ordered life, because it is incompatible with humility.

We can be humble only so long as we give attention to all our own infirmities. The consciousness of these should be predominant; the soul should feel burdened by them and groan under them, and that groaning should be as a perpetual prayer to be set free from "its bondage to decay," and admitted into the "glorious freedom of the children of God."[3] Overwhelmed by its own faults, the soul should feel it deserves no deliverance by the great mercy of Jesus Christ. Woe to the soul that is self-satisfied, that treats God's gifts as its own merits, and forgets what is due to God!

Set apart regular seasons for reading and prayer. Involve yourself in outward matters when it is really necessary, and attend more to softening the harshness of your judgment, to restraining your temper, and to humbling your mind than to upholding your opinion even when it is right. Finally, humble yourself whenever you find that an undue interest in the affairs of others has led you to forget the one all-important matter of yourself: eternity.

"Learn from me," Jesus says to you, "for I am gentle and humble in heart, and you will find rest for your souls."[4] Be sure that grace, inward peace, and the blessing of the Holy Spirit will be with you if you will maintain a gentle humility amid all your external uncertainties.

⇒ 16
DEALING WISELY WITH
THE FAULTS OF OTHERS

Self-love cannot bear to see itself. The sight would overwhelm it with shame and irritation, and if it catches an accidental glimpse, it seeks some false light that may soften and condone what is so hideous. Therefore, we always keep up some illusion as long as we retain any self-love. In order to see ourselves perfectly, self-love must be rooted up, and the love of God must reign solely in us. Then the same light that shows our faults will remove them. Till then we only half know ourselves, because we are only half given to God, clinging to self a great deal more than we think or dare to admit to ourselves.

When we receive all truth, we will see clearly. Then, loving ourselves only with the love of charity, we will see ourselves as we see our neighbor, without self-interest, and without flattery. Meanwhile, God spares our weakness, showing us our true hideousness only in proportion to the courage he gives us to bear the sight. He shows us first one bit, and then another, as he gradually leads us on to changing for the better. Without this merciful preparation of light and strength in due proportion, the sight of our frailty would only lead to despair.

Those to whom spiritual guidance is entrusted should lay bare people's faults only as God prepares the heart to see them. Spiritual guides must learn to watch a fault patiently, and take no external measure until God begins to make it felt by the inward conscience. Indeed, spiritual guides must imitate God's own way of dealing with the soul, softening his rebuke, so that the person who has been reprimanded feels as if it was rather self-reproach, and a sense of wounded love, than God rebuking. All other methods of guidance—correcting impatiently, or because the spiritual guide is agitated by the other's infirmities—smack of earthly judgments, not the correction of grace. This is imperfection rebuking the imperfect: this is a subtle, clinging self-love that cannot see anything to forgive in the self-love of others. The greater our own self-love, the more severe critics we will be.

Nothing is so offensive to a haughty, sensitive self-conceit as the self-conceit of others.

But, on the contrary, the love of God is full of consideration, forbearance, voluntary descent from one's rank, and tenderness. It adapts itself, waits, and never moves more than one step at a time. The less self-love we have, the more we know how to adapt ourselves to curing our neighbor's failings of that kind; we learn better never to lance without applying plenty of healing ointment to the wound, never to purge the patient without feeding him, never to risk an operation except when nature indicates its safety. We learn to wait years before giving a beneficial warning. We learn to wait till Providence prepares suitable external circumstances, and grace opens the heart. If you persist in gathering fruit before it is ripe, you simply waste your labor.

Since most of our moods are passing and complicated, our explanations are apt to become untrue before we finish making them. Something quite different takes over, and that in its turn seems unreal. So it is best to be content to say about ourselves what seems to be true at the moment we are opening our hearts. It is not necessary to tell everything methodically; let it be enough to keep back nothing intentionally, and to soften nothing with the flattering touches of self-conceit. God supplies what is lacking to an upright heart according to its needs; and spiritual guides who are enlightened by grace easily perceive what people do not know how to tell when the penitent is honest and simple, and holds nothing back.

Since our friends, too, are imperfect, they can know us only imperfectly. They often judge only from the external failings that make themselves felt in company, and that jar their own self-conceit. Self-conceit is a very sharp, harsh, unforgiving critic, and the same self-conceit that softens their view of their own faults makes them magnify ours. Their point of view being completely different from ours, they see what we do not perceive in ourselves, and overlook much that we see. They are quick to discern many things that wound their sensitive, jealous self-love, things that our self-love equally conceals. But they do not see those secret faults that stain our virtues more, because they offend no one but God. And so their maturest judgment may be very superficial.

My conclusion is that it is best to listen attentively to God in a profound inward silence, and in all simplicity to say for or against ourselves whatever his light discloses to us at the moment we seek to open our heart.

17
THE DANGERS OF SELF-CHOSEN PLANS

You have withered your heart by so eagerly pressing your own wishes regardless of God's will. This is the cause of all your suffering. You have spent a great deal of time in making plans that were mere cobwebs, and a breath of wind has blown them away. You withdrew gradually from God, and he has withdrawn from you. You must return to him and give yourself up unreservedly to him. There is no other way to regain your peace.

Let go all your plans. God will do as he pleases with them. Even if they were to succeed through earthly means, he would not bless them. But if you offer them unreservedly to him, he will turn everything to his own merciful purposes, whether he does what you wish or not.

The important thing is to practice prayer and communion with God, whatever dryness, distraction, or weariness you may find in it. You deserve to be rejected by God after having rejected him for the world so long. Your patience will win him again.

Meanwhile, persevere in your communions to strengthen your weakness. The weak need to be fed above all with Bread. Do not argue, or give heed to your fancies, but receive communion as soon as you can.

18
USING EAGER ASPIRATIONS

It is not to be wondered at that you should have a sort of jealous eagerness and ambition to advance in the spiritual life, and to be in the confidence of noteworthy servants of God.

Self-love naturally seeks this kind of success, which is flattering to it. The real thing that matters, however, is not to satisfy your ambition by some brilliant advance in virtue, or by being taken into the confidence of distinguished persons, but to mortify the flattering tendencies of self-love, to humble yourself, to love obscurity and contempt, and to seek God only.

People cannot become perfect by hearing or reading about perfection. The chief thing is not to listen to yourself, but silently to give ear to God. It is to renounce all vanity, and apply yourself to real virtue.

Talk little, and do much without caring to be seen. God will teach you more than all the most experienced persons or the most spiritual books can do. What is it you want so much to know? What do you need to learn but to be poor in spirit and to find all wisdom in Christ crucified? "Knowledge puffs up." Only "love builds up."[5] Be content to aim at charity. Do you need any such great knowledge in order to love God and deny yourself for his love? You already know a great deal more than you practice. You do not need fresh knowledge half as much as you need to put into practice what you already know.

How people delude themselves, when they expect to advance by means of argument and inquisitiveness! Be lowly, and never expect to find in people those things that are God's only.

⇌ 19
THE NEED OF CALMING NATURAL ACTIVITY

Do not let your natural activity consume you amid the irksome details around you. You cannot take too many pains to subdue your natural temperament by prayer, and by a frequent renewal of God's presence throughout the day. A Christian who grows anxious over worldly trifles and suddenly awakes to the sense of God's presence amid such eagerness is like a child whose mother catches him suddenly having lost his temper over a game—he is quite ashamed at being found out.

Let it be our concern to abide peacefully, fulfilling all outward duties as well as we can, while inwardly we are absorbed by him who is the only one worthy of all our love. Whenever we become conscious of the impulses of our nature, we must throw them aside so that grace may possess us completely. It is well to stop immediately when we find nature getting the upper hand. Such fidelity to grace is almost as beneficial to the body as to the soul—there is no neglect of duty, and yet we have none of Martha's trouble.[6]

⇌ 20
DOING EVERYTHING FOR GOD

St. Augustine says that whatever we love outside God, so much the less do we love him. It is like a brook from which part of the waters is turned aside. Such a diversion takes away from what belongs to God and gives rise to harassment and trouble. God desires to have everything, and his jealousy cannot endure a divided heart. The slightest affection apart from him becomes a hindrance and causes indifference and consequent separation. The soul can expect to find peace only through love that holds nothing back.

Disintegration, the great foe of recollection, activates all human feelings, distracts the soul, and drives it from its true resting place. Further still, it kindles the senses and the imagination, and to quiet them again is a hard task, while the very effort to do so is in itself inevitably a distraction.

Give a quiet, calm attention to those things assigned to your care by Providence at proper seasons, and be sure that we can accomplish a great deal more by quiet, thoughtful work done as in God's sight, than by all the busy eagerness and overactivity of our restless nature.

⤳ 21
THE DANGER OF COMPROMISE

The first commandment of the law alone is enough to banish all excuse for any reserve with God: "Love the Lord your God with all your heart and with all your soul and with all your strength and with all your mind" (Luke 10:27). Observe how our Lord heaped together expressions that would forestall all the soul's evasions and reservations concerning God's jealous love, requiring not merely the heart's strength and power, but that of the mind and thought. Who can be so self-deceived as to think one loves God if one does not willingly ponder God's law or try diligently to fulfill God's holy will?

Be sure that all those who are reluctant to perceive fully what God's love requires are still a long way off from it. There is only one true way of loving God, namely to do nothing except with and for him, and to obey his call with a free spirit. Those who aim at a compromise, who would like to hold onto the world with one hand, cannot believe this, and so they run the risk of being among those "lukewarm"[7] persons whom God will reject.

Surely those careless souls who say, "I will go this far, but no farther," must be most displeasing to God. Is it fitting for the clay to dictate to the potter? What would people of the world think of servants or subjects who presumed to offer such a half-service to their master or monarch, who shrank from a too hearty fulfillment of their duty, and were ashamed to let their loyalty be seen? And if that is the case, what will the King of kings say if we pursue such cowardly conduct?

The time is at hand; he will soon come; let us prepare his way. Let us adore that eternal beauty that never grows old, and that imparts perpetual youth to those who love no one else. Let us turn from this miserable world, which is already beginning to crumble away. How many great people we have seen pass away beneath the cold hand of death! We, too, will soon be called to leave this world we love so dearly, and which is nothing but vanity, weakness, and folly—*a mere shadow passing away!*

22
THE LIFE OF PEACE

Go on amid the shadows in the simplicity spoken of in the Gospels, not stopping short either in feelings, or tastes, or the light of reason, or any extraordinary gifts. Be content to believe, to obey, to die to self, according to the state of life in which God has placed you.

You must not be discouraged by your involuntary distractions. It is enough if you do not encourage such distractions in times of prayer by yielding too easily to a voluntary disintegration and scattering of your thoughts all through the day.

People pour themselves out too much. They perform even good works with too much eagerness and excitement. They indulge their tastes and fancies, and then God punishes all this in their times of prayer. You must learn to act calmly and in continual dependence on the Spirit of grace, mortifying all the hidden works of self-love.

Habitual intention, which is a reaching forth of the inmost soul to God, will suffice. This is to live in the presence of God. Be still, and do not forfeit what you have at home by turning to seek elsewhere what you will not find. Try to make your intentions more definite, but meanwhile your undefined, undeveloped intentions are good.

A peaceful heart is a good sign, provided that you heartily and lovingly obey God, and are watchful against self-love.

Make use of your imperfections to learn detachment from yourself, and adhere firmly to God alone. Try to grow in all goodness, not that you may find a dangerous self-satisfaction in doing so, but that you may do the will of your Beloved.

Try to be single-minded. Avoid looking backward anxiously, a fault that self-love encourages under various pretexts. This will only disturb you and prove a snare. Those who lead a recollected and mortified life through real desire to love God will be quickly warned by that love whenever they sin against it. As soon as you feel such warnings, pause. I repeat my injunction: be at rest.

23
TO ONE IN SPIRITUAL DISTRESS

When you say, "It is impossible to do what is required of me," this is a temptation to despair. Despair of yourself as much as you please, but not of God. He is both loving and powerful, and he will deal with you in keeping with your faith. If you believe all, you will attain all—you will move mountains. But if you believe nothing, you will receive nothing, only it will be your own fault. Remember Abraham, who hoped against hope. Imitate the blessed Virgin, who, when what seemed completely impossible was set before her, answered unhesitatingly, "May it be to me as you have said."

So do not shut up your heart. It is not that you *cannot* do what is required of you, so restricted is your heart. It is that you do not *want* to be able to do it. You do not wish to have your heart enlarged. You are afraid that it will be done. How can you expect grace to win entrance into a heart so resolutely closed against it? All that I would ask of you is to acquiesce calmly and in a spirit of faith, and not give ear to your own suggestions. Provided you will yield meekly and gradually regain peace through recollection, everything will be achieved by degrees. What seems impossible in your present state of temptation will become easy. Then we will hear you saying, "What? Is this all?" Why so much despair and outcry for so simple a matter that God is bringing about and preparing so lovingly?

Be careful not to resist him, for this can cause you to become indifferent and hostile toward him. All your religion would prove hollow if you should fail in this essential point—all would lapse into mere indulgence of tastes and tendencies. May God not allow you to fall away! There is more danger in the risk of resisting God than in the heaviest of other sorrows. Crosses borne with quiet endurance, lowliness, simplicity, and self-denial unite us to Jesus Christ crucified, and work untold good. But crosses that we reject through thinking too highly of ourselves and through self-will separate us from him, contract the heart, and by degrees dry up the fountain of grace. Yield humbly, therefore, without trusting yourself, mere broken reed that you are, and say, "To him nothing is impossible." He asks only one "Yes," spoken in pure faith.

⤳ 24
BEARING THE BAD OPINIONS OF THE WORLD

The world, always too ready to think evil of good people, assumes that there are no good people on the earth. Some rejoice to think this way, and triumph maliciously. Others are troubled, and in spite of a certain desire for what is good, they hold aloof from piety out of mistrust of the pious.

People are astonished to see a person who has seemed to be religious, or who, more correctly speaking, has been really converted while living in solitude, relapse into old ways and habits when confronted once more with the world. Did they not know before that mortals are frail, that the world is full of contagion, and that weak human beings can stand upright only by deliberately avoiding occasions of falling? What new thing has happened? Surely this is a great fuss about the fall of a rootless tree, on which every wind blew! After all, are there not hypocrites in honesty as well as in religion to be found in the world? And ought we to conclude that there are no honest people because we find some to be false? When the world rejoices over the scandal of a person falling, it shows how little it knows about humankind or about virtue.

We may well be grieved at such a scandal, but those who know how deep is human frailty, and how even the little good we do is but a borrowed thing, will be surprised at nothing. Let those who stand upright tremble for fear that they too will fall; let those who wallow in the mire not rejoice because they see one fall who seemed able to stand alone.

Our confidence is neither in frail mortals nor in ourselves, who are as frail as others. Our confidence is in God alone, the one unchanging Truth. Let all humankind prove themselves to be mere mortals—that is to say, nothing but falsehood and sin. Let them be carried away by the torrent of iniquity. Still God's truth will not be weakened, and the world will only show itself as more hateful than ever in having corrupted those who were seeking after virtue.

As for hypocrites, time always unmasks them, and they are sure to expose themselves one way or another. They are hypocrites only with the object of enjoying the fruits of their hypocrisy. Either their life is sensual and pleasure-seeking, or their conduct is self-interested and ambitious. They can be seen cajoling, flattering, playing all kinds of roles, whereas real virtue is simple, single-minded, free from impressive airs or mystery. It does not rise and fall, it is never jealous of the success or reputation of others. It does the smallest amount of wrong that it can, lets itself be criticized in silence, is content with small things, and is free from plots, maneuverings, and pretensions. Take it or leave it, it is always the same. Hypocrisy may imitate all this, but only very roughly.

People will be deceived by it only through their lack of discernment or of experience in real virtue.

People who do not understand diamonds, or who do not examine them closely, may take false stones to be real. But all the same there are such things as real diamonds, and it is possible to distinguish them.

In order to trust fair-seeming people, we should be able to recognize their conduct as single-minded, steadfast, solid, and well-tried under difficulty, free from affectation, while firm and vigorous in all that is essential to real virtue.

25
CHRISTIAN PERFECTION

Christian perfection is not the strict, wearisome, constrained thing many suppose it to be. It requires us to give ourselves to God with our whole heart, and as soon as this is accomplished, whatever we are called upon to do for God becomes easy. Those who are completely God's are always satisfied, for they desire only what he wills, and are ready to do whatever he requires. They are ready to strip themselves of all things, and are sure to find a hundred times as much in that nakedness. This hundredfold happiness that the true children of God possess amid all the troubles of this world consists in a peaceful conscience, freedom of spirit, a welcome resignation of all things to God, the joyful sense of his light ever growing stronger within their heart, and a thorough deliverance from all tyrannical fears and longings after worldly things. The sacrifices they make are for him whom they love best. They suffer willingly, realizing such suffering is better than any worldly joy. Their body may be diseased and their mind weak and shrinking, but their will is firm and steadfast, and they can say a hearty Amen to every blow that it pleases God to deal them.

What God requires is an undivided will—a yielding will, desiring only what he desires, rejecting only what he rejects, and doing both unreservedly. Where such a mind is, everything turns to good, and its very amusements become good works. Such people are happy indeed! They are delivered from all their own passions—from the judgments of others, from their unkindness, their slavish maxims, and their cold, heartless mockery. They are freed from the troubles of what the world calls fortune, from the treachery or forgetfulness of friends, from the snares of enemies, from their own weakness, and from the weariness of this brief life. They are delivered from the terrors of an unholy death, from the bitter remorse that follows sin, and from the eternal condemnation of God. From all these endless evils, Christians are set free. They have resigned their will to God and know no will except God's, and as a result, faith and hope are their comfort amid all possible sorrows.

Is it not a grievous mistake to be afraid to give yourself to God and to commit yourself to so blessed a state of things? Blessed are they who throw themselves headlong and blindfolded into the arms of "the Father of compassion and the God of all comfort."[8] Nothing remains for them except to know him better and better. Their only fear is that they may not be quick enough to see what he requires. Immediately upon discovering any fresh light from his word, they "rejoice as one who finds a hidden treasure." Whatever may happen to true Christians, all is well to their minds. They seek only to love God more, and the further they learn to walk in the way of perfection, the lighter they feel God's yoke.

Can you not see that it is mere folly to be afraid of giving ourselves too entirely to God? It merely means that we are afraid of being too happy, of accepting his will in all things too heartily, of bearing our inevitable trials too bravely, of finding too much rest in his love, of letting go too easily of the worldly passions that make us miserable. Let us try to despise all that is of the world so that we may be completely God's.

I do not say that you should cut yourself off from all earthly affections. To one who is leading a good, well-regulated life, all that is needed is for the motivating power to become that of love. You would then do very much the same things that you do now, for God does not usually alter the condition he has assigned to each of us or the duties of that condition. The alteration would be this: Whereas now we fulfill our duties for our own satisfaction and that of the world around, we would then pursue the same line as now. However, instead of being eaten up by pride or passion, instead of living in bondage to the world's malicious criticism, we would act freely and bravely in the fullness of hope in God. We would be full of trust, and looking forward to eternal blessings would comfort us for the earthly happiness that seems to slip from under our feet. God's love would give wings to our feet in treading his paths and lifting us up beyond all our cares. If you doubt me, try this Scripture: "Taste and see that the LORD is good"!⁹

The Son of God says to all Christians without any exception, "If anyone would come after me, he must deny himself and take up his cross and follow me."¹⁰ The broad road leads to destruction; strive to follow that narrow path on which so few enter. Only "forceful people lay hold of the kingdom of heaven." You must be born anew, renounce and despise yourself, become as a little child, mourn that you may be comforted, and not be of this world, which is condemned because of unbelief.

These truths frighten many because they only see what religion requires without realizing what it offers or the loving spirit by which it makes every burden light. They do not understand that such religion leads us to the very highest perfection by filling us with a loving peace that lightens every woe. Those who have given themselves unreservedly to God are always happy. They realize that the yoke of Jesus Christ is light and easy, that in him they do indeed find rest, and that he lightens the load of all that are weary and heavy laden, as he promised.

But what can be more wretched than those hesitating, lax souls that are divided between God and the world? They will and will not; they are torn apart both by their own passions and by remorse at their indulgence. They are usually afraid of God's judgments and those of other people. They are afraid of what is evil and ashamed of what is good. They have all the trials of goodness without its comfort. If they only had the courage to despise idle talk, petty ridicule, and the rash judgments of others, what peace and rest they might enjoy in the bosom of God!

Nothing is more perilous to your own salvation, more unworthy of God, or more hurtful to your ordinary happiness than being content to remain as you are. Our whole life is given us with the object of going boldly on toward the heavenly home. The world slips away like a deceitful shadow, and eternity draws near. Why delay to push forward? While it is time, while your merciful Father lights up your path, make haste and seek his kingdom!

🖎 26
THE BURDEN OF PROSPERITY

Chains of gold are no less chains than those of iron. And while their wearers are objects of envy, they are worthy of compassion. Their captivity is in no way preferable to that of one kept unjustly in prison—the only real comfort is that it is God who deprives them of liberty, and this is the same comfort by which the innocent prisoner would be upheld. So all they have more than such a person is a phantom of glory, which gives them no real advantage, but exposes them to the risk of being dazzled and deceived.

But, after all, the consolation of knowing that we are where we are by God's providence is quite inexhaustible: while we have that, nothing can matter. By it the iron chains are transformed, I will not say to gold—for we have just agreed that golden chains are nothing better!—but into freedom and happiness.

What is the good of that natural freedom of which we are so jealous? It sets us free only to follow our own unruly inclinations even in lawful things, to indulge pride and presume on independence, and to carry out our own will, which is the very worst thing that can happen to us. Well it is for those whom God cuts off from their own will that they may follow his, and woe indeed to those who are bound by their passions! They are just as miserable as the others are blessed.

Those who are so bound cannot please themselves. From morning to night they do what God would have done, not what they like—so much the better! He holds them bound, so to speak, hand and foot by his will. He never leaves them a moment to themselves. He is jealous of that tyrannous "I" that wants everything its own way. He leads them on from one sacrifice to another, from one trouble to another, and trains them to fulfill his noblest plans amid commonplace annoyances, frivolous society, and trivialities of which they feel ashamed. He urges the faithful soul till it has scarce time to draw breath: No sooner has one interruption ceased than God sends another to carry on his work. The soul would like to be free to think about God, but all the while, it is far more really united to him by yielding to the cross he sends than by the most glowing, tender emotions. This soul would like to be more its own in order to belong more to God! It forgets that one never belongs to God so little as when self asserts its claim. The self by means of which we fancy we can unite ourselves to God puts a wider gulf between him and us than the most ridiculous frivolity, for there is a venom in self that does not exist in mere childish amusement.

Of course, we should make use of all available moments to loosen our bonds, and specially try to secure certain hours for the refreshment of body and mind by recollection. As to the rest of the day, however, if the stream carries us away in spite of ourselves, we must yield without regret. We learn to find God amid the stream of distractions, and all the more readily in that it is not a self-chosen path.

Some he leads by bitter privations. Others he seems to lead by over-whelming them with the enjoyment of great prosperity. He makes their lot hard and difficult by use of those very things that blind outsiders imagine to be the most perfect enjoyment of life! And so he carries on two good works in them—he teaches them by experience and causes them to die to self by the very things that foster evil and wickedness in many people.

They are like that king we read of, whose hand turned whatever he touched to gold, and whose riches were his misery. But you can turn your worldly prosperity into a blessing by leaving everything to God, not even seeking to find him except where and when he chooses to reveal himself to you.

You must not wait for freedom and retirement to learn to let go. The prospect of such a time is very visionary—it may never come. We must all be ready, should it so please God, to die in harness. If he forestalls our plans for retirement, we are not our own, and he will require of us only what it is in our power to give. The Israelites by the waters of Babylon longed for Jerusalem, yet how many were there among them who never saw their own beloved country again, but ended their lives in Babylon! How great would their delusion have been if they had postponed hearty, true service to God until they could once more see their native land! It may be that our lot will be like that of those Israelites.

We think we are missing God, but it is self we really miss, for the most trying side of this exciting life of constraint is that we are never free as regards ourselves. It is the lingering spirit of self that would like a quieter state of things in which to enjoy its own intellect and gifts. The self would like to air all its good qualities in the company of a chosen few who would soothe its self-satisfaction. Or, perhaps, the spirit of self makes us wish to enjoy the consolations of religion in peace, just when God wills to send nothing but disturbance and contradiction, the more to mold us to his will.

⇌ 27
GOD'S VARIOUS CROSSES

God is very ingenious in making crosses for us. Some he makes of lead and iron, which are overwhelming in themselves. And some he makes of straw, which seem so light and yet are no less heavy to bear. Others he makes of gold and jewels, the glitter of which dazzles those around and excites the world's envy, but which all the while are as crucifying as the most despised of crosses.

He makes crosses for us of whatever we love best, and turns all to bitterness. High position involves constraint and harassment. It gives things we do not care for, and takes away the things we crave.

The poor man who does not have bread to eat finds a leaden cross in his poverty, but God mingles trouble very much akin to his with the cup of the prosperous. The rich man hungers for freedom and ease just as the poor man hungers for bread. Whereas the poor person can freely knock at every door and call upon every passerby for pity, the person of high estate is ashamed to seek compassion or relief. God very often adds bodily weakness to this moral servitude among the great. Nothing can be more profitable than two such crosses combined: they crucify such persons from head to foot, and teach them their own lack of power and the uselessness of all they possess.

Providence tests us in all manner of ways according to our position. Truly, it is very possible to drink the cup of bitterness amid grandeur and without enduring calamity—indeed, to drink it to the very bitterest dregs out of the golden vessels that adorn the tables of kings! It is God's pleasure in this way to confound human greatness, which is really no more than disguised powerlessness.

Happy are those who seek these things with that illumination of heart of which St. Paul speaks. The trials of high position are more acute than rheumatism or headache! But faith turns them all to good account. It teaches us to look upon all such things as mere bondage, and in our patient acceptance of them it shows us real freedom, which is all the more real because it is hidden to our outward gaze.

The only good point of worldly prosperity is one to which the world is blind—its cross! An elevated position does not save us from any of the ordinary afflictions common to the human condition. Indeed, it has its own special trials, and furthermore, it involves a bondage that prevents people from seeking the relief open to those in a less exalted place. Those who are not in a high place can at least, when ill, see whom they will, and be sheltered from outward disturbance. But public persons must carry their whole cross. They must live for others, when they would prefer to consider their own comfort. In this way God turns the good things that the world covets into trouble and toil, and allows those whom he has raised to earthly grandeur to be an example to others. It is his will to perfect their cross by concealing it beneath the most splendid worldly riches, in order to show what little value there is in prosperity.

Let me repeat, happy are those who in such circumstances learn to see God's hand bruising them in mercy. Surely, it is a blessed thing to find one's purgatory in what seems a paradise to the worldly. In seeking that false paradise, many too often forfeit the hope of a true paradise after this brief life ends.

The one real treasure of great seeming prosperity is its hidden cross.

O cross! Holy cross! May I cling firmly to you! May I worship my Lord as he hangs upon you, and may I die with him to sin and the world forever! Amen.

28
SIMPLICITY AND SELF-CONSCIOUSNESS (I)

There is a simplicity that is merely a fault, and there is a simplicity that is a wonderful virtue. Sometimes it comes from a lack of discernment and an ignorance of what is due others. In the world when people call anyone simple they generally mean a foolish, ignorant, credulous person. But real simplicity, far from being foolish, is almost sublime. All good people like and admire it. They are conscious of sinning against it, observe it in others, and know what it involves, and yet they could not precisely define it. One may apply to it what blessed Thomas à Kempis says in *The Imitation of Christ* about compunction of heart: "I would rather feel it than know how to define it."[11]

I should say that simplicity is an uprightness of soul that prevents self-consciousness. It is not the same as sincerity, which is a much humbler virtue. Many people are sincere who are not simple. They say nothing but what they believe to be true, and do not aim at appearing anything but what they are. But they are continually in fear of passing for something they are not, and so they are forever thinking about themselves, weighing their every word and thought and dwelling upon themselves in fear of having done too much or too little. These people are sincere, but they are not simple. They are not at ease with others, or others with them. There is nothing easy, frank, unrestrained, or natural about them. We feel that we would like less admirable people better, people who are not so stiff! This is how people feel, and God's judgment is the same. He does not like souls that are self-absorbed, and are always, so to speak, looking at themselves in a mirror.

One extreme as opposed to simplicity is to be absorbed in the world around us, never turning a thought within, as is the blind condition of some who are carried away by what is present and tangible. The other extreme is to be self-absorbed in everything, whether it is duty to God or other people, and as a result making us wise in our own conceits—reserved, self-conscious, uneasy at the least thing that disturbs our inward self-complacency. Such false wisdom, in spite of its solemnity, is hardly less vain and foolish than the folly of those who plunge headlong into worldly pleasure. The first are impassioned by their outer surroundings, the others by what they believe themselves to be doing inwardly. But both are in a state of intoxication, and the last is a worse state than the first, because it seems to be wise, though it is not really—and so people do not try to be cured. They rather pride themselves on this state, and feel exalted above others by it. It is a sickness somewhat like insanity—a person may be at death's door while claiming to be well.

Those who are so carried away by outer things that they never look within are in a state of worldly intoxication; and those who dissect themselves continually become affected, and are equally far from being simple.

Real simplicity lies in a happy medium, equally free from thoughtlessness and affectation, in which the soul is not overwhelmed by external things so that it can look within, nor is it given up to the endless introspection that self-consciousness induces. The soul that looks where it is going, without losing time arguing over every step, or looking back perpetually, possesses true simplicity.

⇒ 29
SIMPLICITY AND
SELF-CONSCIOUSNESS (2)

The first step to real simplicity is for the soul to put away outward things and look within so that it can know its own real interests. So far, all is right and natural. This much is only a wise "self-love" that seeks to avoid the intoxication of the world.

In the next step, the soul must add contemplation of God, whom it fears, to contemplation of self. This is a faint approach to real wisdom, but the soul is still greatly self-absorbed. It is not satisfied with fearing God. It wants to be certain that it does fear him, and is afraid that it does not fear him, going round in a perpetual circle of self-consciousness. All this restless dwelling in self is very far from the peace and freedom of real love—that is yet in the distance. The soul must go through a season of trial, and if it were suddenly plunged into a state of rest, it would not know how to use it.

The first humans fell through self-indulgence, and their descendants have to go through much the same course, gradually coming from out of self to seek God. For a while, then, it is well to let the penitent soul struggle with itself and its faults, before attaining the freedom of the children of God. But when God begins to open the heart to something higher and purer, then it is time to follow on the workings of his power step by step until the soul attains true simplicity.

The third step is that, ceasing from a restless self-contemplation, the soul begins to dwell upon God instead. By degrees it forgets itself in him. It becomes full of him and ceases to feed upon itself. Such a soul is not blinded to its own faults or indifferent to its own errors. It is more conscious of them than ever, and increased light shows them in plainer form. But this self-knowledge comes from God, and therefore it is not restless or uneasy.

Much anxious contemplation of its own faults hinders the soul just as travelers are hindered by an excessive quantity of bulky wraps that prevent their walking freely. Superstition and scruples, and even, contrary as it seems at first sight, *presumption*, grow readily out of such self-consuming processes. Real Christian simplicity is generous and upright and forgets itself in unreserved resignation to God. If we mortals expect our earthly friends to be free and open-hearted with us, how much more will God, our best Friend, require a single-hearted, open, unreserved exchange of thoughts and feelings?

Such simplicity is the perfection of God's true children, the object at which we should all aim. The greatest hindrance to its attainment is the false wisdom of the world that is afraid to trust anything to God—that wants to achieve everything by its own skill, to settle everything its own way, and indulge in ceaseless self-admiration. This is the wisdom of the world that St. Paul tells us is foolishness with God.[12] Yet true wisdom, which lies in yielding one's self up unreservedly to God's Holy Spirit, is mere foolishness in the eyes of the world.

In the first stages of conversion, we are forced continually to urge wisdom upon Christians. When they are thoroughly converted, we have to be afraid that they will be "wise," and we need to warn them to "think . . . with sober judgment,"[13] as St. Paul says. When at last they crave a nearer approach to God, they must lose themselves in order to find themselves again in God. They must lay aside that worldly wisdom that is so great a stay to self-reliant natures. They must drain the bitter cup of the "foolishness of the cross," which has so often been the substitute for martyrdom for those who are not called on to shed their blood like the primitive Christians.

Once all self-seeking and brooding is overcome, the soul acquires indescribable peace and freedom. We may write about it, but only experience can really teach anyone what it is. The person who attains it is like a child at its mother's breast, free from fears or longings, ready to be turned this way and that. It is indifferent as to what others may think, except so far as charity always would deliberately avoid scandal. It is always doing everything as well as possible, cheerfully, heartily, but not worried about success or failure. Such a person embodies St. Paul's words: "I care very little if I am judged by you or by any human court; indeed, I do not even judge myself."[14]

⤳ 30
SIMPLICITY AND
SELF-CONSCIOUSNESS (3)

How far most of us are from real simplicity of heart! Still, the farther we are, the more urgently we should seek it. Far from being simple, the greater number of Christians are not even sincere. They are not merely artificial, but often false and dissimulating toward their neighbors, toward God, and toward themselves. What endless little maneuvers and unrealities and inventions people employ to distort truth! The pity is that "all men are liars!"[15] Even those who are naturally upright and sincere, whose disposition is what we call frank and simple, are often jealously self-conscious and foster a pride that destroys all real simplicity. Real simplicity consists in genuine forgetfulness of self.

How can you help being constantly self-engrossed when a crowd of anxious thoughts disturbs you and sets you ill at ease? Do only what is in your own power to do! Never voluntarily give way to these disturbing anxieties. If we are steadfast in resisting them whenever we become conscious of their existence, by degrees we will get free. But do not hunt them out with the notion of conquering them! Do not seek a collision—you will only feed the evil. A continual attempt to repress thoughts of self and self-interest is practically continual self-consciousness, which will only distract us from the duties incumbent on us and deprive us of the sense of God's presence.

The great thing is to resign all our interest, pleasures, comfort, and fame to God. Those who unreservedly accept whatever God may give them in this world—humiliation, trouble, and trial from within or without—have made a great step toward self-victory. They will not dread praise or censure. They will not be sensitive. Or, if they find themselves wincing, they will deal so roughly with their own sensitiveness that it will soon die away. Such full resignation and unfeigned acquiescence is true freedom, and from this arises perfect simplicity. The soul that knows no self-seeking, no hidden motives, is thoroughly candid. It goes straight ahead without any hindrance. Its path opens daily more and more to "perfect day." And its peace, amid whatever troubles beset it, will be as boundless as the depths of the sea. But the soul that still seeks self is constrained, hesitating, smothered by the risings of self-love. Blessed indeed are those who are no longer their own, but have given themselves completely to God!

The world takes the same view as God in relation to a noble, self-forgetting simplicity. The world knows how to appreciate among its own worldly people the easy, simple manners of unselfishness, because there is really nothing more beautiful and attractive than a thorough absence of self-consciousness. But this is out of keeping for worldly people. They rarely forget self unless it is when they are altogether absorbed by still more worthless external interests. Yet, even such simplicity of heart as the world can produce gives us some faint idea of the beauty of the real thing. Those who cannot find the substance sometimes run after the shadows, and shadow though it may be, it attracts them for lack of better things.

Take persons who are full of faults, but not seeking to hide them, not attempting to hide their sin, claiming neither talent, goodness, nor grace, not seeming to think more of themselves than of others, not continually remembering that self to which most of us are so alive. Such persons will be generally liked in spite of many faults. Their spurious simplicity passes as genuine. On the contrary, very clever persons, full of acquired virtues and external gifts, will always be jarring, disagreeable, and repulsive if they seem to be living in perpetual self-consciousness and affectation. So we may safely say that even from the lower point of view, nothing is more attractive or desirable than a simple character free from self-consciousness.

But you will say, am I never to think of myself, or of what affects me? Am I never to speak of myself? No indeed, I would not have you so confined: such an attempt at being simple would destroy all simplicity. What is to be done, then? Make no rules at all, but try to avoid all affectation. When you are disposed to talk about yourself from self-consciousness, thwart the itching desire by quietly turning your attetion to God or to some duty that he sets before you.

Remember, simplicity is free from false shame and mock modesty as well as from ostentation and self-conceit. When you feel inclined to talk about yourself out of vanity, the only thing to be done is to stop short as soon as possible. But if, on the other hand, there is some real reason for doing so, then do not perplex yourself with arguments, but go straight to the point.

You may say, "But what will people think of me? I will seem to be boasting foolishly, to be putting myself forward!"

All such anxious thoughts are not worthy of a moment's attention; learn to speak frankly and simply of yourself as of others when it is necessary, just as St. Paul often speaks of himself in his Epistles. He alludes to his birth and to his Roman citizenship. He says that he is not "in the least inferior to those 'super-apostles.'" He says that he has done even more than all of them, and that he "opposed [Peter] to the face, because he was clearly in the wrong." He says that he was "caught up to paradise, and heard inexpressible things." He says that he strove "always to keep [his] conscience clear before God and man," and that he "worked harder than all of them." He bids the faithful, "Follow my example, as I follow the example of Christ." See with what dignity and simplicity he always speaks of himself, and is able to say even the loftiest things without displaying any emotion of self-consciousness. He describes what concerns himself just as he would describe something that had happened a thousand years ago.

I do not mean that we can or ought all to do the same, but what I do mean is that whenever it is right to speak concerning one's self, it should be done simply. Of course, not everyone can attain to St. Paul's sublime simplicity, and it would be dangerous indeed to affect it. But when there is any real call to speak about yourself in ordinary life, try to do so in all straightforwardness, neither yielding to mock modesty nor to the shamefacedness that belongs to false pride, for indeed false pride often lurks behind a seemingly modest, reserved manner. We do not want to show off our own good points exactly, but we are very glad to let others find them out, so as to get double credit both for our virtues and our modesty in concealing them.

If you want to know how far you are really called upon to think or speak of yourself, consult someone who knows you thoroughly. By doing so, you will avoid self-opinionated decisions, which it is always a great thing to do. A wise spiritual guide will be much more impartial than we can ever be toward ourselves in judging how far we are justified in bringing forward our own good deeds. As for unforeseen occasions rising up suddenly, all you can do is to look to God for immediate guidance, and do unhesitatingly what he seems to indicate. You must act promptly, and even if you are wrong, he will accept your right intention if you have sought with a single heart to do what you believe to be right in his eyes.

As to speaking of one's self in condemnation, I can say little. If a person does so in real simplicity, through a sense of abhorrence and contempt inspired by God, the results have been very marvelous among saints. But ordinarily for us who are not saints, the safest course is never to speak needlessly of one's self either good or bad. Self-love would rather find fault with itself than abide silent and ignored. As to your faults, you should be watchful to correct them. There are many ways of doing this, but as a rule, nothing is more helpful in the attempt than a spirit of recollection, a habit of checking eager longings and impulses, and entire resignation of yourself into God's hand without a constant fretting self-inspection. When God undertakes the work and we do not frustrate him, it goes swiftly.

Such simplicity as this influences all things, including outward manners, and makes people natural and unaffected. You get accustomed to act in a straightforward way, something that is incomprehensible to those who are always self-occupied and artificial. Then even your faults will turn to good, humbling you without depressing you. When God intends to make use of you for his glory, either he will take away your failings or overrule them to his own ends, or at all events, he will so order things that they should not be an obstacle to those among whom he sends you. And practically, those who attain such real inward simplicity generally acquire with it a candid, natural manner, one that may even sometimes appear somewhat too easy and careless, but that will be characterized by a truthful, gentle, innocent, cheerful and calm simplicity, which is exceedingly attractive.

Truly such simplicity is a great treasure! How will we attain it? I would give all I possess for it; it is the costly pearl of Holy Scripture.[16]

31
RULES FOR A BUSY LIFE

You greatly need certain free hours to be given to prayer and recollection. Try to steal some such hours, and be sure that such little parings of time will be your best treasures. Above all, try to save your mornings; defend them like a besieged city! Make vigorous sallies upon all intruders, clear out the trenches, and then shut yourself up within your keep! Even the afternoon is too long a period to let go by without taking a breath.

Recollection is the only cure for your haughtiness, the sharpness of your contemptuous criticism, the onslaughts of your imagination, your impatience with inferiors, your love of pleasure, and all your other faults. It is an excellent remedy, but it needs frequent repetition. You are like a good watch that needs constant winding. Read again the books that moved you: they will do so again, and with greater profit than the first time.

Bear with yourself, avoiding both self-deception and discouragement. This is a medium that is rarely attained. Either people look complacently on themselves and their good intentions, or they despair utterly. Expect nothing of yourself, but expect all things of God. Knowledge of our own hopeless, incorrigible weakness, with unreserved confidence in God's power—these are the true foundations of all spiritual life.

If you do not have much time at your own disposal, do not fail to make good use of every moment you have. It does not require long hours to love God, to renew the consciousness of his presence, to lift up the heart to him or worship him, to offer him all we do or bear. This is the true kingdom of God within us, which nothing can disturb.

32
GOD'S CROSSES ARE SAFER THAN SELF-CHOSEN CROSSES

The crosses that we make for ourselves by overanxiety about the future are not the heaven-sent crosses. We tempt God by our false wisdom, seeking to forestall his arrangements, and struggling to supplement his providence by our own provisions. The fruit of our wisdom is always bitter. God allows it to be so that we may be frustrated when we forsake his fatherly guidance. The future is not ours. We may never have a future, or, if it comes, it may be completely different from all we foresaw. Let us shut our eyes to what God hides from us in the hidden depths of his wisdom. Let us worship without seeing. Let us be silent and lie still.

The crosses actually laid upon us always bring their own special grace and consequent comfort with them. We see the hand of God when the cross is laid upon us. But the crosses brought about by anxious foreboding are altogether beyond God's appointments. We meet them without the special grace adapted to the need—indeed, rather in a faithless spirit, which renders grace impossible. And so everything seems hard and unendurable. All seems dark and helpless, and the soul that indulges in inquisitively tasting forbidden fruit finds nothing but hopeless rebellion and death within.

All this comes from not trusting God, from prying into his hidden ways. "Tomorrow will worry about itself," our Lord has said, and the worry and trouble of each day become good if we leave them to God. What are we that we should ask him, "Why are you doing this?" It is the Lord, and that is enough. It is the Lord: let him do as seems good to him. Let him lift up or cast down. Let him wound or heal. Let him smite or soothe. Let him give life or death: he is always the Lord. We are only his work. Let us throw self aside, and then God's will, unfolding hour by hour, will satisfy us as to all he does in or around us. The contradictions of mortals, their inconstancy, their very injustice will be seen to be the results of God's wisdom, justice, and unfailing goodness. We will see nothing but that infinitely good God, hidden behind the weakness of blind, sinful humanity.

The greatest persons are nothing of themselves, but God is great in them. He uses their caprices, their pride, their pretensions, their vanity, and other wild passions to set forward his everlasting purposes for his elect. He turns everything within and without, the sins of others and our own failings, to our sanctification. Everything in heaven and earth is designed to purify and make us worthy of him. So let us be glad when our heavenly Father puts us to the test with various inward and outward testing. When he surrounds us with external adversities and internal sorrows, let us rejoice, for in this way our faith is tried as gold in the fire. It is this crucial experience that snatches us from self and the world. Let us rejoice, for by such painful work the new self is born in us.

In the trials of life we learn the hollowness and falseness of all that is not God: Hollowness, because there is nothing real where the one sole Good is not present. And falseness, because the world promises and kindles hopes, but gives nothing but emptiness and sorrow of heart.

Unreality must be unreal everywhere. It excites desires and kindles hope, but can never fill the heart. That which is itself empty cannot fill another. The weak, wretched idols of earth cannot impart a strength or happiness that they do not possess themselves. Do people seek to draw water from a dry well? Surely not. Then why should they look for peace and joy from famous or great people who themselves cannot find amusement, and who are consumed with inward weariness amid all their outward display? "Those who make them will be like them,"[17] as the psalmist says of idolaters. Let us fix our hopes higher, further from the casualties of this life.

All that is not God will be found to be vanity and falsehood, and consequently we find both of these in ourselves. What is so vain as our own heart? With what delusions do we not deceive ourselves? Happy is the person who is thoroughly undeceived, but our heart is as vain and false as the outer world. We must not despise that without despising ourselves. We are even worse than the world, because we have received greater things from God. Let us endure patiently if the world fails or misuses us, since we have so often failed or misused God, grieving his Spirit of grace. The more the world disgusts us, the more it is furthering God's work, and while seeking to harm us, it will help us.

"And the peace of God, which transcends all understanding, will guard your hearts and your minds in Christ Jesus."[18] Cut away every root of bitterness, and cast aside whatever disturbs the simple peace and trust of a child of God. Turn to your Father in every care; bury yourself in that tender heart, where nothing can fail you. Rejoice in hope, and casting aside the world and the flesh, taste the pure joys of the Holy Spirit.

May your faith be unmoved amid every storm, and may you ever remember the words of the great Apostle, "In all things God works for good to those who love him, who have been called according to his purpose."[19]

ᔈ 33
LUKEWARMNESS

Nothing is harder to bear than lukewarmness and lack of a conscious inward life. But it seems to me you have only two things to do, one of which is to avoid whatever excites and scatters you. In this way you can cut off the source of dangerous distractions, which dry up prayer.

You cannot expect to find interior nourishment if you live only for what is exterior. Strict watchfulness in giving up whatever makes you too eager and impetuous in conversation is an absolute necessity if you want to gain the spirit of recollection and prayer. No one can have a relish for both God and the world simultaneously, and whatever spirit you have carried about with you through the day's occupations you will carry to the appointed hours of prayer.

Then, after cutting down whatever excesses distract your mind, you must try very often to renew the presence of God, even amid those occupations that are right and necessary, guarding against your self-will. Try continually to act by the leadings of grace and in the spirit of self-renunciation. By degrees you will come to it, by frequently checking your impulsiveness and listening attentively to God's voice within, letting him possess you completely.

⇒ 34
THE USE OF SEASONS OF SPIRITUAL PEACE

When God gives you inward as well as outward peace, I pray that he who has begun this good work in you may fulfill it to the day of the coming of Christ. What you need then is to make use of these peaceful days to grow in recollection. You ought to sing with your whole heart the Amen and Alleluia that reecho in the heavenly Jerusalem. This is a token of continual acceptance of God's will, and the unreserved sacrifice of your will to his.

At the same time, you should hearken inwardly to God with a heart free from all flattering prejudices of self-love, so that you may faithfully receive his light as to anything that needs correction. As soon as he points these out, yield without argument or excuse, and give up whatever touches the jealous love of the Bridegroom without reserve.

Those who yield in this manner to the Spirit of grace will see imperfection in their purest deeds and an inexhaustible fund of refined evil in their hearts. All this leads us in dismay at ourselves to cry out that God alone is good. We strive to correct ourselves calmly and simply, but continuously and steadfastly, and we do so even more because our heart is undivided and peaceful. We reckon on nothing as of ourselves, and hope only in God. We give way neither to self-delusion nor to laxity. We know that God never fails us, though we often fail him. We yield ourselves completely to grace, and above all things dread any resistance to it. We blame ourselves without being discouraged. We bear with ourselves while striving to amend.

ꙅ 35
THE DANGERS OF INTELLECTUAL ATTRACTIONS

In your obedience, do not trust too much in your intellect. Do not obey an advisor because he can argue more forcibly or speak more feelingly than others, but because he is providentially ordered for you and has been set over you naturally, or because apart from all else you feel that he more than others is able to help you conquer your infirmities and lead you to self-renunciation.

Would that I could teach you true poverty of spirit! Remember what St. Paul says, "We are fools for Christ, but you are so wise in Christ!"[20] I would like to see in you no wisdom but that of grace, which leads faithful souls in the sure way when they do not yield to temper, to passions or self-will, or to any merely natural impulse. To such faithful souls, all that the world calls talent, taste, and good reasoning is as nothing.

Let me repeat: beware of your own intellectual gifts and those of others. Judge no one according to them. God, the only wise Judge, takes a very different tack: he gives preference to children and the childlike mind. Read nothing out of mere curiosity or in order to confirm your own opinions. Rather, read with a view to foster a hearty spirit of meekness and submission.

Be as frank as a child toward those who counsel you. Make no count at all of your enlightenments or your extraordinary graces. Abide in simple faith, content to be obscure and unremitting in obedience to God's commandments. Act on whatever God may make known to you through others, and accept meekly whatever may seem strange to you.

Self-forgetfulness should take the shape of crushing out self-will, not of neglecting the watchfulness that is essential to the real love of God.

The greater your love, the more jealously you will watch over yourself, so that nothing may creep in that is unworthy of that love.

⤳ 36
THE USE OF TIME

There is a wide difference between the mind's conviction and the right disposition of the heart, resulting in diligent, dutiful practice.

One meets with many souls who are most perfect and saintly in what they believe, but "by their fruit you will recognize them,"[21] the Savior of the world has said. This is the only sure rule, if it is fairly dealt with, and by this we must judge ourselves.

Time bears a very different aspect at different seasons of one's life, but there is one maxim that applies equally to all seasons: No time should go by uselessly. All time forms a part of the order, a link in the chain of God's providence. Every season carries with it various duties of God's own appointing, and we must give account to him of how we have done them, since from the first to the last moment of life, God never means us to look upon any time as purposeless.

The important thing is to know how he would have us use it. And this is to be learned, not by restless, fidgety eagerness, which is more likely to confuse than enlighten us, but by a pure, upright heart, simply seeking God and being diligent in resisting the deceits and wiles of self-love as quickly as we recognize them. For remember, we waste time not only by doing nothing or doing amiss, but also by doing things that are in themselves right yet are not what God would have us do. We are strangely ingenious in perpetual self-seeking; and the things that worldly people do overtly, those who want to serve God sometimes do with more refinement, under some pretext that hides the faultiness of their conduct.

One general rule for the right use of time is to accustom yourself to live in continual dependence upon God's Holy Spirit, receiving whatever he wills to give from one moment to another, referring all doubts to him. Where an immediate course of action has to be taken, seek strength in him—lift up your heart to him whenever you become aware that outward things are leading you away, or tending toward forgetfulness of God.

Blessed is the soul that by sincere self-renunciation abides always in its Creator's hands, ready to do whatever he wills, not weary of saying a hundred times daily, "Lord, what will you have me do? Teach me to do your will, for you are my God. Send forth your light, Lord, to guide me; teach me to use the present time to your service. Forgive the misuse of what is past, and may I never blindly count on an uncertain future."

As to business and outward duties, we need only to give straightforward, diligent heed to the ordering of God's providence. As all such duties are the result of his plans, we have only to accept them dutifully, submitting our own dispositions, fancies, and inclinations, our self-will, perfectionism, and restless anxieties, our hurry—in short, all our own natural impulses to do what we like. Take care not to let yourself be overwhelmed by outer things or be utterly immersed in external interests, however important.

Every undertaking should be begun with a definite view to God's glory, continued quietly, and ended without excitement or impatience.

Time spent in society and amusement is generally the time that is most dangerous to one's self, though it may be very useful to others. Be on your guard, that is to say, be more faithful in remembering the presence of God at such times. You need then especially to cultivate the watchfulness so often urged by our Lord—to use aspirations and liftings up of your heart to him, as the only source of strength and safety; otherwise you can scarcely hope to be kept from the subtle venom so often lurking amid society and its pleasures, or to be really useful to others.

Spare time is often the most pleasant and the most useful as concerns one's self. It can hardly be put to a better use than that of renewing your strength (bodily as well as mentally) through secret communion with God. Prayer is so necessary and is the source of so much blessing, that when once the soul has realized its gifts, it will hardly fail to seek them over and over as often as it is free to do so.

⤺ 37
THE LOVING SEVERITY OF GOD

Strict as God seems to be in his dealings with us, he never inflicts any suffering solely to give pain. He always has the purification of the soul in view. The severity of the operation is caused by the depth of the malady to be cured. God would not cut if there were no sore. He only probes the ulcerated proud flesh. So, after all, it is our own destructive self-will that is the cause of what we suffer, and God's hand deals as gently with us as possible. But how deep our malady, how malignant our souls must be, since all the time he spares us so tenderly, yet puts us to such grievous pain!

Again, just as God wounds only for our healing, in the same way he never deprives us of any of his gifts, except to restore them a hundred times over. In his love, he takes away even his purest gifts if we are using them wrongly; and the purer those gifts the more jealous he is that we should not reckon them as our own or take credit to ourselves for them. The most notable graces turn to deadly poison if we rest upon them in self-complacent security. This was the sin of the fallen angels. As soon as they looked upon their exalted state as their own assured possession, they became the enemies of God and were driven away from his kingdom.

We may learn from this how little we humans understand the real nature of sin. Presumption is the greatest of all sins, yet there are only a few souls who are so pure as to enjoy God's gifts without any intermixture of selfish complacency. In thinking of God's graces, self is almost always uppermost. We are troubled when we realize our own weakness. We take delight in conscious strength. We seldom weigh our own perfection solely with a view to God's glory, as we might do that of another person. We are saddened and depressed when conscious sweetness and grace forsake us. In short, we are almost always thinking not of God, but of self.

And so all our good things need purifying, so that they will not foster a merely natural life in us. Our corrupt nature finds a very subtle food in the graces that are most opposed to nature. Self-love is fed, not merely by humiliations and austerities, by fervent prayer and mortification—but even by the fullest self-renunciation and utter sacrifice. There is an infinite amount of moral strength in the thought that we have no strength at all and that amid such a horrible trial we are still yielding ourselves up unreservedly. And so, to make the sacrifice real, we must give up even our satisfaction in our sacrifice!

The only way to find God truly is in this readiness to part with all his gifts, this thorough sacrifice of self and of all inward resources. God's exceeding jealousy exacts it, and you can easily see how we never lose ourselves in him until all else fails us. A man who is falling into an abyss is not completely cast down as long as he can clutch hold of the sides. And self-love, even when God overthrows it, clutches in its despair at every gleam of hope, like a drowning person grasping at straws.

You must learn to realize the necessity of this deprivation of all God's gifts, which he gradually works out. There is no gift, however precious, that, after having been a help, will not become a snare and a hindrance to the soul that rests in it; and so God often takes away what he has given. However, he does not take it away completely. He often deprives us of something only in order to restore it more fully and without the evil spirit of self-satisfaction that had unconsciously gained possession of us. The self-satisfaction is overthrown by the loss, and then he restores the gift a hundred times over. Then the soul loses sight of the gift and sees only God.

⇒ 38
DRYNESS AND DEADNESS IN PRAYER

The soul, being diseased through self-love, cannot receive and rightly use a conscious strength. It is necessary therefore for God to conceal its strength, its growth, and its good desires. Or, if it is permitted to see these things, they must be seen as only a faint perception, so vague that the soul cannot rely on them. Even though it sees these gifts only faintly, it is prone to view them with vain self-satisfaction, in spite of the humiliating uncertainty.

What would the soul not do if it were really able to see clearly the grace that fills it? Therefore, God does two things for the soul, while he does only one for the body. To the body, he gives nourishment together with the hunger and pleasure in eating, all of which are conscious. To the soul, however, he gives the hunger of desire and food, but while giving these gifts, he hides them, so the soul will not derive self-satisfaction through them. In this way, when purifying us through testing, he deprives us of delight, of conscious zeal, of acutely felt desires. As the soul in its pride turned all conscious power to poison, God reduces it to feel nothing but dullness, distaste, weakness, temptation. Notwithstanding these feelings, the soul always receives real help. It is warmed, kindled, upheld in perseverance—but without the conscious enjoyment of all this.

St. Teresa observes that many souls give up prayer as soon as they cease to find conscious pleasure in it, whereas this is to give up prayer just when it is on the way to being perfected. True prayer is not a matter of sense or imagination, but of the mind and will. But one may easily make mistakes in speaking of pleasure and delight. There is a pleasure that is altogether vague and indeliberate, that does not proceed from the will. And there is a deliberate pleasure, which is nothing more than a steadfast will. And this delight that comes of the deliberate will is that of which the psalmist says, "Delight yourself in the LORD and he will give you the desires of your heart."[22] This delight is inseparable from all real prayer, because it is in itself prayer.

This is not always accompanied by that other delight, the involuntary one that we can feel. The "deliberate pleasure" may be most real, and yet not give any emotional consolation. Sometimes souls that are the most severely tested may retain the delight of the will in an utterly dry prayer without conscious pleasure. Otherwise we would be reduced to saying that souls are perfected in God's ways only to the degree to which they feel their pleasure in virtue increasing, and that all souls deprived of conscious pleasure by a time of trial have lost the love of God and are under delusion.

This would be to upset everything, and measure all piety by the imagination, which would lead to the most dangerous fanaticism, with everyone deciding our own degree of perfection by the degree of our pleasure and taste. Moreover, this is really done consciously by some souls. They seek nothing but pleasure and satisfaction in prayer, and give themselves up to feeling, believing nothing to be real but what they feel and imagine—becoming mere enthusiasts. If they have a fit of fervor, they will enter upon and deal with anything. Nothing stops them. No authority can restrain them. But if this conscious fervor dies out, immediately such souls are disheartened, grow slack, and fall away.

Such souls feel that they have to be perpetually beginning again. They turn like a weather vane with every wind. They follow Jesus Christ only for the miraculous loaves and fishes. They demand quails in the desert. They are forever crying out like St. Peter on the Mount of Transfiguration, "It is good for us to be here."[23] Happy is the soul that is faithful equally in conscious abundance and in the most severe privation. That soul will be "like Mount Zion, which cannot be shaken but endures forever."[24]

Such a soul eats the daily bread of pure faith, neither seeking the enjoyment of anything that God denies it nor the sight of anything he conceals. It is content to believe what the church has taught it, to love God with a simple will, and to do, at all costs, whatever the Gospel commands or counsels. If satisfaction—in prayer and communion with God—is given, it accepts it as a help to its own weakness. If not, it bears the privation quietly and keeps on loving.

Clinging to what is perceptible to the senses or to the intellect leads at one time to discouragement, at another to illusion. Those who lose their conscious enjoyment of spiritual things without any fault of their own suffer just as a child does when its mother weans it. Dry bread is less pleasant, but more strengthening than milk. A tutor's correction is more profitable than the pampering of a nurse.

We may be sure that we never need to pray so earnestly as when we cannot lay hold of any pleasure in prayer. That is the season of testing and trial, and consequently the time for the most earnest recourse to God in urgent prayer. On the other hand, it is good to accept all feeling of devotion very simply, as being given in order to feed, comfort, and strengthen the soul. The soul must never count on such sweetness, for in such feelings the imagination often has its share in flattering us. Let us follow Jesus to his cross like St. John. In so doing we will never be deceived. It is easy to say to ourselves, "I love God with all my heart," when we are conscious of nothing but pleasure in such love. But true love is the one that suffers while loving: "Though he slay me, yet will I hope in him!"[25]

⮌ 39
PEACE OF CONSCIENCE

There is never any peace for those who resist God. If there is any happiness in this world, it belongs to those whose conscience is pure. The whole earth is only pain and anguish to the evil conscience.

How different God's peace is from the one that the world assumes, but cannot really give! God's peace quiets all passion and ensures purity of conscience. It unites a soul to God, and strengthens us against temptation. This purity of conscience is preserved by partaking frequently of the sacrament. All temptation, when resisted, bears its fruit for good. Peace of heart lies in perfect acceptance of God's will.

"Martha, Martha, you are worried and upset about many things, but only one thing is needed."[26] True simplicity, the calmness that results from complete submission to whatever God wills, patience and forbearance toward the faults of others, frankness in confessing your faults, accepting reproof, and receiving counsel—these are the solid graces that will serve as helpful resources toward your sanctification.

Anxiety comes from not sufficiently accepting whatever happens as coming from God. From the moment you give up all self-will, and seek absolutely nothing but what he wills, you will be free from all your restless anxiety and calculating the future. There will be nothing to conceal. Short of that you will be uneasy, changeable, easily upset, dissatisfied with yourself and with others, full of reserve and mistrust. Your talents, unless chastened and humbled, will only torment you. Your piety, though sincere, will do more in the way of inward reproach than of support and consolation. But once you give yourself up to God, you will be at rest, and you will be filled with the joys of his Holy Spirit.

We are constrained to love God because he first loved us, and that with a tender love, as a Father who pities his children, knowing their frailty and the clay out of which he has formed them. He sought us in our own paths, which are sin. He followed us as a shepherd wearies himself in seeking his lost sheep. He is not content with finding us. Having found us, he carries us and our weariness. He loved us unto death, and his obedience can be measured only by his love.

When a soul is filled with that love, it will enjoy peace of conscience and be content and happy. It will need neither greatness, nor fame, nor pleasure, nor anything that passes away. It will crave nothing but the will of God, but will watch continually in a blessed expectation of the Bridegroom's coming.

40
SLACKNESS

St. John wrote to the Church at Ephesus: "Yet I hold this against you: You have forsaken your first love. Remember the height from which you have fallen! Repent and do the things you did at first. If you do not repent, I will come to you and remove your lampstand from its place."[27] It is in this way that God's Holy Spirit loves mortals without flattering them. He loves, yet threatens, but his very threats are love. He holds out a penalty, so that we may not force him to inflict it.

How easily the best people fall gradually away without noticing it! Here is Timothy—said to be Bishop of Ephesus—whom St. Paul addresses as a "man of God,"[28] the angel of one of the holiest churches in the East in those days of religious prosperity. Yet this angel falls. He has forsaken his first love,[29] his recollection, his prayer, his good works. He grows lax and careless. At first he does not perceive his wanderings or his fall. He says to himself, "What harm am I doing? Is not my conduct upright and regular in the world's eyes? Must one not have some pleasure? It is hardly worth living without something to cheer and amuse myself!" It is in this way that people cleverly deceive themselves, and disguise their backsliding. But the Holy Spirit invites them to hasten to open their eyes, and see "the height from which they have fallen."

How far you are below your former standard! Remember the fervency of your prayers, your love of solitude, your jealous watch over your quiet time, and the strictness with which you deliberately avoided whatever could interfere with it. If you do not remember, others have not forgotten, and do not fail to ask, "What has become of all that fervor? There is nothing to be seen now but the love of amusement and pleasure, and a restless inward boredom when there is a pause in these things. This is not the same person."

This is how, without being aware of it, people fall by degrees. Under plausible pretenses they go from a state of sincere self-denial into a laxity that revives all the worst forms of selfishness. You should try to "remember the height from which you have fallen,"[30] and mourn over the "first love" that fostered you. You must try to resume those "things you did at first," which you have exchanged in such a slothful way for mere vanities. You must gaze from afar on the desert in which you dwelt at peace with the true Comforter. You must say with the prodigal son,

"I will set out and go back to my father and say to him: Father, I have sinned against heaven and against you. I am no longer worthy to be called your son."[31] If you fail in returning swiftly to his fatherly breast, you heard what he would do: "I will come to you and remove your lampstand from its place."[32] He would take away the light that you do not use, and leave you in darkness. He would transfer his precious gifts that you have trodden underfoot to some truer, more obedient soul. You must resume your reading, your prayers, your silence, your former simplicity and lowliness.

41
OPENNESS AND CANDOR

Nothing is more useful than speaking out freely. Open your heart; we heal our woes by not holding them fast. We learn simplicity and yieldedness, for people are reserved only about things that they do not mean to give up. Finally, we humble ourselves, for nothing is more humbling than to open our hearts and lay bare all our weaknesses, yet nothing draws down a greater blessing.

I do not mean that you should always tell everything you may be thinking with scrupulous exactness. This would be endless, and you would be forever uneasy for fear of having forgotten something. Simply keep back nothing out of untruthfulness or false shame of self-love, which would never willingly show anything but its fair side. So if you never intend to keep back anything, you may safely say less or more, as seems best for the occasion.

It is not a question of feelings, but of the will. Often our feeling does not depend at all upon ourselves. God takes it away purposely that we may feel our poverty, that we may learn to accept the cross of inner dryness, and that we may undergo the purification of clinging to him without any conscious consolation. Then he restores to us the comfort of warm feelings from time to time out of pity for our weakness.

Try to take an attitude toward God, not of forced conversation such as you maintain with persons toward whom you stand on ceremony and address in a mere complimentary fashion, but such as you observe toward a dear friend with whom you are under no restraint, and who is under none with you. Such friends meet and talk and listen, or are silent, content to be together saying nothing. They do not weigh what they will say. They insinuate nothing and have no hidden agenda. Everything comes out in truth and love regardless of how it is said. Nothing is held back, perverted, or dressed up. They are just as well satisfied one day when a little has been said as another when there was plenty to say.

We can never be as real with our best earthly friends as fully as we could wish, but we can be so to any extent with God, if only we will not hem ourselves in with our own self-love. It will not do to pay him visits, as if we were discharging a debt due to society. We must abide with him in the privacy of servants, or better still, of children. Be with him as you would have your child be with you, and then you will never be weary.

⇒ 42
PATIENCE
UNDER CONTRADICTION

A heated imagination, strong feelings, a world of argument, and a flow of words are really useless. The practical thing is to act in a spirit of detachment, doing what we can by God's light, and being content with such success as he gives.

Such continuous death to self is a blessed life that only a few bring into concrete existence. A single word quietly spoken under such influences will go further, even in worldly matters, than the most eager, bustling exertions. It is the Spirit of God, speaking with his own strength and authority. He enlightens, persuades, touches, edifies. Scarcely anything has been said, but everything has been done.

On the contrary, when people let loose their natural excitability, they talk interminably, and indulge in endless, subtle, superfluous imaginations. They are afraid of not saying or doing enough. They get warm and excited. They exhaust themselves without anything being the better for it.

Let the river flow beneath its bridges. Let people be themselves: weak, vain, inconstant, unjust, false, presumptuous. Let the world be the world, in other words. You cannot hinder it. Let everybody follow their natural disposition and habits. You cannot remold them. It is easier to leave them alone and bear with them. Accustom yourself to put up with unreasonableness and injustice.

Abide tranquilly in God's bosom.* He sees all these evils more clearly than you do, yet he allows them. Be content with doing well what little depends upon you, and let everything else be as though it did not exist.

---

*We must keep such advice in perspective. This is not counsel to irresponsible passivity, but to letting go of the urge to control, or to fret uselessly over what we cannot change.

⇒ 43
BEARING INSULTS

You greatly need God's Holy Spirit to guide you in your difficulties, and to moderate your natural vehemence under circumstances that are calculated to excite it.

As to those who have caused this difficulty, I think you should speak of that to no one but God in prayer on behalf of the person who insulted you. People are not killed by a blow on the extremities—the nails or the hair—but by an injury to the vital parts. When God purposes to make us die to self, he always touches the thing that is the very essence of our life. He adapts our cross to each one of us.

Let yourself be humbled. Calm and silence under humiliation are a great benefit to the soul. We are sometimes tempted to talk about humility, and it is easy to find plenty of opportunities for doing so, but it is better to be humbly silent. Talkative humility is always suspicious: talk is a certain relief to self-conceit.

Do not get angry about what people say. Let them talk while you try to do God's will. As to the will of other people, you could never come to an end of satisfying it, nor is it worth the trouble. Silence, peace, and union with God ought to comfort you under whatever people may falsely say. You must be friendly to them without counting on their friendship. They come and go. Let them go—they are just like chaff scattered by the wind.

Only see God's hand in what they do. He wounds or comforts us by using them. You need all your resolution, but at the same time your quickness of temper requires checks and impediments. Possess your soul in patience.

Frequently recall the presence of God, so as to calm yourself, to humble and adapt yourself to the humble of heart. Nothing is really great except lowliness, charity, mistrust of self, and detachment from one's own opinions and will. All stiff, harsh goodness is contrary to Jesus Christ.

⇒ 44
FREEDOM FROM SELF

As long as we are centered in self, we will be prey to the contradiction, the wickedness, and the injustice of others. Our temper brings us into collision with other tempers. Our passions clash with those of our neighbors. Our wishes are so many tender places open to the shafts of those around. Our pride, which is incompatible with our neighbors', rises like the waves of a stormy sea. Everything arouses, attacks, and rebuffs us. We are exposed on all sides by the sensitiveness of passion and the jealousy of pride.

We cannot look for peace within when we are at the mercy of a mass of greedy, insatiable longings, and when we can never satisfy that "me" that is so keen and touchy as to whatever concerns it. Hence in our dealings with others we are like a bedridden invalid who cannot be touched anywhere without pain. A sickly self-love cannot be touched without screaming—the mere tip of a finger seems to terrify it! Then add to this the roughness of neighbors in their ignorance of self, their disgust at our infirmities (which is at least as great as ours toward theirs), and you soon find all the children of Adam tormenting each other, each embittering the other's life.

And this martyrdom of self-love you will find in every nation, every town, every community, every family, often between friends.

The only remedy is to renounce self. If we set self aside and lose sight of it, we will have nothing to lose, to fear, or to consider. Then we will find that true peace that is given to people of good will, that is, those who have no will except God's, which has become theirs.

Then no one will be able to harm us. They can no longer attack us through hopes or fears, for we will be ready for everything, and we will refuse nothing. And this is to be inaccessible, invulnerable to the enemy. People can do only what God permits, and whatever God permits them to do against us becomes our will, because it is God's. By doing this, we will store our treasure so high that no human hand can reach to assail it. Our good name may be tarnished, but we consent, knowing that if God humbles us, it is good to be humbled. Friendship fails us: Well! it is because the one true Friend is jealous of all others, and sees fit to loosen our ties. We may be worried, inconvenienced, distressed—but it is God, and that is enough. We love the Hand that delivers the blow; there is peace beneath all our woes, a blessed peace.

We desire nothing that is denied us; and the more absolute this self-renunciation, the deeper our peace. Any lingering wishes and clingings disturb it. If every bond were broken, our freedom would be boundless. Let contempt, pain, or death overwhelm me, still I hear Jesus Christ saying, "Do not be afraid of those who kill the body but cannot kill the soul."[33] They are powerless indeed. Even though they can destroy life, their day is soon over. All they can do is break the earthen vessel, and kill that which voluntarily dies daily. Anticipate somewhat the welcome deliverance, and then the soul will escape from their hands into the heart of God, where all is unchanging peace and rest.

⤙ 45
THE PRESENCE OF GOD

The real mainspring of all perfection you will find contained in the precept given in ages past by God to Abraham: "Walk before me, and be blameless."[34] The presence of God will calm your spirit—it will give you peaceful nights, and tranquilize your mind even amid the hardest day's work. But then, for this to happen, you must give yourself up unreservedly to God. When once you have found God, you will realize that you need not seek anything more among people. You must be ready to sacrifice even your dearest friendships, for the best of friends is the One who indwells hearts. He is like a jealous bridegroom, who will tolerate no rival near him.

You do not need much time to love God, to renew the thought of his presence frequently, to lift up your heart to him and worship him in the depths of your heart, to offer him all you do and all you suffer. This is the real kingdom of God within you,[35] and nothing can disturb it.

If outward distractions and your own lively imagination hinder your soul from conscious recollection, in any case you must practice it in your will. In doing this the *desire* for recollection will become in itself a kind of recollection that will be of advantage, especially if you turn resolutely toward God and to whatever he requires of you with a steadfast intention.

Try at intervals to kindle within yourself a hearty desire to give yourself to God to the fullest extent of all your powers. Give your mind to know and think about him, and your will to love him. Endeavor to consecrate all your outward actions to him. Be on your guard not to let yourself be engrossed too entirely, or for any length of time, with anything external or interior that so distracts your heart and mind as to make it difficult for you to turn fully toward God.

The moment you feel that any outside object causes you too much pleasure or delight, sever your heart from it, and for fear that you might stop short in the world, turn yourself at once to your only true end and sovereign good, God himself. If you are steadfast in breaking off all worship of created things, and in reserving to God alone the love and reverence that he requires, you will soon experience the true happiness that he never fails to give to the soul that holds loosely to all earthly affections. When you are conscious that you are longing very earnestly for anything whatsoever, or that you are too keenly excited about anything in which you are engaged, whether great or small, try to pause and remember that God himself tells us his Holy Spirit is not to be found in the storm or the whirlwind. Be watchful not to throw yourself too actively into all that is going on or to let yourself become too engrossed by it, for this is one great source of distractions.

As soon as you have made certain what the Lord would have you to do in each matter as it arises, stop there, and pay no attention to all the rest. By doing this you will be able to keep your mind calm and composed, and you can shake off an infinity of useless matters that hamper the soul and hinder it from turning fully to God.

One excellent method of maintaining inward calmness and freedom is to keep putting aside all useless reflections on the past, whether of regret or self-satisfaction. When one duty is accomplished, go steadily on with the next, confining your attention entirely to the one thing God gives you to do, and not putting off difficulties for the future any more than dwelling on regrets for the past. Again, accustom yourself to make frequent brief acts of God's presence through the day amid all your activities. Whenever you are conscious that anxiety or disturbance are springing up within, calm yourself in this way: Cut yourself off from all that is not of God. Cut short useless thoughts and broodings. Avoid unprofitable talk. If you seek for God within your heart, you will find him without fail, and with him you will find peace and happiness.

As to your activities, try even in those to let God have the largest share. If you would fulfill your most common duties well, you must do them as in his presence and for his sake. The sight of his majesty and love will calm and strengthen you. A word from the Lord stilled the raging of the sea,[36] and a glance from us to him, and from him to us, will do the same in our daily life.

Lift up your heart continually to God. He will purify, enlighten, and direct it. Try to be able to say with the holy King David, "I have set the LORD always before me,"[37] and again, "Whom have I in heaven but you? And earth has nothing I desire besides you. . . . God is the strength of my heart and my portion for ever."[38] Do not wait till you can be alone to seek a recollected mind. The moment you become conscious of having lost recollection, strive to renew it.

Turn to God simply, familiarly, trustfully. This can be done even amid the greatest interruptions, even when you are wearied and pestered with uncongenial society. In all things, to be sure, "God works for the good of those who love him."[39]

You must be regular with such spiritual reading as is suited to your needs, making frequent pauses to hearken to the Voice that will help to call your inner self to recollection. A very few words studied in this way are a true manna to the soul. You may forget the actual words, but they are taking root all the time secretly, and your soul will feed upon them and be strengthened.

⁓ 46
SEEING OURSELVES IN GOD'S LIGHT

Forgetfulness of self does not interfere with gratitude for God's gifts. Such forgetfulness does not lie in being unmindful of anything we possess, but rather in never confining ourselves to the contemplation of self, or dwelling upon our own good or evil in an exclusive or personal fashion. All such self-occupation severs us from pure and simple love, narrows the heart, and sets us further from true perfection.

But though we may forget ourselves, we will not fail often to see ourselves as we truly are. We will not contemplate self out of egotism, but as we contemplate God there will often be a side light, so to speak, thrown upon ourselves. This is what happens when we stand looking at the reflection of another person in a large mirror: while looking for that other person we also see ourselves without seeking to do so. And in this way we often see ourselves clearly in the pure light of God. The presence of God in purity and simplicity, sought after in very faithfulness, is like that large mirror, in which we discern even the tiniest spot that flecks our soul.

A peasant who has never passed beyond his own poor village only faintly realizes its poverty. But set him amid splendid palaces and courts, and he will perceive how squalid his own home is and how pathetic his rags are compared with such magnificence. Even so we realize our own loathsomeness and unworthiness when brought face to face with the beauty and greatness of God.

Talk as much as you will of the vanity and emptiness of the world, the shortness and uncertainty of life, the inconstancy of fortune and friends, the delusions of grandeur, life's inevitable and bitter disappointments, the failure of bright hopes, the emptiness of all we attain, and the pain of the evils we endure: all these things, true and just as they are, do not touch the heart. They do not reach far enough or alter people's lives. People sigh over the bondage of vanity, yet they do not seek to break their bonds.

But let one ray of heavenly light penetrate within, and immediately seeing the depth of goodness, which is God, they likewise see the depth of evil, and know what fallen creatures they are. Then they despise themselves, and they hate, shun, fear, and renounce self. They throw themselves upon God and are lost in him. Truly such people's loss is a blessed one, for they find themselves without seeking. They have no more selfish interests, but everything turns to their profit, for everything turns to good to those who love God. They see the mercies that flow into their weakness, sin, and nothingness. They see and rejoice.

And here observe that those who have not as yet made any great progress in self-renunciation still see all these mercies very much in relation to their personal interests. For a thorough setting aside of self-will is so rare in this life that very few souls are able to look at the mercies they have received from anything but their own point of view. They rejoice in the all-powerful hand that has saved them, so to speak, in spite of themselves.

But really pure, completely self-detached souls, such as are the saints in heaven, would feel the same joy and love over the mercies poured forth on others as on themselves. For, completely forgetting self, they would love the good pleasure of God, the riches of his grace, and his glory, as displayed in the sanctification of others as much as in their own. Everything would be the same, because "I" ceased to be. It would be no more "I" than another, but God alone in everything, to be loved, adored, and the sole joy of true, disinterested love. Such souls are rapt in wonder at God's mercies, not for their own sake, but for love of God. They thank him that he has done his will and glorified himself, even as in the Lord's Prayer we ask that his will may be done, and that his kingdom may come.

But short of this blessed state, the soul is touched with gratitude for the benefits of which it is conscious. And just as nothing is more dangerous than any attempt to soar beyond what God has called us to, so nothing is more harmful to the spiritual life than to lose sight of such sustenance as is suitable to our actual needs by aiming at a higher standard of perfection than is suited to us. When the soul feels deeply moved with gratitude for all God has done for it, such gratitude should be cherished carefully, waiting till the time when God may see fit to purify it still more from all elements of self.

The child who attempts to walk alone before its time is sure to fall. Let us be content to live on gratitude, being sure that though there may be a mingling of self-interest in it, it will strengthen our heart. Let us love God's mercies, not merely for himself and his glory, but for ourselves and our eternal happiness. If eventually God should enlarge our hearts to contain a purer, more generous love, a love more unreservedly his, then we may safely and unhesitatingly yield to that more perfect love.

Therefore while you adore God's mercy and are filled with wondering admiration at it, while you long above all things to fulfill his will, while you marvel at the goodness with which he has made a lump of clay that seemed "for common use" into pottery for noble purposes,[40] pour out the most abundant thanksgiving of which you are capable. And remember that the purest of all God's gifts is the power to love them all for his sake, not for your own.

47
BEING DEPRIVED OF CONSCIOUS SWEETNESS

You must accustom yourself to privation: the great trouble it causes shows how much it is needed. It is only because we cling to light, sweetness, and enjoyment that it is so necessary that we should be stripped of all these things. As long as the soul clings to any consolation, it needs to be stripped of it. Undoubtedly the God we feel to be beneficent and indulgent is still God, but it is God with his gifts. God surrounded with darkness, privation, and desolation is God without anything else. When a mother wants to attract her little one, she comes to him, her hands full of toys and sugarplums. But the father approaches his grownup son without any presents. God goes still further: he veils his face, he hides his presence, and often he visits only those he seeks to perfect through the utter darkness of simple faith.

God does not intend either to spoil or discourage you. Give yourself up then to the changes that so upset your soul. By accustoming the soul to having no enduring condition, these changes make it supple and plastic to receive whatever impression God wills. It is God's way of melting and molding your heart so that all the outlines of self are lost. Pure water has neither color nor form: it always takes the form and color of the vessel containing it. Let this be your case with God.

≈ 48
CONFORMITY TO THE WILL OF GOD (1)

In *The Imitation of Christ* you will find several marvelous chapters on conformity to God's will. The whole gist of the matter lies in our will, and this is what our dear Lord meant by saying, "The kingdom of God is within you."[41] It is not a question of how much we know, how clever we are, nor even how good. It all depends upon the heart's love. Actions are the results of love—they are the fruit it bears. But the source, the root of love lies in the deep recesses of the heart. Some virtues are suitable to one condition in life, some to another. Some are suitable to one season, some to another. But at all seasons and in all places we need a will that is good.

That kingdom of God within us consists in always willing whatever God wills, completely and unreservedly. It is in this way that our prayer "thy kingdom come" is fulfilled. It is in this way that "his will is done in earth as in heaven." It is in this way that we become identified with him. Blessed are the poor in spirit. Blessed are those who strip themselves of all they can call their own, even their will, for this it is to be truly poor in spirit.

But how, you ask, are you to acquire this saintly will? By absolute conformity to that of God. By willing what he wills and desiring nothing that he does not will. By nailing, so to speak, your feeble will to his all-powerful will. If you do this, nothing can happen that you do not will, nor can anything happen except what God orders. And you will find unfailing comfort and rest in submitting to his will and pleasure. Such a life within is indeed a foretaste of the blessedness of the saints, and their everlasting song, Amen, Alleluia!

As you learn to worship, praise, and bless God for all things—to see his hand everywhere—you will feel nothing to be an unbearable evil, for everything, even the most cruel sufferings, will turn to good for you. Who would call evil the sorrows that God lays on us with a view to purify and make us fit for himself? Surely what achieves such exceeding good cannot be evil. Cast all your cares into the bosom of your loving Father. Let him do as he sees fit with you. Be content to obey his will in all things, and to align your will concerning everything in his.

What right have you, who are not your own, to any intrinsic possession? A slave has no proprietary rights; how much less the creature, which in itself is mere sin and nothingness, and which can possess nothing except by the gift of God? God has endowed us with free will in order that we may have something real to offer him. We have nothing to call our own except our will. Nothing else is ours. Sickness takes away health and life. Riches melt away. Mental powers depend upon a person's bodily strength. The one and only thing really ours is our will.

Consequently, it is of this that God is jealous, for he gave it, not for us to use it as our own, but for us to restore it to him, completely and undividedly. Any one of us who holds back any particle of reluctance or desire as our right defrauds our Maker, to whom everything is due.

⌁ 49
CONFORMITY TO THE WILL OF GOD (2)

What a deep pity it is that we meet so many self-asserting souls, people who would like to do right and love God, but only after their own habitual manner and choice, who practically lay down the law to God as to his dealings with them! They wish to serve him and possess him and let him possess them. As a natural result, how much resistance God meets with from such people, even when they seem full of zeal and ardor for his service! To a certain degree, indeed, their spiritual abundance becomes a hindrance, because they look upon it as their own, and self-assertion mingles in their best works. Truly, the soul that is utterly impoverished, incapable of willing anything at all from hour to hour except what God sets before it in the precepts of his gospel and the ordering of his providence, is far ahead of all those enlightened people who persist in traveling to heaven by their own self-chosen path.

This is the real meaning of those words of Jesus Christ, "If anyone would come after me, he must deny himself and take up his cross and follow me."[42] We must follow him step by step, not strike out a new road of our own, by "denying" self. And what is it to deny self but to renounce all rights over self? It is even as St. Paul says, "You are not your own."[43] Woe to those who take back the gift once they have given it!

Pray to the Father of mercies, the God of consolation, that he would tear out all that is of self in you, leaving no remnant behind. So painful an operation must be hard to bear. It is very difficult to lie still under God's hand while he cuts to the quick, but this is the patience of saints, the offering of pure faith. Let God do as he will with you. Never resist him voluntarily even for a moment. The instant you become conscious of the revulsion of nature and inclination, turn trustfully to him. Take his side against your own rebellious nature. Give it up to God's Holy Spirit, and ask him to put it by degrees to death. Watch, as in his sight, over your most trifling faults. Strive never to grieve the Holy Spirit, who is so jealous over your hidden life. Make use of past faults to attain a humble consciousness of your own weakness, only without weariness or encouragement.

How could you give more glory to God than by absolutely setting aside self and all its longings, and letting him send you where he pleases? It is in this way that he will be your God and that his kingdom will come in you—if, paying no heed to all outward hindrances and helps, you look to nothing, within or without, except God's hand governing all things.

If you persist in serving him in one place or one way rather than another, you are serving him according to your will, not his. But if you are ready to go anywhere and do anything, if you leave yourself to be entirely molded by his providence and put no limits to your submission, this is indeed taking up your cross and following him.

Then you would be perfectly happy if he were to lay the heaviest trials on you for his great glory.

Open your heart wide, unboundedly wide, and let God's love flow in as a torrent. Do not be afraid of anything on your way. God will lead you by the hand, if only you trust him completely, and are filled with love for him rather than fear for yourself.

∽ 50
SEEKING HELP IN INNER TROUBLE

When you feel that your heart is sinking under trouble, be simple and frank in saying so. Do not be ashamed to let your weakness be seen, or to ask help in your urgent need. By doing this you will advance in simplicity, in humility, and in trustfulness. You will go far to root out self-love, which keeps up a perpetual disguise in order to seem cheerful when it is really in despair.

If you nurse your troubles in silence they will grow stronger and finally overpower you, and the unreal courage that self-love creates will cause you a world of harm. The poison that goes into the system is deadly. The poison that comes out does no great injury. You must not be ashamed of seeing a free discharge from the sore in your heart.

I would give no consideration whatever to certain expressions that escape you, and that are merely the utterances of suffering in spite of your real self. It is enough if such expressions teach you that you are weak, and if you learn not to hide and cherish your weakness, but bring it to the light so that it may be cured.

51
LEGALISM AND FREEDOM

You should combine great exactitude with great freedom. The first will cause you to be faithful, the latter courageous. If you aim at being exact without freedom, you will fall into scruples and bondage. If, on the other hand, you achieve freedom without exactness in duty, you will soon yield to negligence and laxity. Mere exactness in the fulfillment of duty narrows heart and mind; mere freedom stretches them too widely.

Those who have no experience in God's ways do not believe it is possible to combine these two virtues. By being exact they understand living in a state of constraint and exhaustion, in a restless, scrupulous timidity that deprives the soul of all freedom. They look for sin lurking everywhere, and they narrow the soul's vision so much that it frets about every trifle and scarcely dares to breathe. By freedom they mean having a very lax conscience, ready to pass over detail. They mean being content to avoid serious faults, and calling serious nothing except gross crimes. They mean indulging freely in whatever is acceptable to self-love, and taking considerable license as to the passions, thinking that they meant no great harm. This was not the freedom St. Paul contemplated when he wrote to his children in grace, children whom he was trying to train up to Christian perfection, "You, my brothers, were called to be free. But do not use your freedom to indulge the sinful nature."[44]

It seems to me that real freedom consists in obeying God in all things. It consists in following the light that points out our duty, and in following the grace that guides us. We should take as our rule of life the intention to please God in all things. We should make it our rule not only always to do what is acceptable to him, but if possible to do what is *most* acceptable. It is good not to trifle with petty distinctions between great and small sins, imperfections, and faults, for although it may be very true that there are such distinctions, they should have no weight with a soul that is determined to keep back nothing it possesses from God.

It is in this sense that St. Paul says, "That law is not made for the righteous"[45]—a burdensome, hard, threatening law, one might almost say a tyrannical, enslaving law. But there is a higher law that rises above all this, and that leads St. Paul into the true "freedom of the children of God." This is the law that makes him strive always to do what is most pleasing to his heavenly Father, in the spirit of those beautiful words of St. Augustine, "Love, and then do what you will."

Yield completely to the grace with which God sometimes draws you closer to him. Do not be afraid to lose sight of self, to fix your gaze solely and as closely upon him as he will permit, and to plunge completely into the ocean of his love—happy if you could do it so entirely as never to come out again.

⌒ 52
THE RIGHT USE OF CROSSES

The more we are afraid to bear crosses, the more we need them. Let us not, therefore, fall into hopeless discouragement when the hand of God lays crosses heavily upon us. We should be fully aware of the magnitude of our disease by seeing the severity of the remedies that our spiritual Physician sees good to apply. Truly we must be extremely diseased, and God must be extremely merciful, since, despite our opposition, he reaches down to heal us. Surely, we should find in our very crosses a supply of love, comfort, and confidence, saying with the Apostle, "For our light and momentary troubles are achieving for us an eternal glory that far outweighs them all."[46] Happy are those who weep, and who, having sown in tears, will with indescribable joy reap the harvest of eternal life.[47]

"I have been crucified with Christ,"[48] says St. Paul. It is with our Savior that we are bound to the cross, and it is his grace that binds us there. It is for Jesus' sake that we would not depart from the cross, since without it we cannot have him.

Adorable and suffering Body, in and with which we are forever united, give me, together with your cross, your spirit of love and self-denial. Teach me rather to think of the privilege of suffering with you, than of the pangs of that suffering. What can I suffer that you have not endured? or rather, how do I dare to presume to speak of suffering, when I remember what you bore for me? Weak mortal, be silent, see your Master and be silent! Lord, teach me to love you, and I will not be afraid of any cross. Then, whatever grievous and bitter pangs may come, I will never have more to bear than I am glad and willing to bear.

PART TWO

Talking
with God

INTRODUCTION TO PART TWO
Talking with God

How does one "hear" God? The Bible speaks over and over again about listening and hearing his voice. The psalmist said, "Our God comes, he does not keep silence. . . . Hear, O my people, and I will speak."[1] Yet for the most part, do we expect to hear him speak to us?

Fénelon has been a trusted counselor for myriads of Christians for more than three centuries. He came to believe strongly that God is a living, active presence and voice in the Christian's life. He did not hesitate to give the wisest word he knew to those who asked his advice. He was frank in sharing his own difficulties and struggles as life dealt him unexpected and difficult blows. But out of that crucible of suffering and misunderstanding, he listened for God's word, God's will, God's message to him.

More often than not, God is speaking to us in the so-called circumstances of life. If we look at them on a merely human plane, we may become confused, discouraged, and totally disillusioned with life. Self-pity and accusation of others may be our daily bread. If we look at them as being part of God's loving dealing with us, weaning us away from what is false, binding us more firmly to what is eternal, we begin to "hear" God's word coming through these conditions.

This compilation of Fénelon's letters and words of counsel can encourage us as it has generations before to *listen* and *hear* the voice of the Good Shepherd.

1
HOW TO TALK WITH GOD

Talk with God with the thoughts that your heart is full of. If you enjoy the presence of God, if you feel drawn to love him, tell him so. Such conscious fervor will make the time of prayer fly without exhausting you, for all you will have to do is to pour forth from your abundance and say what you feel.

But what, you ask, are you to do in times of dryness, inner resistance, and coldness? Do just the same thing. Say equally what is in your heart. Tell God that you no longer feel any love for him, that everything is a terrible blank to you, that he wearies you, that his presence does not even move you, that you long to leave him for the most trifling activity, and that you will not feel happy till you have left him and can turn to thinking about yourself. Tell him all the evil you know about yourself.

So how can we even ask what there is to talk to God about? The pity is that there is only too much! But when you tell him about your miseries, ask him to cure them. Say to him, "Dear God, see my ingratitude, my inconstancy, my infidelity. Take my heart, for I do not know how to give it to you. Give me an inner distaste for external things; give me crosses necessary to bring me back under your yoke. Have mercy on me in spite of myself!" In this way, either God's mercies or your own miseries will always give you enough to talk to him about. The subject will never be exhausted!

In either of these two states I have described, tell him without hesitation everything that comes into your head, with the simplicity and familiarity of a little child sitting on its mother's knee.

⮌ 2
DESIRING GOD'S WILL

Love desires that God would give us what we need and that he would have less regard to our frailty than to the purity of our intentions. Love even covers our trifling defects and purifies us like a consuming fire. "The Spirit intercedes for the saints in accordance with God's will," for "We do not know what we ought to pray for,"[2] and in our ignorance, we frequently ask for things that would be detrimental. We would, for instance, like to have fervor of devotion, distinct emotions of joy, and perfections that others could see. But these would serve to nourish the life of self within us and develop a confidence in our own strength. Love, however, leads us on and abandons us, so to speak, to the operations of grace, putting us entirely at the disposal of God's will. In this way it prepares us for all his secret designs.

Then we will have everything and yet nothing. What God gives is precisely what we should have desired to ask. For we will have whatever he wills, and only that. In this way, this state contains all prayer: it is a work of the heart that includes all its desire. The Spirit prays within us for those very things that the Spirit himself wills to give us. Even when we are occupied with outward things, when our thoughts are drawn off by what our duties or position may require, we still carry within us a constantly burning fire that is not, and cannot be put out. It nourishes a secret prayer and is like a lamp continually lighted before the throne of God. "I slept but my heart was awake."[3] "Blessed are those servants whom the master finds awake when he comes."[4]

3
TRUE PRAYER OF THE HEART

True prayer is simply another name for the love of God. Its excellence does not consist in the multitude of our words, for our Father knows what we need before we ask him.[5] True prayer is prayer of the heart, and the heart prays only for what it desires. *To pray*, then, is *to desire or long for*, but to desire what God would have us desire. Those who ask, but not from the bottom of their hearts, are mistaken in thinking that they are praying. Even though they spend days in reciting prayers in meditation, or in forcing themselves in religious exercises, they do not truly pray even once if they really do not *desire and yearn for* the things they claim to be asking for.

Oh, how few there are who pray! How few there are who desire what is truly good! Crosses, external and internal humiliation, the renunciation of our own wills, the death of self, and the establishment of God's throne upon the ruins of self-love—these are indeed good. If we do not desire these, we are not truly praying. To desire them seriously, soberly, constantly, and with reference to all the details of life, this is true prayer. Not to desire them, and yet to suppose we are praying, is an illusion like that of the wretched souls who delude themselves that they are happy. How distressing it is that so many souls, full of self and of an imaginary desire for perfection in the midst of hosts of willful disobediences, have never yet uttered this true prayer of the heart. It is in reference to this that St. Augustine says, *One who loves little, prays little; one who loves much, prays much.*

On the other hand, the heart in which the true love of God and true desire exist never ceases to pray. Love, hidden in the depths of the soul, prays without ceasing, even when the mind is drawn another way. God continually sees the desire that he has himself implanted in the soul. Though we may at times be unconscious of its existence, the heart is touched by it. Such a hidden desire in the soul ceaselessly draws God's mercies. It is that Spirit who, according to St. Paul, helps us in our weakness and intercedes for us "with sighs too deep for words."[6]

⮑ 4
MAINTAINING A
LIFE OF PRAYER

Two main points of attention are necessary to maintain a constant spirit of prayer that unites us with God. We must continually seek to nurture it, and we must avoid everything that tends to make us lose it.

In order to nurture it, we should follow a regular course of reading. We must have appointed times of secret prayer and frequently recall our minds consciously to God during the day. We should make use of quiet days or retreats when we feel the need of them or when they are advised by those more experienced than we whose counsel we seek, and when our other responsibilities allow for them.

We should be very afraid of all things that have a tendency to make us lose this state of prayer and be very careful to avoid them. Therefore, we should avoid worldly activities and associates that turn our minds in the wrong direction, and the pleasures that excite the passions. We should avoid everything calculated to awaken the love of the world and the old inclinations that have caused us so much trouble.

There are many details that might apply in dealing with nurturing the spirit of prayer and avoiding anything that works against it. Because each individual case has features peculiar to itself, only general directions can be given here.

We should choose books that instruct us in our duty and in our faults. Such books, while they point to the greatness of God, teach us what our duty is to him and how very far we are from perfecting it. We should not seek emotional publications that melt and sentimentalize the heart. The tree must bear fruit. We can judge the life of the root only by the fruit it bears.[7]

The first effect of a sincere love is an earnest desire to know all that we ought to do to gratify the one we love. Any other desire is an indication that we love ourselves under a pretense of loving God. It shows that we are seeking an empty and deceitful consolation in him and that we want to use God for our pleasure, instead of sacrificing that pleasure for his glory. God forbid that his children should love him that way! No matter what it costs us, if we truly want to love him, we must know what he requires of us and try to do it without reservation.

Periods of secret prayer must be determined by the time available, the disposition, the condition, and the inward leading of each individual.

A necessary foundation to prayer is meditating and thinking on the great truths that God has revealed. We should be familiar with all the mysteries of Jesus Christ and the truths of his gospel. Our souls should be colored by them and penetrated by them as wool is by dye. These truths should become so familiar to us that we acquire the habit of never forming any judgment except in their light, so that they may be our only guide in what we do, as the rays of the sun are our only light in what we see.

It is when these truths are inwardly incorporated in us that our praying begins to be real and fruitful. Up to that point, prayer was only a shadow. We thought we had penetrated to the inmost depths of the gospel, when in truth we had barely set foot upon its border. All our most tender and ardent feelings, our firmest resolutions, our clearest and most distant visions were, in reality, only the rough and shapeless mass from which God wishes to hew his likeness in us.

When his celestial rays begin to shine within us, then we see in the true light. Then we instantaneously assent to every truth in the same way we admit, without any process of reasoning, the splendor of the sun the moment we see its rising beams. Our union with God must be the result of our faithfulness in doing and enduring all that he wills for us.

Our meditations should become deeper and more inward every day. I say *deeper*, because by frequent and humble meditation upon God's truth, we penetrate further and further in search of new treasures. And I say *more inward*, because as we seek more and more to enter into these truths, they penetrate into the very substance of our souls. Then it will be that a simple word will go further than a whole sermon.

Our meditation should not be subtle or composed of lengthy reasoning. Simple and natural reflections based on the subject of our thoughts are all that is required. We need to take just a few truths and meditate upon these without hurry, without effort, and without seeking for far-fetched reflections. Every truth should be considered with reference to its practical bearing in our lives. To receive it without using all means to put it faithfully into practice at whatever cost is to "hold the truth in unrighteousness."[8] It is a resistance to the truth that has been impressed upon us and, of course, is resistance to the Holy Spirit. This is the most terrible of all unfaithfulness.

As to a method of praying, each person must be guided by his or her own experience. If some find themselves aided in using a strict method, they do not need to depart from it. Those who cannot so confine themselves may make use of their own mode without judging what has proved helpful to so many others. A method is intended to assist.

Growth in prayer is indicated by growth in simplicity and steadiness in our attitude. Our conversation with God resembles that with a friend. At first, there are a thousand things to be told, and just as many to be asked. After a time, however, these diminish, while the pleasure of being together does not. Everything has been said, but the satisfaction of seeing each other, of feeling that one is near the other, can be felt without conversation. The silence is eloquent and mutually understood. Each feels that the other is in perfect harmony with him, and that their two hearts are continuously being poured into each other, becoming one.

It is the same way in prayer. Our communion with God becomes a simple and familiar union, far beyond the need of words. But let it be remembered that God must initiate this kind of prayer within us. Nothing would be more rash or more dangerous than to dare to attempt it in ourselves. We must allow ourselves to be led step by step, by someone who has frequent and familiar association with the ways of God and who may lay the immovable foundations of correct teaching and of the complete death of self in everything.

Our practice of prayer in seclusion or private retirement must be regulated by our leisure and our other needs. We must attend to duty before we seek enjoyment in spiritual exercises. People who have public duties and spend time meditating when they should be attending to those duties will miss God while they seek to be united to him. True union with God is to do his will without ceasing in every duty of life, in spite of all natural disinclination, and however disagreeable or mortifying it may be to our self will.

We must, however, reserve the necessary time to seek God alone in prayer. Those who have positions of importance to fill usually have so many indispensable duties to perform, that without the greatest care in the management of their time, there will be none left to be alone with God. If they have ever so little inclination for foolish amusement, the hours that belong to God and their neighbor disappear altogether.

We must be firm in observing our rules. This strictness seems excessive, but without it everything falls into confusion. We will become dissolute, relaxed, and spiritually weak. We will be unconsciously drawn away from God. We will surrender ourselves to all our pleasures, and begin to see that we have wandered only when it is almost hopeless to think of trying to return.

Prayer, prayer! this is our only safety. "Praise be to God who has not rejected my prayer, or withheld his love from me!"[9] To be faithful in prayer it is indispensable that we arrange all the activities of the day with a regularity that nothing can disturb.

⇒ 5
CHOOSING COMPANIONS WISELY

Whoever walks with the wise becomes wise,
but the companion of fools suffers harm.[10]

Do you want to truly know a person? Observe who that person's companions are! How can one who loves God and who loves nothing except in and for God enjoy the intimate companionship of those who neither love nor know God, and who look upon love of God as a weakness? Can a heart full of God and deeply aware of its own state of weakness ever rest and be at ease with those who do not have feelings in common with it—who, indeed, are constantly seeking to rob it of its treasure? Their delights are incompatible with the pleasures that faith brings.

I am well aware that we cannot, indeed, *ought not* to break with those friends to whom we are bound by our appreciation of their natural good nature, by their assistance, by ties of sincere friendship, or by the regard that grows out of mutual helpfulness. Friends whom we have treated with a certain familiarity and confidence would be wounded to the quick if we were to separate from them entirely. We must gently and imperceptibly diminish our association with them without declaring abruptly our alteration of feeling. We may see them in private and relate to them more closely than to less intimate friends. We may confide to them those matters in which their integrity and friendship enable them to give us good advice and share our thoughts. In short, we may continue to serve them and show them a cordial friendship without allowing our hearts to be hindered or confused by them.

Without this precaution, our state is perilous indeed! If we do not from the outset boldly make our commitment to the Lord entirely free and independent from our unregenerate friends, that commitment is threatened with a speedy downfall. If we are of a yielding disposition and passionate nature, it is certain that such friends, even the best-intentioned ones, will lead us astray. They may be good, honest, and faithful, and they may have all those qualities that make friendship perfect in the eye of the world, but for us they are infected, and their good-naturedness only makes them more dangerous. Those friendships that do not have this valuable character should be sacrificed at once. We are blessed when a sacrifice that ought to cost us so little may serve to give us such a precious security for our eternal salvation.

◈ 6
THE PRACTICE OF HUMILITY

Always be afraid of blatant, disdainful pride. Be afraid of overconfidence in your own ideas, and of determination in your way of speaking. Be meek and humble of heart. That is to say, your meekness—your willingness to endure injury with patience and without resentment—should come from a sincere humility. Bitterness and lack of moderation come only from pride.

If you wish to become meek, you must humble yourself. Make yourself little in the depths of your heart. A humble heart is always gentle and capable of being easily led in its center, even if on the surface it may seem rough through unexpected outbursts of a sharp and irritable temper. Watch, pray, and work at this. Bear with yourself without flattering yourself. Let your spiritual reading and your prayer help you to know yourself better, to correct yourself, and to overcome your natural temperament in the presence of God.

◈ 7
CONFORMING TO THE LIFE OF JESUS

We are called to imitate Jesus: to live as he lived, to think as he thought, and to be conformed to his image. This is the mark of our sanctification.

What a contrast! Nothingness strives to be something, and the Almighty becomes nothing! I will be nothing with you, Lord! I offer you the pride and vanity that have possessed me. Help my will in this resolve! Protect me from occasions of stumbling. Turn away my eyes from beholding vanity.[11] Let me see nothing but you, and myself in your presence, that I may understand what I am and what you are.

Jesus Christ was born in a stable. He had to flee into Egypt. Thirty years of his life were spent in a workshop. He suffered hunger, thirst, and weariness. He was poor, despised, and miserable. He taught the truths of heaven, and no one would listen to him. The great and the wise persecuted and took him, subjected him to frightful torments, treated him as a slave, and put him to death between two criminals. They chose to give liberty to a robber rather than allow him to escape. Such was the life that our Lord chose. We, on the other hand, are horrified at any kind of humiliation and cannot bear the slightest appearance of contempt.

Let us compare our lives with that of Jesus, remembering that he was the Master and we are the servants, that he was all-powerful and that we are only weakness, that he was abased and that we are exalted. Let us so constantly bear our wretchedness in mind in such a way that we may have nothing but contempt for ourselves. With what face can we despise others and dwell on their faults, when we ourselves are filled with nothing else but faults? Let us begin to walk in the path that our Savior has marked out, for it is the only one that can lead us to him.

How can we expect to find Jesus if we do not seek him in the states of his earthly life, in loneliness and silence, in poverty and suffering, in persecution and contempt, in becoming of no effect, and in the cross? The saints find him in heaven, in the splendors of glory, and in unspeakable pleasures, but only after having dwelt with him on earth in reproaches, in pain, and in humiliation. To be a Christian is to be an imitator of Jesus. In what can we imitate him if not in his humiliation? Nothing else can bring us near to him. We may adore him as all-powerful, fear him as just, and love him with all our heart as good and merciful. But we can imitate him only as humble, submissive, poor, and despised.

Let us not imagine that we can do this by our own efforts. Everything in us is opposed to it, but we may rejoice that God is present within us. Jesus has chosen to be made partaker of all our weaknesses. He is a compassionate High Priest, who has voluntarily submitted to be tempted in all points as we are.[12] Let us, then, derive all our strength in him who became weak so that he might strengthen us. Let us make ourselves rich out of his poverty, confidently exclaiming, "I can do everything through him who gives me strength."[13]

Let us earnestly occupy ourselves with this work, and let us change our hard hearts, which are so rebellious, to become like the heart of Jesus Christ.

Lovely Jesus! You suffered so many injuries and reproaches for my sake. Let me cherish and love them for your sake, and help me desire to share your life of humiliation.

⮽ 8
THE USES OF HUMILIATION

What a mercy humiliation is to a soul that receives it with steadfast faith! There are a thousand blessings in it for ourselves and for others, for our Lord bestows his grace upon the humble.

Humility makes us charitable toward our neighbor. Nothing will make us so generous and merciful to the faults of others as seeing our own faults.

Two things produce humility when they are put together. The first is the sight of the bottomless gulf of wretchedness from which the all-powerful hand of God has snatched us, and over which he still holds us, so to speak, suspended in the air. The other is the presence of that God who is *All.*

Our faults, even those that are the most difficult to bear, will all be of service to us if we make use of them for our humiliation without relaxing our efforts to correct them. It does no good to be discouraged. That is only the result of a disappointed and despairing self-love. The true method of profiting from the humiliation of our faults is to see them in all their deformity without losing our hope in God and without having any confidence in ourselves.

We must bear with ourselves without either flattery or discouragement, although we seldom achieve this happy medium. We either expect great things of ourselves and of our good intentions, or else we completely despair. We must hope for nothing from self, but wait for everything from God. Convicted of our helplessness, we have no confidence in ourselves, and yet we have unbounded confidence in God. These are the true foundations of the spiritual structure.

Those who are truly humble will be surprised to hear any kind of praise given them. They are calm and peaceful, of a contrite and humble heart, merciful and compassionate. They are quiet, cheerful, obedient, watchful, fervent in spirit, and incapable of strife. They always take the lowest place, rejoice when they are despised, and consider everyone better than themselves. They are lenient to the faults of others in view of their own. They are very far from preferring themselves before anyone. We may in this way judge our progress in humility by the delight we have in humiliations and contempt.

[handwritten notes in margin: Oh my Jesus]

[handwritten notes: — beneath consideration — scorn, despicable — worthless]

9
BEARING OUR FAULTS PATIENTLY

I pray God that he may preserve you in complete faithfulness to his grace. May the one who began a good work among you bring it to completion by the day of Jesus Christ.[14] We must bear with ourselves patiently, without flattering ourselves, and we must continually subject ourselves to everything that can overcome our natural inclinations and our inner dislikes, so that we may become more adaptable to the impressions of divine grace in living out the gospel.

This work, however, must be peaceful and untroubled. It must even be moderate, and we must not attempt to do all the work in a single day. We must try to reason little and to do much. If we do not take care, our whole life may be spent in reasoning, and we will require a second life to practice! We run the risk of believing that we have advanced in proportion to our understanding of perfection. All these fine ideas, far from advancing us in dying to ourselves, may serve only to secretly nourish the life of the old Adam within us by giving us confidence in our own opinions. *Be extremely distrustful of your intellect and your own ideas of perfection.* That will be a great step toward becoming perfect. Humility and distrust of yourself, with simplicity, are fundamental virtues for you.

10
WHEN FEELINGS FAIL US

Many people are tempted to believe that they no longer pray when they cease to enjoy a certain pleasure in the act of prayer. But if they will remember that perfect prayer is only another name for love of God, their eyes will be open to the truth.

Prayer does not consist in sweet feelings, or in the appeal of an excited imagination, or in the illumination of mind that traces the most sublime truths in God with ease. It does not even consist in a certain consolation in our vision of God. All these things are external gifts from his hand. If they are withheld from us, our love may become more pure, as the soul may then attach itself immediately and solely to God instead of to his mercies.

This is that love by plain faith that is the death of nature, because it leaves it no support. When we are convinced that all is lost, that very conviction is the evidence that all is gained.

Pure love is in the will alone. It is not sentimental love, for imagination has no part in it. It loves, if we may so express it, without feeling, as faith believes without seeing. We do not need to fear that this love is an imaginary thing. Nothing can be less so than the mere will when it is separated from all imagination. Without such emotional feeling, faith is in full exercise while humility is preserved.

Such love is chaste, for it is the love of God, in and for God. We are attached to him, but not for the pleasure that he bestows on us. We follow him, but not for the loaves and fishes.

Someone may indeed object that this "will" is a mere idea, a trick of the imagination instead of a true willing of the soul. I would indeed believe that it was a deception if it did not engender faithfulness on all proper occasions. A good tree brings forth good fruit, and a true will makes us truly earnest and diligent in doing the will of God. But it is still compatible in this life with little failings that are permitted by God so that the soul may be humbled. If, then, we experience only these little daily frailties, let us not be discouraged, but extract their proper fruit from them.

True virtue and pure love reside in the will alone. Is it not a great matter always to desire the supreme good wherever he is seen, to keep our mind steadily turned toward him, and to bring it back whenever it wanders? Is it not a great thing to will nothing but what is according to his order? In short, is it not a great matter to remain the same in the spirit of a yielded, irreclaimable burnt offering when all earthly enjoyment is gone? Do you think it is nothing to deny all the uneasy reflections of self-love, and to press forward continually without knowing where we are headed—yet to go on without stopping? Is it a small thing to cut off satisfying thoughts of self, or at least to think of ourselves as we would of another, and to obey the Spirit's leadings for the moment without trying to look ahead?

It is a kind of betrayal of simple faith to continually demand to be assured that we are doing well. It is the will of God that we should be ignorant, and to reason about the way is to waste time trifling along it. The safest and shortest course is to renounce, forget, and abandon the demands of self, and through faithfulness to God to think no longer about such demands. This is what commitment means: to get out of self and self-love in order to get into God.

11
WHEN WE FEEL ABANDONED BY GOD

We should never abandon ourselves to God so fully as when he seems to abandon us. Let us enjoy light and consolation when it is his pleasure to give them to us, but let us not attach ourselves to his gifts, but to him. When he plunges us into the night of pure faith, let us still press on through agonizing darkness.

Moments are worth days in this tribulation. The soul is troubled and yet at peace. Not only is God hidden from it, but the soul is hidden from itself, so that *everything* may be of faith. The soul is discouraged but feels nevertheless an immovable will to bear everything that God may choose to inflict. It wills everything and accepts everything, even the troubles that test its faith, and so in the very height of the tempest, the waters beneath are secretly calm and at peace, because its will is one with God's will.

Blessed be the Lord who performs such great things in us, notwithstanding our unworthiness!

⌒ 12
LIVING IN THE PRESENT

One of the cardinal rules of the spiritual life is that we are to live in the present moment. You remember that the Israelites in the desert followed the pillar of fire or cloud, not knowing where it was leading them. They had a supply of manna for only one day, and any they gathered for the next day became useless.

There is no need to move in haste. Think only of laying a solid foundation. See that this foundation is deep and broad by absolutely renouncing yourself, and by abandoning yourself without reserve to the requirements of God. Then let God raise upon this foundation whatever type of building he pleases. Shut your eyes and commit yourself to him. How wonderful is this walking with Abraham in pure faith, not knowing where we are going! And how full of blessings is the path!

God will be your Guide. He himself will travel with you, as we are told he did with the Israelites, to bring them step-by-step across the desert to the Promised Land. Now, how blessed you will be if only you will surrender yourself into the hands of God, permitting him to do whatever is his will, not according to your desires, but according to his own good pleasure!

13
PURE LOVE

"The LORD hath made all things for himself,"[15] says the Scripture. Everything belongs to him, and he will never release his right to anything. Free and intelligent creatures are as much his as are those that are otherwise. He directs every unintelligent thing totally and absolutely to himself, and he desires that his intelligent creatures should voluntarily make the same disposition of themselves. It is true that he desires our happiness, but that is neither the chief end of his work, nor an end to be compared with that of his glory. It is for his glory alone that he wills our happiness. Happiness is a subordinate consideration that he assigns to the final and essential end of his glory.

In order that we may align ourselves with his purpose in this respect, we must prefer God before ourselves, and we must seek to will our own happiness for his glory. In any other case, we invert the order of things. We must not desire his glory on account of our own salvation, but on the other hand, we should see that our own happiness is a thing that he has been pleased to make a part of his glory. It is true that all holy souls are not capable of exercising this explicit preference for God over themselves, but there must be at least an implicit preference.*

We human beings have a great distaste for this truth, and consider it to be a very hard saying, because we are lovers of self. We understand, in a general and superficial way, that we must love God more than all his creatures, but we have no conception of loving God more than ourselves, and loving ourselves only for him. We can utter these great words without difficulty, because we do not fully comprehend their meaning. But we shudder when it is explained to us that we are to prefer God and his glory before ourselves and everything else to such

---

* By this I understand Fénelon to mean that we cannot, except by a supernatural act of God's grace, *be happy* and feel good about this choice. We can, however, by an act of our will, give God permission to advance his glory, even at the cost of our happiness, trusting him to change our feelings in due time, in full assurance that our true happiness advances his glory.

a degree that we must love his glory more than our own happiness, and must refer our happiness to his glory as merely a means to an end.

14
THE REFINEMENTS OF SELF-LOVE

The origin of our trouble is that we love ourselves with a blind passion that amounts to worshiping an idol. If we love anything beyond, it is only for our own sakes. We must be undeceived about all those generous friendships in which it seems as though we have forgotten ourselves so far as to think only of the interests of our friend. If the motive of our friendship is not base and unrefined, it is nevertheless still selfish. And the more delicate, the more concealed, and the more proper such friendship is in the eyes of the world, the more dangerous it becomes, and the more likely it is to poison us by feeding our self-love.

In those friendships that appear so generous and unselfish, we seek the pleasure of loving without receiving anything in return. By indulging such a noble sentiment, we raise ourselves above the weak and sordid members of our race. Together with that tribute that we pay to our own pride, we seek from the world the reputation of unselfishness and generosity. We want to be loved by our friends even though we do not desire to be served by them. We hope that they will be pleased with what we do for them without expecting any return from them. In this way we get the very return that we seem to despise, for what is more delicious to a delicate self-love than to hear itself applauded for not being self-love?

You may have seen people who seemed to think of everyone but themselves, who were the delight of good people, who were well disciplined, and who seemed entirely unmindful of self. This self-denial is so great that self-love would even imitate it, and find no glory equal to that of seeming to seek none at all. This moderation and self-renunciation that, if genuine, would be the death of the old natural self become, on the other hand, the most subtle and imperceptible food of a pride that despises all ordinary forms of glory and desires only the glory that is to be secured by trampling all the unrefined objects of ambition that captivate ordinary minds.

It is not difficult to unmask this modest arrogance—this pride that seems not to be pride at all because it appears to have renounced all the ordinary objects of pride's ambition. Condemn it and it cannot bear to be found fault with. Let those whom it loves fail to repay it with friendship, esteem, and confidence, and it is stung to the quick! It is easy to see that it is not disinterested, though it tries so hard to seem so. It does not indeed accept payment in such gross coins as others may. It does not desire empty praise, or money, or the repayment that consists in office and dignities. It must be paid, nevertheless. It is greedy of the esteem of good people. It loves so that it may be loved in return and admired for its unselfishness. It *seems* to forget self, so that it may draw the attention of the world to self alone.

Of course it does not make all these reflections in full detail. It does not say in so many words, "I will deceive the whole world with my generosity in order that the world may love and admire me." Of course it would not dare address such unworthy language to itself! *It deceives itself along with everyone else.* It admires itself in its generosity, as a beautiful woman admires her beauty in a mirror. It is moved by thinking that it is more generous and unselfish than the rest of humanity. The illusion it prepares for others it extends to itself, and this is what pleases it more than anything else.

However little we may have looked within ourselves to study the occasions of our pleasure and our grief, we will have no more difficulty in admitting that pride has various tastes, whether it is more delicate or less so. But give it what taste you will, it is still pride, and the thing that appears the most restrained and the most reasonable is the most devilish. In esteeming itself, it despises others. It pities those who are pleased with foolish vanities. It recognizes the emptiness of greatness and rank. It cannot abide with those who are impassioned by good fortune. It would, by its moderation, be *above* fortune, and in this way raise itself to a new height by putting under foot all the false glory of humankind. Like Lucifer, it would become like the Most High. And it does not perceive that it seeks to place itself above others by this deceitful pride that blinds it.

We may be sure, then, that it is only the love of God that can make us come out of self. If his powerful hand did not sustain us, we would not know how to take the first step in that direction.

There is no middle course: we must refer everything either to God or to self. If we refer it to self, we have no god other than self. If we refer it to God, we are then in order, and we regard ourselves only as one among the other creatures of God, without selfish interests. With a single eye to accomplish his will, we enter into the self-abandonment that our Lord calls us to make.*

* Self-abandonment should be here understood only in the light of the Gospel word: "If anyone would come after me, he must deny himself and take up his cross daily and follow me" (Luke 9:23, NIV). And the word of our Lord, "Whoever finds his life will lose it, and whoever loses his life for my sake will find it" (Matthew 10:39, NIV; see also Matthew 16:25; Mark 8:35; Luke 9:24; John 12:25). There is no annihilation of identity or personhood, but the placing of our life—every part of it—under the Lordship of Christ.

⤚ 15
LISTENING TO GOD
RATHER THAN SELF

You allow yourself to be led away too much by your inclination and your imagination. Apply yourself again to listen for the voice of God in prayer, and listen less to yourself. Self-love speaks less when it sees that we pay no attention to it.

The words of God to the heart are simple and peaceful. They nourish the soul, even if they bring death to it. On the contrary, the words of self-love are full of unevenness, of disturbance, and of emotion, even when they flatter us. To listen for the voice of God without making any plans of our own is to die to our own judgment and to our own will.

⤳ 16
THE MIRACLE OF SELF-DENIAL

The greater our natural gift of frankness, the more we have pleasure in doing good, the more we love honor and generous friendship, the more we should distrust ourselves, and the more we should fear that we might take complacency in these natural gifts.

The reason no created thing or person can draw us out of ourselves is that there is nothing on earth that deserves to be preferred before ourselves. There is no one who has the right to claim such unqualified denial of self. From this it follows that we love nothing outside our selves without the reference it has to our self-interest. If we are coarse and boorish, that will be the direction our self-love takes. If ours is a refined desire for glory, self cannot be satisfied with what is unrefined and vulgar.

But God does two things that only he has the power to do. He reveals himself to us, with all his rights over the creature and in all the appeals of his goodness. Then we feel that since we did not make ourselves, we are not made for ourselves. We begin to see that we were created for the glory of the One who has been pleased to form us, and that he is too great to make anything except for himself. It follows that we begin to realize that all our perfection and our happiness should be lost in him.

Created things, dazzling though they may be, cannot do this for us. Far from finding in them the infinity that so fills and satisfies us in God, we discover only a void, an inability to fill our hearts, an imperfection that continually drives us back into ourselves.

God's second miracle is to work in our hearts what he pleases after he has enlightened our understanding. He is not satisfied with simply revealing his own charms. Rather, by his grace, he makes us love him by producing his love in our hearts. In this way, he himself performs within us what he has caused us to see that we owe him.

There is little difficulty in comprehending that we must reject unlawful pleasures, dishonest gains, and unrefined vanities, because the very renouncement of these things involves a contempt that repudiates them absolutely and forbids us to derive any enjoyment from them. It is not, however, so easy to understand that we must abandon property honestly acquired, the pleasures of a modest and well-spent life, and the honors derived from a good reputation and a virtue that elevates us above the reach of envy.

The reason we do not understand that we must give up these things is that we are not required to discard them with aversion. On the contrary, we are to preserve them to be used according to the responsibilities God places on us.

We need the consolation of a mild and peaceful life to console us under its troubles. As for honors, we are to regard what is fitting. We must keep the property we possess in order to supply our needs. How then are we to renounce these things at the very moment we are occupied in preserving them? We are to make a sober use of them in moderation, without placing our hearts on them.

I say a *moderate use* of them, because when we are not attached to a thing for the purposes of self-enjoyment and of seeking our happiness in it, we use only as much of it as we need.

The abandonment of evil things, then, consists in refusing them with intense dread and aversion. The abandonment of good things consists in using them for our needs in moderation, continually seeking to refuse those *imaginary* needs with which greedy nature would flatter itself.

Remember that we must forsake not only evil, but also good things, for Jesus has said, "Whoever of you does not renounce all that he has cannot be my disciple."[16]

It follows then, that the Christian must forsake everything that he has, however innocent. For if we do not forsake it in our heart, it ceases to be innocent. This includes those things that it is our duty to guard with the greatest possible care, such as the good of our family, or our own reputation. We must not have our heart on any of these things. We must be ready to give them all up whenever it is the will of providence to deprive us of them.

Our renunciation of them consists in this: we are to love them for God alone. We are to make use of the consolation of their love and friendship soberly, and for the supply of our needs. We are to be ready to part with them when God wills it. We should never seek in them the true peace and tranquility of our heart. That is the chastity of true Christian friendship that seeks in the mortal and earthly friend only the heavenly Bridegroom. It is in this way that we use the world and the things of creation without abusing them, according to St. Paul. He says, "[Let] those who deal with the world [live] as though they had no dealings with it. For the form of this world is passing away."[17] We do not desire to take pleasure in them. We use only what God gives us, what he wills that we should love, with the reserve of a heart that is keeping itself for a more worthy Object.

It is in this sense that Christ would have us leave father and mother, brothers and sisters, and friends. It is in this sense that he comes to bring a sword upon earth.

God is a jealous God. If in the recesses of your soul you are attached to any creature, your heart is not worthy of him. He must reject it as a bridegroom would reject a spouse who divided her affections between him and a stranger.

17
BEARING THE CRITICISM OF OTHERS

Go on your spiritual journey naturally, and what others say will not harm you. A moderate, simple, decided course of conduct will impose silence upon them. Even if you have to bear some unkind mockeries, you will get off very cheaply. Having been approved by the world for so long, when you wished to please those who were blind, is it not just that you should have to suffer something from the folly of the world, so that you may acquire true wisdom? We are too jealous of a vain reputation when we fear the comments of those whom we do not admire and whose irregular conduct we know well. The main thing for you is to reserve to yourself hours for withdrawal, when by your exercise of devotion you can provide yourself with a good antidote against all their poisonous errors.

Read the truth in the words of eternal life. Pray, watch, and be detached from yourself. Love God with a generous love. Let what was created only for him belong only to him. Expect all things from him without neglecting yourself, so that you may be faithful to his gifts.

After saying all this, you can see by the language that this letter contains how much I am interested in all that concerns you.

⌒ 18
MEETING TEMPTATIONS

I know of only two resources against temptations. One is faithfully to follow the interior light, instantly and immediately cutting off everything that we are at liberty to dismiss that may excite or strengthen temptation. I say everything that we are at liberty to dismiss, because we are not always permitted to avoid the occasions of evil. Those that are unavoidably connected with the particular position in which providence has placed us are not within our power to dismiss.

The other resource against temptation consists in turning to God whenever temptation comes, without being disturbed or anxious to know if we have not already yielded a sort of half consent, and without interrupting our immediate recourse to God. By examining too closely whether we have not been guilty of some unfaithfulness, we incur the risk of being again entangled in the temptation. The shortest and surest way is to act like a little child at its mother's breast. When we show it a frightening monster, it shrinks back and buries its face in its mother's bosom, that it may no longer see it.

The sovereign remedy is the habit of dwelling continually in the presence of God. He sustains, consoles, and calms us.

We must never be astonished at temptations, however outrageous they may be. On this earth all is temptation. Crosses tempt us by irritating our pride, while prosperity tempts us by flattering it. Our life is a continual combat, but one in which Jesus Christ fights for us. We must pass on unmoved while temptations rage around us, as the traveler, overtaken by a storm, simply wraps his cloak more closely about him and pushes on more vigorously toward his destined home.

If the thought of former sins and wretchedness should be permitted to come before us, we must remain confounded and abashed before God, quietly enduring in his adorable presence all the shame, all the deep personal humiliation and disgrace of our transgressions. We must not, however, seek to entertain or to call up so dangerous a recollection.

In conclusion, it may be said that in doing what God wills there is very little to be done by us. And yet, there is a wonderful work to be accomplished; it is nothing less than that of keeping nothing back, making no resistance, even for a moment, to the jealous Love that searches inexorably into the most secret recesses of the soul for the smallest trace of self, for the slightest intimations of an affection of which Divine Love is not the Author. On the other hand, true progress does not consist in a multitude of self-searching, or of austerities, troubles, and strife. It means simply to will nothing of self and everything of God, cheerfully performing each day's round as God appoints it for us, seeking nothing, refusing nothing, finding everything in the present moment, and allowing God, who does everything, to do his pleasure in and by us without the slightest resistance on our part.

Oh, how happy is the person who has attained this state! How full of good things is that soul, when it appears to be emptied of everything!

Let us pray the Lord to open to us the whole infinitude of his fatherly heart, that our own may be submerged and lost there, and so that it may be as one with his. Such was the desire of St. Paul for the faithful, when he longed for them "with the affection of Christ Jesus."[18]

19
THE GIVER OR THE GIFTS?

The best rule we can ever adopt is to receive with the same submission everything that God sends us, both within ourselves and from outside ourselves.

There are many things in our circumstances that must be met with courage, and pleasant things that must not be allowed to capture our affections. We resist the temptations of the disagreeable by accepting them at once, and the temptations of the pleasant by refusing to admit them into our hearts.

This same course is necessary in regard to our interior life. Whatever is bitter serves to crucify us and works all its benefit in our souls if we receive it simply and with a willingness that knows no bounds, and with a readiness that seeks no alleviation.

Pleasant gifts, which are intended to support our weakness by giving us conscious consolation in our outward activities, must be accepted with equal satisfaction, but in a different way. They must be received because God sends them, rather than because they are agreeable to our own feelings. They are to be used like any other medicine, without self-complacency, without attachment to them, and without taking them for our own. We must accept them, but not hold on to them, so that when God sees fit to withdraw them, we may be neither dejected nor discouraged.

The root of presumption lies in our attachment to these passing and material gifts. We imagine we have no regard to anything but to the gift of God, while we are really looking to self, taking as our own possession his mercy and mistaking it for himself. In this way we become discouraged when we find that we have been deceived in ourselves. The soul that is sustained by God, however, is not surprised at its own wretchedness. It is delighted to find new proof that it can do nothing of itself and that God must do everything. We are never in the least troubled at being poor when we know that our Father has infinite treasures that he will give us. We will soon become free of trust in ourselves if we allow our hearts to feed upon absolute confidence in God.

We must count less on conscious delights and the measures of wisdom that we devise for our own perfection. We must count more upon simplicity, lowliness, renunciation of our own efforts, and our perfect pliability to all the designs of grace. Everything else tends to focus on *our* virtues and in this way inspires a secret reliance on our own resources.

Let us humbly ask God to root out of our hearts everything of *our* planting, and set there, with his own hands, the Tree of Life, bearing all manner of fruits.

20
WHEN UNDERGOING GREAT WEAKNESS

You are in God's hands. You must live each day as if you were going to die. Then you will be quite ready, for our preparation for death simply consists in detaching ourselves from the world in order to attach ourselves to God.

While you are so weak, do not put the constraint upon yourself of making your prayer time so regularly.* Such exactitude and such application of mind might do harm to your feeble health. It is quite enough for you in your present state of weakness if you again place yourself in the presence of God when you perceive that you are no longer there. A simple and familiar companionship with God, in which you can tell him all your troubles with perfect trust in him, and in which you can ask him to comfort and strengthen you, will never exhaust you. It will nourish your heart.

* The recipient of this letter was undergoing an undisclosed illness.

~ 21
THE INTERIOR VOICE OF THE SPIRIT

It is certain from the Holy Scriptures that the Spirit of God dwells within us. There he acts, there he prays without ceasing with sighs too deep for words, there he desires and asks for us what we do not know how to ask for ourselves. The Spirit urges us on, animates us, speaks to us when we are silent, suggests to us all truth, and so unites us to him that we become one spirit.[19] This is the teaching of faith, and even those teachers farthest removed from the interior life cannot avoid acknowledging it to be so. To be sure, there are some who strive to maintain that in practice we are illuminated by the external law or by the light of learning and reason, and that as a result our understanding acts of itself from that instruction. They do not rely sufficiently upon the interior Teacher, the Holy Spirit, who does everything within us. We could not form a thought or desire without him. What a pity this is! What blindness is ours! We suppose ourselves to be alone in the inner sanctuary, when God is more intimately present there than we are ourselves.

You may say, "What then! Are we all inspired?" Yes, without a doubt! But not in the same way the prophets and apostles were. Without the actual inspiration of the Spirit of grace, we could neither do, nor will, nor believe any good thing. Therefore we are always inspired, but we incessantly stifle the inspiration. God does not cease to speak, but the noise of the world outside us, and the noise of our passions within, prevent our hearing him. We must silence every creature, including self, in order to perceive the ineffable voice of the Bridegroom—that voice that cannot be expressed in words—in the deep stillness of the soul. We must lend an attentive ear, for his voice is soft and quiet, and is heard only by those who hear nothing else!

How rare it is to find a soul that is quiet enough to hear God speak! The slightest murmur of our vain desires, or of a love fixed upon self, confounds all the words of the Spirit of God. We hear well enough that he is speaking and that he is asking for something, but we cannot distinguish what is said, and often we are glad enough that we cannot. The least reserve, the slightest act rooted in self-consideration, the most imperceptible fear of hearing too clearly what God demands interferes with the still, small voice.

Is it any wonder, then, that many people, religious people, are full of false wisdom, amusements, vain desires, and confidence in their own virtues, and that they cannot hear the voice of the Spirit within? Should we be surprised that they consider its very possibility as a dream of fanatics? What good would be the spoken word of pastors and preachers, or even of the Scriptures themselves, if we did not have within us the word of the Holy Spirit giving to those other words all their life and vitality? The spoken word, even of the gospel, without the life-giving interior word of the Spirit is only an empty sound.

"For the letter kills,"[20] and the Spirit alone can give life.

Eternal and all-powerful Word of the Father, it is you who speak in the depth of our soul.

The words that proceeded from the mouth of our Savior during the days of his mortal life have had energy to produce such wondrous fruits only because they have been given life and spirit by the Spirit of life, which is the Word itself. That is why St. Peter says, "Lord, to whom shall we go? You have the words of eternal life."[21]

It is not the outward law of the gospel alone that God shows us by the light of reason and faith. It is his Spirit within us who speaks, touches, operates in, and moves us to action. So it is the Spirit who does in us and with us whatever we do that is good, just as it is our soul that gives life to the body and regulates all its movements.

It is true that we are continually inspired and that we do not lead a godly life except so far as we act under this inward inspiration. But what a pity it is that so few Christians feel it! How few there are who do not render it of no consequence through their voluntary distractions or by their resistance!

God is continually speaking to us.[22] He speaks to the unrepentant also, but, stunned by the noise of the world and their passions, they cannot hear him. The interior voice to them seems to be a fable.

He speaks to awakened sinners, and they feel gnawing distress of conscience, which is the voice of God inwardly reproaching them for their sins. When they are deeply moved, they have no difficulty in understanding this inner voice, for it is this voice that pierces them so sharply. It is to them that "two-edged sword" of which St. Paul speaks as "piercing even to the dividing asunder of soul and spirit."[23] God causes himself to be perceived, enjoyed, and followed. They hear that sweet voice that sends a reproach to the bottom of the heart and causes it to be torn to pieces. Such is true and pure sorrow and remorse for sin.

God speaks, too, to wise and enlightened persons, whose outwardly correct lives seem adorned with many virtues. But such persons are often too full of themselves and their own standards and opinions to listen to God. Everything is turned into reasoning. They substitute the principles of natural wisdom and the plans of human prudence for what would come infinitely better through the channel of simplicity and a willingness to be taught by the Word of God. They seem good, sometimes better than others, and perhaps they are, up to a certain point, but it is a mixed goodness. They are still in possession of themselves and always want to be so. They love to be in the hands of their own counsel and to be strong and great in their own eyes.

I thank you, dear God, with Jesus Christ, that you hid your ineffable secrets—your secrets that cannot be described or uttered—from these great and wise ones. You take pleasure in revealing them to feeble and humble souls! It is with babes alone that you are completely unreserved: the others you treat in their own way. They desire knowledge and great virtues, and you give them dazzling illuminations and convert them into heroes. But this is not the better part. There is something more hidden for your dearest children. They lie with John on your breast.

As for these great ones who are constantly afraid of becoming lowly, you leave them in all their greatness. They will never share your caresses and your familiarity, for to deserve these, they must become as little children and play upon your knees.

⟳ 22
JUDGE CAUTIOUSLY

In all things judge as little as you possibly can. It is a very simple matter to hold back all decisions that are not necessary for us. This is not lack of resolution. It is a simple distrust of ourselves and a very practical detachment from our own ideas. And this distrust and detachment extend to everything, even to the commonest things.

When we are truly detached, we believe what we ought to believe and we act when necessary with a simple determination and without thinking about ourselves or trusting in ourselves. When there is no necessity, we do not judge, and we allow all appearances and all reasons for believing to pass before our eye. Instead, we are so empty of self and of our own opinions that we are always ready to receive light from others. We are willing to believe that we are mistaken, and ready to retrace our steps like a little child whom its mother leads back by the hand.

This emptiness of spirit, this childlike readiness and willingness to be taught, will bring peace to your heart—peace with yourself and with your neighbor.

⟳ 23
THE LAST SHALL BE FIRST

I have often observed that a rough, ignorant sinner who is just beginning to be touched by a lively sense of the love of God, is much more disposed to listen to the inward language of the Spirit of grace than those enlightened and learned persons who have grown old in their own wisdom. God's sole desire is to impart himself. He cannot, so to speak, find where to set his foot in souls so full of themselves, who have grown fat upon their own wisdom and virtues. But, as the Scriptures say, "His secret is with the simple."[24]

But where are they? I do not know who they are, but God sees them and loves to dwell in them. "My Father and I," says our Lord Jesus Christ, "will come to him, and make our home with him."[25] How astounding! A soul delivered from self, and abandoned to grace, counting itself as nothing, walking without its own thought, moving at the will of the pure love that is its perfect Guide—that soul has an experience that the wise can neither receive nor understand!

I was once as wise as any. Thinking I saw everything, I saw nothing. I crept along, feeling my way by a succession of reasonings, but there was no ray to enlighten my darkness. I was content to reason. But when we have silenced everything within us in order to listen to God, we know everything without knowing anything. Then we perceive that before this took place, we were utterly ignorant of everything we thought we understood. We lose all that we once had, and we do not care for it, because we then have nothing else that belongs to self. Everything is lost, and ourselves with it. There is something within us that joins with the spouse in the Song of Solomon in saying, "Show me your face, let me hear your voice; for your voice is sweet, and your face is lovely."[26] How sweet is that voice—it makes me tremble within! Speak, my Beloved! Let no other being dare to speak but you. Be still, my soul! Speak, Love!

Then it is that *we know everything without knowing anything.* Not that we have the presumption to suppose that within ourselves we possess all truth. No! On the contrary, we feel that we see nothing, can do nothing, and are nothing *in ourselves.* We feel this and are delighted at it. But in this state we find everything we need from moment to moment in the infinity of God. There we find the daily bread of knowledge and of everything else, without storing it up. Then the anointing from above teaches us all truth, while it takes away our own wisdom, glory, self-interest, even our own willfulness. It makes us content with our weakness and with a position below every creature. We are ready to yield to the lowest, and to confess our most secret wretchedness before the whole world, fearing unfaithfulness more than punishment and shamefacedness.

Here it is that the Spirit teaches us all truth: for all truth is inherently contained in this sacrifice of love, where the soul strips itself of everything in order to present itself to God.

⋑ 24
WHEN SPIRITUALLY DISHEARTENED

It is indeed good to see only the friends whom God gives us, and to be protected from all the rest! In the midst of my difficulties I often feel inclined to long for the freedom that solitude brings. But we must stay in the path marked out for us, and go on our way without listening to our own preferences.

Avoid weariness, and give some satisfaction to your natural activity. Seek a certain number of persons whose company is not disagreeable to you and who can refresh your mind when there is need of it. We do not need a great deal of company, and we must accustom ourselves not to be too particular. It is sufficient if we find some good people who are quiet and moderately reasonable. Vary your occupations so that you may not be fatigued with any one of them.

I am not at all surprised that your feelings of lukewarmness and your lack of attraction to the spiritual life should cast you down. Nothing can be more disheartening. You have to do only two things, it seems to me: One is to avoid all that distracts or absorbs you. By doing this you will cut off the source of everything that can be a dangerous distraction and can dry up your prayer. We must not expect to be nourished inwardly when we are always taken up with external things. Faithfulness in renouncing things that make you too excited and too unreserved in conversation is absolutely necessary to draw down upon yourself the spirit of tranquility and prayer. We cannot enjoy God and the world at the same time. We keep regular in our prayers, and for two hours we keep the same disposition that we have in our hearts during the rest of the day.

Having cut off the things that distract you, you must try frequently to renew your sense of the presence of God, even in the midst of the things that are necessary for you, so that you may not throw into them too much of your purely natural action. You must try to act always by grace in the spirit of death to self. We can gradually arrive at this by often suspending our impulsiveness, in order to listen to the voice of God within the soul, and to let him take possession of us.

≈ 25
DEALING WITH OUR FAULTS

Many of our faults are voluntary in different degrees, though we may not commit them with a deliberate purpose of failing God. One friend sometimes reproaches another for a fault that is not expressly intended to offend, and yet is committed with the knowledge that it might do so. In the same way, God lays this sort of fault to our charge. Such faults are voluntary, for although we do not do them with an express intention, we still commit them freely and against a certain inner light of conscience that should have caused us to hesitate and wait. Godly souls are often guilty of these offenses. As for faults that are committed deliberately, it would be strange indeed if a soul consecrated to God should fall into such things.

Little faults become great and even monstrous in our eyes, to the extent that we increase in the pure light of God. Just as the rising sun reveals the true size of objects that were seen dimly during the night, the increase of inward light will show our imperfections to be far greater and more deadly in their roots than we had thought them. We witness, in addition, a host of other faults, of whose existence we did not have the slightest suspicion. We find the weaknesses necessary to deprive us of all confidence in our own strength. This discovery, however, far from discouraging us, serves to destroy our self-reliance and to raze to the ground the edifice of pride. Nothing so decidedly marks the solid progress of a soul as being able to view its own depravity without being disturbed or discouraged.

It is an important precept to abstain from doing a wrong thing whenever we perceive it in time, and when we do note that we have done it, to bear the humiliation of the fault courageously. If we perceive a fault before committing it, we must see to it that we do not resist and quench the Spirit of God warning us of it inwardly. The Spirit is easily offended and very jealous. He desires to be listened to and obeyed. He withdraws if he is displeased. The slightest resistance to him is a wrong, for we must yield everything to him the moment we perceive him. Faults of haste and frailty are nothing compared with those of shutting our ears when the voice of the Holy Spirit begins to speak in the depths of the heart.

Restlessness and an injured self-love will never mend those faults that we do not recognize until after we have committed them. On the contrary, such feelings are simply the impatience of wounded pride at seeing what frustrates it. We must quietly humble ourselves in peace. I say *humble ourselves in peace*, for we have not become humble if we do so in a vexed and spiteful way. We must condemn our faults, mourn over them, and repent of them without seeking the slightest shadow of consolation in any excuse. We must see ourselves covered with shame in the presence of God, and all this without being bitter against ourselves or discouraged, but peacefully reaping the profit of being humbled. In this way, we draw from the serpent itself the antidote of his venom.

It often happens that what we offer to God is not what he most desires to have of us. *That* we are frequently the most unwilling to give, and the most fearful that he will ask. He desires the sacrifice of *Isaac*, the well-beloved son. All the rest is as nothing in his eyes, and he permits it all to be offered in a painful, unprofitable manner, because he has no blessings for a divided soul. He will have everything, and until then there is no rest. "Who has resisted him and come out unscathed?"[27] Would you prosper and secure the blessing of God upon your labors? Reserve nothing, cut to the quick and burn without sparing anything, and the God of peace will be with you! What comfort, what freedom, what strength, what enlargedness of heart, what increase of grace will follow when there remains nothing between God and the soul, and when the last sacrifices have been offered up without hesitation!

We must be neither amazed nor disheartened. We are not more wicked than we were. We are really less so, but while our evil diminishes, our light increases, and we are struck with painful dismay at its extent. But let us remember, for our consolation, that becoming aware of our disease is the first step in its cure. When we have no sense of our need, we have no curative principle within us. We are in a state of blindness, presumption, and apathy, in which we are delivered over to our own counsel, and commit ourselves to the current whose fatal speed we do not realize until we are called to struggle against it.

We must not be discouraged either, by our weakness or by our dislike of the constant activity that may be a part of our life. Discouragement is not the fruit of humility, but of pride. Nothing can be worse. Suppose we have stumbled, or even fallen. Let us rise and run again. All our falls are useful if they strip us of a disastrous confidence in ourselves, while they do not take away a humble and saving trust in God.

The dislikes we feel toward our duties come from our imperfections. If we were perfect and mature, we would love everything in the order of God. Since we are born corrupt, however, and with a nature revolting against his laws, let us praise him that he knows how to bring good from evil, and can use even our dislikes as a source of virtue. The work of grace does not always progress as evenly as that of nature, says St. Teresa.

Carefully purify your conscience, then, from daily faults. Allow no sin to dwell in your heart. Small as a sin may seem, it obscures and dims the light of grace, weighs down the soul, and hinders the constant communion with Jesus Christ that it should be your pleasure to cultivate. You will become lukewarm, forget God, and find yourself growing in attachment to the world. A pure soul, on the other hand, that is humbled and rises promptly after its smallest faults, remains fervent and upright.

God never makes us aware of our weakness except to give us his strength. Do not be disturbed by what is not deliberate. The great point is never to act in opposition to the inner light, and to be willing to go as far as God would have us go.

26
FAITHFULNESS IN SMALL THINGS

St. Francis de Sales says that great virtues and faithfulness in small things are like sugar and salt. Sugar is more delicious, but of less frequent use, while salt enters into every article of our food. Great virtues are rare. They are seldom needed, and when the occasion comes, we are prepared for it by everything that has gone before. We are excited by the greatness of the sacrifice involved, and sustained, either by the brilliancy of the action in the eyes of others, or by self-confidence in our ability to do such wonderful things.

Small occasions, however, are unforeseen. They recur every moment and place us constantly in conflict with our pride, our laziness, our self-esteem, and our passions. They are calculated to subdue our wills thoroughly, and leave us no retreat. If we are faithful in them, the old nature will have no time to breathe. It must die to all its inclinations. It would please us much better to make some great sacrifices, however painful and violent, on the condition that we could then be free to follow our own pleasure and to keep our old habits in little things. However, it is only by faithfulness in small matters that the grace of true love is sustained and distinguished from the fleeting excitements of a purely human nature.

We may compare the godly life with our temporal goods: there is more danger from the little expenses than from larger expenditures, and one who understands how to take care of little things will soon accumulate more. Everything great owes its greatness to the small elements that compose it. One who wastes nothing soon will be rich.

Consider, on the other hand, that God does not so much regard our actions as he does the motive of love from which they spring and the pliability of our wills to his. Other people judge our deeds by their outward appearance. With God, things that are the most dazzling in human eyes are of no account. What he desires is a pure intention, a will that is ready for anything and is ever pliable in his hands. What he seeks is the giving up of self. All this can be manifested much more frequently on small occasions than on extraordinary ones. There will also be much less danger from pride, and the test will be far more searching. Indeed, it sometimes happens that we find it harder to part with something of little substance than with an important interest. It may be more of a cross to us to abandon a vain amusement than to give a large gift to charity.

We are more easily deceived about small matters if we imagine them to be innocent and think that we are indifferent to them. Nevertheless, when God takes them away we may easily recognize, in the pain of their loss, how excessive was our use of them and how inexcusable was our attachment to them. If we are in the habit of neglecting little things, we will be constantly offending our families, our fellow workers, and all who have relationships with us. No one can well believe that our Christian walk is sincere when our behavior is careless and irregular in its little details. What ground do we have for believing that we are ready to make the greatest sacrifices if we fail daily in offering the least?

The greatest danger of all is this: by neglecting small matters, our soul becomes accustomed to unfaithfulness. We grieve the Holy Spirit. We revert to ourselves. We begin to think it a small thing to be lacking toward God. On the other hand, true love can see nothing as small; everything that can either please or displease God seems to be great. It is not that true love disturbs the soul with scruples,* but it puts no limits to its faithfulness. It acts simply with God, and as it does not concern itself about things that God does not require of it, so it never hesitates an instant about those things he does, whether they are great or small.

---

* It is very important that a word of caution be sounded here against taking this chapter as a justification for scrupulous concern for little things. It is the mark of immature and self-righteous spirituality to become anxious about little things and neglect the great ones. Fénelon's word here is spoken to those who excuse themselves in the little things, not to those who are already plagued with the fear of being wrong. See the introduction to Part 1, *The Royal Way of the Cross*, for more about *scruples*.

Therefore it is not by incessant care that we become faithful in the smallest things, but simply by a love that is free from the reflections and fears of a restless and excessively scrupulous soul. We are, so to speak, drawn along by the love of God. We have no desire to do anything but what we do, no will regarding anything that we do or do not do. At the very moment when God is following the soul, relentlessly pursuing it into the smallest details and seemingly taking away all its freedom, the soul finds itself in a spacious place and enjoys perfect peace in him. Happy soul!

Those who are by nature less strict in small matters should apply and preserve inviolate the most rigid laws respecting those small matters. They are tempted to despise small things, habitually thinking they are unimportant. They do not understand the unconscious and hidden progress of our emotions, and even forget their own sad experience on that subject. They prefer to be deluded by the promise of an imaginary future firmness of resolve, and to trust in their own courage that has so often deceived them, rather than to subject themselves to unceasing faithfulness. "It is a small matter," they say. That is true, but it is of amazing consequence to you. It is something you love enough to refuse to give it up to God. It is something you sneer at in words, so that you may have an excuse to keep it: a small matter—but one that you withhold from your Maker, which can prove your ruin.

It is not nobility of the soul that despises small things. On the contrary, it is a constricted, shrunken spirit that regards as unimportant what it cannot project as far as its inevitable result. The more it causes us to be on our guard against small matters, the more we need to fear neglectfulness, to distrust our strength, and to put impregnable barriers between ourselves and the smallest carelessness.

Finally, judge by your own feelings. What would you think of a friend who owed everything to you and who was willing from a sense of duty to serve you on those rare occasions that are called great, but who should manifest neither affection nor the least regard for your wishes in the common, everyday things of life?

Do not be frightened at this attention to small matters. It takes courage at first, but this is a discipline that you need, and it will yield you peace and security. Without it, everything is trouble and relapse. God will gradually make it pleasant and easy to you, for true love is obedient without being forced to be so, and without strife or effort.

⤳ 27
EXACTNESS AND
FREEDOM OF SPIRIT

We should unite great exactness with great freedom. Exactness will make you faithful, and freedom will make you courageous. If you were to attempt to be exact without being free, you would fall into slavery and scruples. If you were to attempt to be free without being exact, you would soon degenerate into negligence and carelessness. Exactness by itself narrows the mind and heart, and freedom by itself loosens them too much.

Those who have no experience in the ways of God do not believe that these two virtues can agree together. They think that being exact means always living under constraint, in distress of mind, and in an uneasy and scrupulous timidity that robs the soul of all its rest and makes it see sins everywhere. They think that being exact hampers the soul so much that it is in constant conflict with itself about everything—down to the merest trifles, scarcely daring to breathe. To be free, they say, is to have a broad conscience, and not to pay too close an attention even to that, to be satisfied with avoiding gross faults, and to count as considerable faults only gross crimes. Excepting only these, they allow themselves everything that can artfully flatter self-love. Whatever license we may give to our passions, we are to calm and console ourselves easily by the simple thought that we did not see any great evil in such things. St. Paul did not speak in this way when he said to those whom he had brought into the life of grace and of whom he was trying to make perfect Christians: *Be free, but with the liberty that Jesus Christ has purchased for you; be free, because the Savior has called you to freedom; but do not let this liberty be for you an occasion or a pretext for doing evil.*[28]

True exactness consists in obeying God in all things. It means to follow the light that shows us our duty and the grace that urges us to do it, having for the principle of our conduct the desire to please God in everything and always to do, not only what is agreeable to him, but if possible, what is *most* agreeable to him without bothering ourselves with quibbling about the difference between great sins and little sins, between imperfections and unfaithfulnesses. For, although it is true that there is a difference between all these things, there ought to be no such distinction any longer for a soul that is determined to refuse nothing to God that it can give him. It is in this sense that the Apostle says that "the law is not made for the righteous."[29] He is talking about the constraining law, the hard law, the threatening law—if we may dare to say so, the tyrannical and enslaving law. But just persons have a superior law that raises them above all this and makes them enter into the true liberty of the children of God. That is, they always wish to do what is most pleasing to their heavenly Father, according to those excellent words of St. Augustine: "Love, and then do what you will."

To a sincere will always to do what seems best to us in the sight of God, we may unite the further intention of doing so with joy, of never allowing ourselves to be discouraged when we have not done it. We may begin over and over again, hundreds of times, resolved to do it better, hoping always that in the end we *will* do it, bearing with ourselves in our unintentional weaknesses as God bears with us. We can wait patiently for the moment that he has marked out for our perfect deliverance, making up our mind meanwhile to walk on with simplicity in the way that is open to us, according to our strength, not wasting time looking behind us. We are to extend our energies and set our faces steadily always, as the Apostle says, "to what lies ahead."[30] At the same time, we are not to make a multitude of useless reflections upon our failures. Doing that would only keep us back, trouble our minds, and cast down our heart. We must humble ourselves because of our failures and grieve over them when we first see them. But afterward we must leave them and go on our way.

We are not to interpret everything against ourselves with a literal and legalistic severity, looking upon God as a spy who is watching us so that he may surprise us, or as an enemy who is laying snares for us, but rather as a Father who loves us and wishes to save us. If we persevere in these intentions, if we are full of confidence in his goodness, if we are careful to invoke his mercy, and if we get rid of all our vain reliance on creatures and on ourselves—if we do all this, we will have found the way to true and perfect freedom, and perhaps its fixed dwelling place.

Aspire to this. Exactness and freedom ought to walk together with even steps. But indeed I think you have more need to lean to the side of confidence in God and a great expansion of heart. It is for this reason that I do not hesitate in telling you that you must give yourself up entirely to the grace that God gives you sometimes in a close union with himself. Do not be afraid at such times to lose sight of yourself, to contemplate him alone, as closely as he will allow you to do so. Do not be afraid to plunge yourself in the ocean of his love. Happy you, if you could do this so perfectly as never to find yourself again! It is good, when God gives you this grace, to always finish with an act of humility and of filial and respectful fear. This will prepare your soul for new gifts. This is the advice of St. Teresa, and I commend it to you.

28
DEALING WITH
CONTRADICTORY FEELINGS

We must not be surprised if we frequently find in ourselves emotions of pride, of self-complacency, of self-confidence, of desire to follow our own inclination against what is right, of impatience at the weakness of others, or even of annoyance at our own condition. In such cases we must instantly let them drop like some stone to the bottom of the sea and place ourselves again in God, and before acting, wait until we are in such a frame of heart as our recollection can bring forth in us. If the distraction of business, or of tenacity of imagination, should keep us from entering calmly and easily into such a state, we must at least try to be quiet by a steady set of the will and by the desire for such refocusing. In such a case, the will to be recollected serves to deprive the soul of its own will and to render it submissive in the hands of God.

If in your excitement, some emotion too nearly like the old fallen nature should come up in you, do not be discouraged. Keep going straight ahead. Quietly bear the humiliation of your fault before God without allowing self-love to be distressed at the betrayal of its weakness. Proceed confidently, without being troubled by the anguish of a wounded pride that cannot bear to see itself imperfect. Your fault will be of service in causing you to die to self and to become nothing before him.

The true method of curing this defect is to become dead to the sensitiveness of self-love, without impeding the movement of grace, which had been slightly interrupted by this fleeting unfaithfulness!

The great point is to renounce your own wisdom by honesty of conduct, and to be ready to give up the favor, esteem, and approval of everyone whenever the path in which God leads you requires it.

We are not to meddle with things that God does not lay upon us, or uselessly utter hard sayings that those about us are not able to bear. We must follow after God, never go before him. When he gives the signal, we must leave everything and follow him. If we hesitate, delay, lose courage, and dilute what he would have us do; if we indulge in fears for our own comfort or safety, desiring to shield ourselves from suffering and a bad reputation; or if we seek to find some excuse for not performing a difficult and painful duty, we are truly guilty in his sight, especially so after we have made an absolute consecration and a conviction in conscience that he is requiring something of us. May God keep us from such unfaithfulness! Nothing is more dreadful than this inward resistance to him.

Other faults committed in the simplicity of your good intention will be of service if they produce humility and make you of less and less account in your own eyes. But resistance to the Spirit of God through pride or a cowardly worldly wisdom, concerned for its own comfort in performing the work of God, is a fault that will imperceptibly quench the Spirit of grace in your heart. God, jealous and rejected after so much mercy, will depart and leave you to your own resources. You will then turn around in a kind of circle instead of advancing with rapid strides along the King's highway. Your inward life will grow dim and dimmer, without your being able to detect the sure and deep-seated source of your disease.

God would choose to see in us a single-heartedness that can contain as much more of his wisdom as it contains less of our own. He desires to see us lowly in our own eyes, and as meek in his hands as a little child. He desires to create in our heart the childlike disposition so distasteful to the spirit of fallen man, but so agreeable to the spirit of the gospel.

By this very singleness and lowliness he will heal all the remnants of haughty and self-confident wisdom in us. And we will say with David, "I will become even more undignified than this, and I will be humiliated in my own eyes,"[31] from the moment we give ourselves to the Lord.

29
MAINTAINING FAITH WITHOUT FEELINGS

You rely a little too much on the concentration of your soul and feelings in the presence of God. God has taken away these conscious gifts in order to detach you from them, to teach you how weak you are in yourself, and to accustom you to serve God without the enjoyment that makes virtue easy. The same service means much more to him when we perform it without pleasure and with distaste. I do very little for my friend when I go on foot to see him, because I love walking, have excellent legs, and take very great pleasure in using them. But if I become gouty, then every step that I take costs me a great deal of pain, and so the same visits that I formerly made to my friend, and that he did not think much of, begin to have a new value. They become signs of a very deep and very strong friendship, and the more pain I have in making them, the more he appreciates it. One step taken in that pain is worth more than a hundred steps taken in pleasure.

I say this to prevent you from falling into a very dangerous temptation, which is discouragement and trouble. When you are enjoying the abundance of grace and interior fervor, then count all your good works as nothing, because they flow, so to speak, from the very Source. But, on the contrary, when you feel yourself to be in dryness, obscurity, poverty, and almost powerlessness of soul, remain humble under the hand of God in a state of bare faith, recognize your own misery, turn yourself toward the all-powerful Lord, and never doubt his assistance. Oh, how good it is for us to see ourselves stripped of all those emotional supports that flatter self-love and reduced to confess the truth of those words of Holy Scripture, "No one living is righteous before you."[32]

Walk on always, in the name of God, although it may seem to you that you have neither strength nor courage to put one foot in front of the other. If human courage fails you, so much the better. If you abandon yourself to God, he will not fail to help your powerlessness. St. Paul exclaims, "When I am weak, then I am strong."[33] And when he prayed to be delivered from his weakness, God answered him, "My power is made perfect in weakness."[34] Allow yourself, then, to be made perfect by experiencing your imperfection and by humbly fleeing to him who is the strength of the weak.

When you are in prayer, engage yourself, in simple freedom, with all that can help you to pray and that will help you to remain focused. Relieve your imagination, which is sometimes impatient and sometimes exhausted. Make use of everything that can calm it and help you to an informal communication with God. All that is to your taste and according to your needs in this loving conversation will be good. "Where the Spirit of the Lord is, there is freedom."[35] This innocent and simple freedom consists in seeking simply and honestly the nourishment of love that can most easily unite us with the Beloved of our soul. Your inner poverty will often recall you to a feeling of your misery. God, who is so good, will not allow you to lose sight of how unworthy you are of him, and the thought of your own unworthiness will bring you back at once to his infinite goodness.

Take courage! The work of God can be done only by the destruction of the self-life. May he sustain you, comfort you, make you poor,
and help you experience the truth of that beautiful word, "Blessed are
the poor in spirit."[36]

⪦ 30
UNDUE ATTACHMENT
TO FEELINGS

Those who are committed to God only so far as they enjoy pleasure
and consolation resemble those who followed the Lord, not to hear
his teaching, but because they ate the loaves and had their fill.[37] They
are ready to say with St. Peter, "Rabbi, it is good for us to be here.
Let us put up three shelters."[38] But they do not know what they say.
After being impassioned by the joys of the mountain, they deny the
Son of God and refuse to follow him to Calvary. Not only do they
desire delights, but they seek illuminations also. The mind is curious
to behold, while the heart demands to be filled with soft and flattering emotions. Is this dying to self? Is this the way in which *the just
shall live by faith?*[39]

Such people desire to have unusual revelations that may be regarded
as supernatural gifts and a mark of the special favor of God. Nothing is
so flattering to self-love. All the greatness of the world at once could
not so inflate the heart. These supernatural gifts nourish in secret the
life of the old nature. It is an ambition of the most refined character,
since it is completely spiritual. But it is merely ambition, a desire to
feel, to enjoy, to possess God and his gifts, to see his light, to discern
spirits, to prophesy—in short, to be an extraordinarily gifted person.
For the enjoyment of revelations and delights leads the soul little by
little toward a secret coveting of all these things.

Yet the Apostle shows us *the most excellent way*,[40] for which he inspires
us to a holy ambition: it is the way of love that is *not self-seeking*.[41] It
is less in search of pleasure than of God, whose will it longs to fulfill.

If this love finds pleasure in devotion, it does not rest in it, but makes it serve to strengthen its weakness, as a convalescent uses a staff to aid her in walking, but throws it aside when she is well again. In the same way tender and childlike souls whom God fed with milk in the beginning, allow themselves to be weaned when they see that it is time for them to be nourished with strong food.

We must not continue to be children, always demanding heavenly consolations. With St. Paul, we must put childish things behind us.[42] Our early joys served well to attract us and to draw us away from unrefined and worldly pleasures toward others of a purer kind. They led us to a life of prayer and commitment. But to demand to be in a state of constant enjoyment takes away the feeling of the cross, and to live in a fervor of devotion that continually keeps paradise open—this is not dying upon the cross and becoming nothing.

This life of revelations and conscious delights is a very dangerous snare if we become so attached to it as to desire nothing more. Those who have no other attraction to prayer will quit both prayer and God whenever these gratifications disappear. St. Teresa says that a great number of people leave off praying at the very moment when their devotion is beginning to be real. How many there are who, in consequence of too soft an upbringing in Jesus Christ, and too great a fondness for the milk of his word, go back and abandon their interior life as soon as God undertakes to wean them! We need not be astonished at this, for they mistake the portico of the temple for the very sanctuary itself. They desire the death of their unrefined external passion, so that they may lead a delicious life of self-satisfaction within. From this it follows that unfaithfulness and disappointment occur even among those who appear the most fervent and the most devoted. Those who have talked the loudest about death to self and about the darkness of faith are often the most surprised and discouraged when they really experience these things and their consolation is taken away.

Souls are earthly in desiring something tangible, so to speak, before they can feel firm. But this is all wrong. It is these very things of sense that produce vacillation. We think, while the pleasure lasts, that we will never desert God. We say in our feeling of security that we will never be shaken.[43] But the moment our intoxication is over, we give up all for lost, in this way substituting our own pleasure and imagination in place of God. Pure and undisguised faith alone is a sure guard against illusion. When our foundation is not upon imagination, feeling, pleasure, or extraordinary illumination; when we rest upon God only in unpretentious and plain faith, in the simplicity of the gospel receiving the consolations that he sends, but dwelling in none of them; when we abstain from judging and ever strive to be obedient, believing that it is easy to be deceived and others may be able to set us right—in short, when we always act with simplicity and an upright intention, following the light of the faith in each present moment—then we are indeed in a way that is not easily subject to illusion.

Experience will demonstrate better than anything else how much more certain this path is than the path of special revelations, illuminations, and emotional delights. Whoever will try it will soon find that this way of simple faith, strictly followed, is the way to the most complete death of self. Interior delights and revelations secure our self-love against loss or harm—despite all our external sacrifices—and lead us to cherish a secret and refined life of the old nature. But to allow ourselves to be stripped inwardly and outwardly at once, outwardly by circumstances and inwardly by this dark night of pure faith*—this is a total sacrifice and least likely to be subject to self-deception.

Those who seek a constant succession of emotions and certainties are by that very course exposing themselves most surely to deception. On the other hand, those who follow the leadings of the love that strips them and leaves them the faith that walks in darkness, without seeking any other support, avoid all the sources of error and illusion. The author of *The Imitation of Christ* (Book III) tells us that if God takes away our inward delights, it should be our pleasure to remain pleasureless. How beloved of God is a soul crucified in this way, a soul who rests calmly upon the cross and desires only to die with Jesus! It is not true to say that on being deprived of feeling we are afraid of

* [without being able to *see* what it is all about!]

having lost God. That fear comes from our impatience under the trial, the restlessness of a pampered and dainty nature, the search for some support for self-love, and the secret return to self after our consecration to God.

Dear God, where are those who do not stop along the way? If they persevere to the end, they will receive a crown of Life!

⇒ 31
THE PROPER USE OF CROSSES

It is hard to convince us of the goodness of God in loading those whom he loves with crosses. "Why," we say, "should he take pleasure in causing us to suffer? Could he not make us good without making us miserable?" Yes, doubtless he could, for all things are possible with God. In his all-powerful hands he holds our hearts, and he turns them as he will, as the skill of the workman can give direction to the stream at the summit of a hill. But able as he may be to save us without crosses, he has not chosen to do so, just as he has not seen fit to create people at once in the full vigor of adulthood, but has allowed them to grow up by degrees amid all the dangers and weaknesses of childhood and youth. In this matter, he is the Master: we have only to adore in silence the depths of his wisdom without understanding it. Nevertheless, we see clearly that we never could become completely good without becoming humble, unselfish, and disposed to give back everything to God without any restless self-concern.

In this process of detaching us from our self-life and in destroying our self-love, it would take a powerful miracle to keep the work of grace from being painful. Neither in his gracious nor in his providential dealings does God work a miracle lightly. It would be as great a wonder to see a person full of self become in a instant dead to all self-interest and all sensitiveness, as it would be to see a slumbering infant wake up in the morning a fully developed adult. God works in mysterious ways in grace as well as in nature, concealing his operations under an unseen succession of events. In this way he keeps us in the darkness of faith. Not only does he accomplish his designs gradually, but also he does so by means that appear the simplest and best designed to accomplish the end in view, in order that human wisdom may ascribe the success to the process, and in this way make his own working be less evident! Otherwise every act of God would seem to be a miracle, and the state of faith, in which it is God's will that we should live, would come to an end.

This state of faith is necessary, not only to stimulate good souls, causing them to sacrifice their reason in a life full of darkness, but also to blind those who, by their presumption, deserve such a sentence. They see the works of God, but they do not understand them. They can see nothing in them but the results of material laws. They are destitute of true knowledge, for that is open only to those who distrust their own abilities. Proud human wisdom is unworthy to be taken into the counsels of God.

God renders the working of grace slow and obscure, then, so that he may keep us in the darkness of faith. He makes use of the inconstancy and ingratitude of the creature, and he makes use of the disappointments, the surpluses, and the excesses that accompany prosperity, in order to detach us from them both. He frees us from self by revealing our weaknesses and corruptions in a multitude of backslidings. All this dealing appears perfectly natural, and it is by this succession of natural means that we are burned as by a slow fire. We would like to be consumed at once by the flames of pure love, but such an end would scarcely cost us anything. It is only an excessive self-love that desires to become perfect in a moment and at so cheap a rate.

Why do we rebel against the length of the way? Because we are so wrapped up in self, and God must destroy this infatuation. It is a constant hindrance to his work. Of what can we complain? Our trouble is that we are attached to creatures and still more to self. The operation is painful, but is made necessary by our corruption, and that same corruption makes it distressing. If our flesh were sound, the surgeon would not use a knife. He cuts only in proportion to the depth of the wound and the diseased condition of the parts. If we suffer greatly, it is because the evil is great. Is the surgeon cruel because he cuts to the quick? No, on the contrary, it is both love and skill. He would use the same treatment on his only and well-beloved son.

It is the same way with God. He never afflicts us except against his own inclination. His fatherly heart is not gladdened at the sight of our misery, but he cuts to the quick, so that he may heal the disease in our souls. He must snatch away from us whatever we cling to too fondly, and all that we love inordinately, contrary to his claim upon us. He acts in this as we do with our children. They cry because we take away the knife that was their amusement but might have been their death. We weep, we become discouraged, we cry aloud. We are ready to murmur against God, as children get angry with their mothers. But God lets us weep and secures our salvation. He afflicts only to amend.

Even when God seems to overwhelm us, he means nothing but good: it is only to spare us the evils we were preparing for ourselves. The things we now lament for a little while would have caused us to mourn forever. What we think was lost was indeed lost when we seemed to have it, but now God has laid it aside for us so that we may inherit it in the eternity that is so near at hand. He deprives us of what we cherish only to teach us how to love it blamelessly, steadfastly, and moderately, and to secure its eternal enjoyment for us in his own bosom. In this way he does us a thousand times more good than we could ask or think by ourselves. With the exception of sin, nothing happens in this world outside of the will of God. He is the Author, Ruler, and Giver of all. He has numbered the hairs of our head, the leaves on the tree, the sand on the seashore, and the drops of the ocean. When he made the universe, his wisdom weighed and measured every atom. He breathes into us the breath of life, and renews it every moment. He knows the numbers of our days, and holds in his all-powerful hand the keys of the tomb to open or to shut.

God is good, tender, and compassionate toward our misery, even when he seems to launch his thunders at us, even when we are open-mouthed in our complaints about his severity.

We exaggerate all our sufferings by our cowardliness. Our sufferings are great, it is true, but they are magnified by fear. The way to lessen them is to abandon ourselves courageously into the hands of God. We must suffer, but the aim of our pain is to purify our souls and make us worthy of him.

⤳ 32
JOY IN BEARING THE CROSS

I cannot help admiring the goodness of the cross. We are worth nothing without it. It makes me tremble and convulses me as soon as I begin to feel it. All that I have said of its helpful operations vanishes away before the agony it brings to my inmost heart. But as soon as it gives me time to breathe, I open my eyes again and I see that it is worthy of praise. Then I am ashamed to have been so overwhelmed by it. The experience of this inconsistency is a deep lesson for me.

In whatever state we may be, whatever consequences God may give, we are blessed in being given over to his hands. If we should die, it is in the Lord. If we should live, it is living to him. As St. Teresa has said, "Either to die, or to suffer."

Nothing is more important than the cross, except the perfect reign of God. Indeed, when we suffer with love, his reign has begun in us, and we must be contented with that as long as God defers the completion of it.

We need the cross. The faithful Distributor of gifts has allotted our portion to us as well. May he be blessed forever. Oh, how good he is to inflict punishment on us for our correction!

⤳ 33
WHAT GOD ORDERS IS BEST

We may desire to be free, so that we may pray to God—and God, who knows so much better than we do what we really want, sends perplexity and restraint so that we are put to confusion. This trial from the hand of God will be far more help to you than the self-sought sweetness of prayer. You know very well that it is not necessary to be always on retreat in order to love God. When he gives you the time, take it and profit by it. But until then, wait in faith, well persuaded that what he orders is best.

Lift your heart to him frequently by pulling away from the world. Speak only when obliged to, and bear with patience whatever happens to cross you. God treats you according to your necessity, and you have more need of humiliation than of illumination!

When you are not permitted to enjoy long seasons of leisure, make the most of the short ones: ten minutes faithfully employed before God in the midst of your distractions will be as valuable to you as whole hours devoted to him in your more unoccupied moments. Moreover, these little odds and ends of time will amount to quite a sum in the course of the day, and will present this advantage, that God will very likely have been more in mind than if you had given it to him all at once. Love, silence, suffering, yielding our own pleasure: such is our lot. We are called to be happy in bearing the burden that God himself lays upon us in the order of his providence.

The crosses that we originate are not nearly as efficient in dealing with self-love as those that come to us in the daily allotments of God. These allotments contribute no food for the nourishment of our own wills, and since they proceed from a merciful providence, they are accompanied by grace sufficient for all our needs. We have nothing to do, then, but to surrender ourselves to God each day, without looking further. He will carry us in his arms as a tender mother bears her child. Let us believe, hope, and love with all the simplicity of little children. In every necessity let us turn a loving and trusting look toward our heavenly Father. For what do the Scriptures say? "Can a mother forget the baby at her breast and have no compassion on the child she has borne? Though she may forget, I will not forget you!"[44]

⮎ 34
KEEPING ALL OUR AFFECTIONS IN GOD

When we love anything out of God, says St. Augustine, we love God the less for it. It is like a stream from which part of the water is turned off. This division of the affections of the heart diminishes what should go to God, and it is from such a division that arise all the disturbances of the heart. God wishes to have everything, and his jealousy will not leave a divided heart in peace. The least affection outside of him complicates our lives and causes us to feel ill at ease. It is only in an unreserved love for him that the heart deserves to find peace.

The divided heart is the opposite of a recollected one. It awakens all our appetites for created things, dragging the soul and tearing it away from the true Center of its rest. Moreover, it excites the emotions and the imagination, requiring painful labor to quiet them again, and this occupation is an additional kind of inevitable distraction.

Busy yourself as little as possible with everything that is external. Give to the concerns that providence lays upon you a quiet and moderate attention at suitable hours. Leave the rest. We do much more by a gentle and tranquil concentration in the presence of God than by the greatest eagerness and all the efforts of our restless nature.

⮎ 35
TWO KINDS OF LOVE

Why do the gifts of God give more pleasure when they exist in ourselves than when they are given to our neighbor? Why, if we are not attached to self? If we prefer to see them in our own possession rather than in the possession of those about us, we will certainly be affected when we see them operating more perfectly in them than they are in us. This constitutes envy. What are we to do? We must rejoice that the will of God is done in us and that his will reigns there not for our happiness and perfection, but for his own good pleasure and glory.

God, in his desire to strip the soul for its own perfection, causes it really to pass through these trials of self, and never leaves it alone until he has put an end to its love of self-concern and support. There is nothing so jealous, so exacting, and so searching as this pure love of God. It cannot abide a thousand things that were unnoticed in our previous state. What other Christians might call insignificant seems a vital point to the soul that is intent on the death of the old self. As with gold in the furnace, the fire consumes all that is not gold, so it seems necessary that the heart should be melted with fervent heat in order for the love of God to be rendered pure. Those being purified in this way are thankful to God for whatever he does in them solely because he does it for his own glory.

God does not pursue every soul in this way in the present life. There are many truly good persons whom he leaves in some degree under the sway of self-love. These remainders of self help support them in the practice of virtue and serve to purify them to a certain degree. There would be almost nothing more harmful or dangerous than to deprive such persons of the contemplation of the grace of God in them as leading to their own personal perfection. This second group is also grateful, but partly because their *own* perfection is secured at the same time. If the first group should try to deprive the second of this interior comfort they have in reference to grace, they would cause them as much injury as they would an infant by weaning it before it was able to eat. To take away the breast would be to destroy it. We must never seek to deprive a soul of the food that still contains nourishment for it, and that God allows to remain as a stay to its weakness. To forestall or hinder grace would be to destroy it.

On the other hand, the second group should not condemn the first because they do not see them as much concerned as they themselves are about their own perfection. God works in everyone as he pleases. The wind blows wherever it pleases,[45] and as it pleases. Forgetfulness of self is a state in which God can do with us whatever most pleases him.

The important point is that those who are still supported somewhat by self should not be too anxious about those who are in pure love, nor should the latter try to make the former pass through new trials before God calls them to it.

⤳ 36
OUR UNION IN GOD

Let us all remain in our only Center, where we can always find each other, and where we are all merely one and the same. Oh, how miserable it is to be separate from one another! We must be only one! I wish to know nothing but that unity. All that goes beyond that comes from division and self-seeking.

Friends are separated and consequently they scarcely love each other at all, or love each other very badly. The "I" loves itself too much to be able to love what is called "him" or "her." Those who have only one single love have stripped off the "I," and love nothing but in God and for God alone.

Those who are engrossed in self-love, love their neighbor only in themselves and for themselves. Let us then be united by being nothing except in our common Center, where everything is blended together without a shadow of distinction. It is there that I will meet you, and we will dwell together. It is at this indivisible point that China and Canada join hands. It is here that all distances are nullified.

In the name of God, be simple, humble, open, unreserved, and distrustful of self. God will give you all you need through others, without giving it to you for yourself. Believe humbly, live by faith alone, and it will be given to you in proportion as you have believed.

⌒ 37
BEARING SUFFERING

Lovingly kiss the Hand that strikes you. Formerly you abused your health, and the pleasures that health gives. The weakness and the pain that now have taken the place of health are your natural penance. May God humble your mind even more than your body, and while he comforts your body according to its needs, may he entirely free you from your deceptions about yourself.

We are truly strong when we cease to believe in our strength, when we feel nothing but the weakness and the limited powers of our own spirit! Then we become ready to think we may be mistaken, and to confess that this is the case by correcting ourselves. Then our minds are open to the opinions of others, and we despise nothing but ourselves and our own ideas. We decide nothing, and we say the most positive things in the simplest tone and in a manner that is most considerate of others. We willingly allow others to judge us, we yield without difficulty, and we give the first comer the right to rebuke or correct us.

At the same time we never judge anyone except from real necessity. We speak only to persons who wish us to speak to them, and while we are telling them of the imperfections we see in them, we do so without laying down the law, as if we would prefer to be silent rather than speaking as if we took pleasure in our criticism.

This is the health I desire for you in your mind, with a real cure in your body. And while you are waiting for this, bear your suffering with humility and patience.

⌒ 38
SUFFERING RIGHTLY

We know that we must suffer, and that we deserve it. Nevertheless, we are always surprised at affliction, as if we thought we neither deserved it nor needed it. Only true and pure love delights to endure, for nothing else is perfectly free from restraint. Resignation induces us to bear pain, but there is something in it that is afflicted in suffering and resists. The resignation that measures out its abandonment to God, selfishly reflecting upon itself, is willing to suffer, but is constantly examining to make sure whether it is suffering acceptably. In fact, the resigned soul is composed so to speak of two persons: one keeping the other in subjection, and watching, so that it will not revolt.

In love that is unselfish and abandoned, the soul is fed in silence on the cross and in its union with the crucified Savior, without any reflections on the severity of its sufferings. There exists only one single, simple will, which permits God to see it just as it is, without trying to see itself. It says nothing, does nothing. What, then, does it do? It suffers. And is this all? Yes, all. It has nothing else to do but suffer. Love can be heard easily enough without speech or thought. It does all that it is required to do, which is to have no will when it is stripped of all consolation. The purest of all loves is a will so filled with the will of God that there remains nothing else.

What a consolation it is that we are then rid of so many anxieties about our exercise of patience and the other virtues in the sight of those around us! It is enough to be humbled and abandoned in the midst of suffering. This is not courage. It is something both more and less: less in the eyes of the ordinary class of Christians, more in the eyes of pure faith. It is a humiliation that raises the soul into all the greatness of God. It is a weakness that strips us of every resource in order to bestow upon us his unlimited power. "When I am weak," says St. Paul, "then I am strong."[46] "I can do everything through him who gives me strength."[47]

When we are undergoing suffering it is enough to feed on some short sentences suited to our condition and our taste, with frequent interruptions to quiet the senses and make room for the inward spirit of recollection. We sometimes suffer, scarcely knowing that we are in distress. At other times we suffer, and know that we are not bearing our suffering well, but we carry this second and heavier cross without impatience. True love goes ever straightforward, not in its own strength, but counting itself as nothing. Then indeed we are truly happy. The cross is no longer a cross when there is no self to suffer under it and to appropriate its good and evil.

⤳ 39
THE USEFULNESS OF DEPRIVATIONS

Follow faithfully the light that God gives you to die to the refinements and sensibilities of your self-love. When we give ourselves entirely to the designs of God for us, we are as willing to be deprived of consolations as to enjoy them. Often a deprivation that disturbs and humbles us is more useful to us than an abundance of comforting.

Why should it not be useful for us to be deprived of the presence and advice of a friend, when it is sometimes very wholesome for us to be deprived of the sense of the presence and of the consoling gifts of God himself? God is very near us when he *seems* far away from us, *if* we bear this apparent absence of his in a spirit of love for him and of death to ourselves.

Accustom yourself gradually to this burden. When children begin to grow, they make a change from the milk of a tender mother who carries them in her bosom, to walking alone and eating dry bread.

⤳ 40
THE VALUE OF MODERATION

Be careful never to become really lax. Avoid acts of self-indulgence and all social contacts and friendships that might bring back your taste for the world, and that might diminish the grace that is within you.

Do not visit with others too much. Do not fatigue yourself, either with too much study or with unhealthy solitude—not even with your exercise of devotion. Take everything with moderation. Change and diversify your activities, and do not become too engrossed in any of them too eagerly. Stop as soon as you feel a certain eagerness that arises from passion. Mistrust your own determined and superior spirit. As soon as a word of haughty disdain escapes from your lips, take a lower tone immediately. Never judge others except from necessity. Never allow yourself any little deception with the view of making yourself appear better to others than you really are. God will be with you if you have in your heart an upright and simple intention of carrying out all this.

You *will* fail, but you must not be discouraged. And while you humble yourself for your faults, you must go on your way again, and repair the false steps where self-love has caused you to stumble.

41
REGARDING PRAYER

In regard to prayer, always propose to yourself some simple and solid subject that is of practical use in attaining the virtues of the gospel. If you find no food for your soul in a given subject, and if you feel an attraction and ability to simply remain in the presence of God, remain there as long as you are so drawn. But never make it a rule for yourself, and always be faithful in proposing a special subject of thought and meditation to yourself, to see if it can occupy and nourish you. Receive without resistance the insights and feelings that may come to you in prayer, but do not trust any of these things that might flatter your pride and fill you with vain self-complacency.

It is better to be very humble and very much ashamed after the faults we have committed than to be pleased with our prayer and think that we are very much advanced after having had many fine feelings and grand thoughts while we were praying to God. Let all such things pass. They may be helps sent to us from God, but we must remember that they may be turned into very dangerous delusions if we dwell upon them ever so little to seek our own pleasure in them.

The great point is to mortify our selves, to obey the Lord, to distrust ourselves, and to carry our cross.

⌇ 42
KEEPING A SPIRIT OF PRAYER

[handwritten margin note: know your faults (page 22]

Never be discouraged about your faults. Bear with yourself while you are trying to correct them, as you would bear with and correct your neighbor. Give up a certain activity of mind that wears out your body and makes you commit many faults. Accustom yourself gradually to extend your prayer over all the outward activities of the day. Speak, act, and work in peace as if you were in prayer, for indeed you should be so.

[handwritten margin note: it probably takes practice]

Do everything without being overly eager, by the spirit of grace. As soon as you perceive that your natural activity is slipping in, enter again quietly within yourself where God reigns. Listen to what the leading of grace demands of you, and then say and do only what that leading inspires. You will be more tranquil for this, and your words will be fewer and more effective for it. While you labor less, you will do many more useful things. It is not a question of a perpetual struggle of the head. That would be impracticable. It is a question of accustoming yourself to a certain peace in which you can easily consult the Beloved of your soul as to what you ought to do. This consultation, very simple and very brief, will be made much more easily with him than the hurried and tumultuous deliberation that we generally have with ourselves when we give way to our natural impetuosity.

When the heart already has a tendency toward God, we can easily accustom ourselves to suspend the hasty movements of nature, and wait for the second moment when we can act through grace by listening to God. It is the continual death of self that constitutes the life of faith. This death is a sweet life, because grace gives peace. It takes the place of nature, nature that only brings us trouble.

Try to accustom yourself to this dependence upon the inner spirit, and then by degrees everything will become prayer. You will still suffer, but a peaceful suffering is only half a suffering.

⋺ 43
WHEN SPIRITUAL
EMOTIONS FADE

It is good to feel how weak we are, and to learn by experience that emotional fervor comes and goes. When we have it, it is God who gives it out of his condescension, to sustain our weakness. It is the milk given to little children. Afterward we must be weaned and eat the dry bread of persons of mature age.

If we were always to have this delight and skill in devotion without any interruption, we would be strongly tempted to look upon it as our permanent possession. We would no longer feel our weakness or our inclination to sin. We would not have sufficient distrust of ourselves, and we would not come to prayer with sufficient humility.

But when this emotional fervor declines or disappears, we feel that we have lost something. We recognize where it came from, and we are forced to humble ourselves, so that we may find it again in God. The less satisfaction we feel in serving him, the more faithfulness we exercise in it. We restrain ourselves. We sacrifice our inclinations. We no longer proceed by the help of winds and sails, but by rowing hard against the current. We take all upon ourselves. We are in darkness, and we have to content ourselves with faith alone. We are in sorrow and bitterness, but we are willing to be so, and it is no longer through pleasure that we hold fast to God. We are ready to receive that pleasure again as soon as God restores it. We recognize our own weakness, and we understand that when God does restore the enjoyment to us, it is in pity for our weakness. But when he deprives us of it, we bear the deprivation in peace, and we are sure that God knows much better than we do what is necessary for us.

What does depend on us, and what ought always to be invariable, is our good will. This will is even purer when it is quite dry and quite bare without ever being lax.

Be as firm in observing your hours of prayer as if you still had the greatest pleasure and ease in them. Profit even by any time in the day when you are only half-occupied in outward activities. It is only in conversation that the practice of this presence is more difficult. Nevertheless, we can often renew within ourselves that general thought of God that can regulate all our words and repress our all-too-lively flashes of wit when we are conversing with others—all our touches of pride or superiority—all the refinements of our self-love.

Bear with yourself, but do not flatter yourself. Labor effectively and constantly to correct your faults, but do so peacefully, and without the impatience that comes of self-love.

44
DEALING WITH SICKNESS AND GRIEF

You know that illness is a precious gift that God gives us to make us feel the weakness of our soul by the weakness of our body. We flatter ourselves that we have no regard for this life and long for the heavenly country, but when age or sickness make us see that the end of our life is much nearer, self-love awakens, feels sorry for itself, and is alarmed. We do not find in the depths of our heart any desire for the kingdom of God. We find only spiritual apathy and inactivity, cowardliness, lukewarmness, disunity, and attachment to all those things from which we thought we had been freed. Such a humiliating experience is often more useful for us than all the emotional feelings upon which perhaps we were relying a little too much. The great point is to give ourselves up to the Spirit of grace, and allow ourselves to be detached from everything here below.

Receive with childlike simplicity all the comforts that you are given. Thinking about God, peace, obedience, the sacrifice of your life, patience in your infirmities—these will be sufficiently great mortifications.

When we have lost someone dear to us and God takes away a great source of comfort, it is because he wishes to deprive us of it through the jealousy of his love. He finds, even in the most lawful and the purest of friendships, certain secret movements of self-love. These he wishes to cut down at their deepest roots. Let him do what he will. Adore this severity that is only love. Enter into his designs. Why should we weep for those who are no longer weeping, and whose tears God has wiped away forever? It is for ourselves that we weep, and we must allow our humanity to be touched in this way with its own grief. But faith assures us that we will soon be reunited with those whom our senses indicate as lost to us.

Live by faith without paying attention to flesh and blood. You will find again the friend who has departed from your eyes, in our common Center, which is the Heart of God. Calm your spirit before God. Do not be afraid to comfort your imagination by the help of some gentle and religiously devoted social contacts. We must not be ashamed to treat ourselves like children when we feel the need of such treatment.

⮌ 45
BEARING SPIRITUAL DRYNESS

Do you no longer find the same peace of mind in your devotions that was so easy and so usual with you earlier? God is accustoming you to a faithfulness that is less sweet and more painful to nature. If such ease in concentrating yourself on God were always equal, it would give you a support that would be too tied to feelings, and, so to speak, too natural. In such a case, you would not experience any interior cross or any weakness. It is necessary for you to feel your state of great unhappiness and emotional distress. The humiliation that follows will be more useful to you than the most comforting spiritual fervor if you bear it patiently without being discouraged.

We must never give up prayer. We must bear the loss of it if it pleases God to take it away from us, but we may not take anything away from ourselves, nor are we allowed to let anything be lost through voluntary negligence.

Continue to pray, but make your prayer in the simplest and freest manner, so that you may not fret over it. Make use of everything that can renew the sense of the presence of God without any uneasy effort.

During the course of the day, avoid everything that might distract you or attract you, or excite your natural liveliness of spirit. Calm yourself as much as you can on every occasion, and pass by all that is not the concern of the present moment. "Each day has enough trouble of its own."[48] Bear your dryness and your involuntary distractions as your principal cross.

It may be helpful in such spiritual dryness to try withdrawing from the world a little, but we must not carry this too far. We may comfort our imagination according to our needs by such things as are compatible with the presence of God.

⤳ 46
USING TIME WISELY

It is essential to put all our time to good purposes. Grace has long since convinced you of this. It is a pleasant thing to come into contact with those who understand this, but there is a tremendous distance between the conviction of the intellect, even combined with the good intention of the heart, and a faithful and exact obedience.

Nothing has been more common in ancient as well as in modern times than to meet souls who are perfect and holy, *theoretically*! "You shall know them by their fruits,"[49] says the Savior. This is the only rule that never deceives, when it is properly understood. It is the one by which we must judge ourselves.

There is a time for everything in our lives, but the maxim that governs every moment is that no moment should be useless. Every moment must enter into the order and progress of our salvation. Every moment must be accompanied by duties that God has allotted with his own hand, and of which he will demand an account. For from the first instant of our existence to the last, he has never designed for us a barren moment, nor one that we can consider as given up to our own discretion.

The great thing is to recognize his will in relation to each moment. This is not to be brought about by seeking eagerly and restlessly—that is much more likely to spoil everything than to enlighten us as to our duty. It is accomplished by true submission to those whom God has set over us and by a clean and upright heart that seeks God in its simplicity and vigorously opposes all the deceit and false wisdom of self as quickly as it is revealed. We misuse our time, not only when we do wrong or do nothing, but also when we do something else than what we *should* have done at that moment, even though it may be the means of good. We are strangely ingenious in perpetually seeking our own interest, and what the world does openly and without shame, those who desire to be devoted to God do in a refined manner under the cover of some pretext that serves as a veil to hide the deformity of their conduct.

In general, the best means to ensure the profitable use of our time is to accustom ourselves to living in continual dependence upon the Spirit of God and his law. It is to receive what he is pleased to bestow at every instant. It is to consult him in every emergency that requires instant action. It is to flee to him in our weaker moments, when strength seems to fail, and to invoke his aid. And it is to raise our hearts to him whenever we are enticed by material things and find ourselves estranged from God and far from the true road.

Happy is the soul that commits itself into the hands of its Creator, ready to do all his will, and continually cries out, "Lord, what wilt thou have me to do?"[50] Teach me to do your will, for you are my God!"[51]

During our necessary activities, we need to pay only an effortless attention to the leadings of divine providence. Since they are all prepared for us and presented by him, our only care should be to receive them with a childlike spirit, submitting everything absolutely to him: temper, will, scruples, restlessness, self-reflections, overflowing emotions of hurry, vain joy, or anything else in the different events of the day that pleases or displeases us. Let us be careful, however, not to allow ourselves to be overwhelmed by the multiplicity of our exterior activities, no matter what they may be.

Let us endeavor to begin every undertaking with the sole aim to commit it to the glory of God, continue it with composure, and finish it with patience.

Intervals of relaxation and amusement are the most dangerous seasons for us, and perhaps the most useful for others. We must be on our guard to be as faithful as possible to the presence of God. We must make use of all the Christian vigilance that was so much recommended by our Lord. We can raise our hearts to God in a simple act of faith and dwell in sweet and peaceful dependence upon the Spirit of grace as the only means of our safety and strength. This is especially necessary for those who are looked up to as an authority, and whose words may be the cause of so much good or evil. Our leisure hours are ordinarily the sweetest and most pleasant for us. No use of them is better than refreshing our spiritual strength by secret and intimate communion with God. Prayer is so necessary and is the source of so many blessings, that those who have discovered this treasure cannot be prevented from having recourse to it whenever they have an opportunity.

47
PRESERVING PEACE WITH OTHERS

To be really pleased even with the best persons, we must be satisfied with little and we must bear with much. The most perfect people have many imperfections. We also have imperfections—big ones. Our faults, joined to theirs, make our bearing with each other very difficult. But carry each other's burdens, and in this way you will fulfill the law of Christ.[52] We must make a charitable allowance in this matter. Frequent silence, habitual recollection, prayer, detachment from ourselves, renunciation of all the carefully crafted criticisms, faithfulness in abandoning all the vain judgments of a jealous, meticulous, demanding self-love—all these things tend very much to preserve peace and union with God. We spare ourselves much trouble by this simplicity. Happy are those who pay no attention to self-love, and who pay no attention to the criticism of others.

Content yourself with leading a simple life according to your circumstances. For the rest, obey the Lord and bear your little daily crosses. You need them, and God gives them to you only out of pure mercy. The great thing is to sincerely make light of yourself, and to consent to be made light of by others if God permits it. Feed on God alone. St. Augustine says that his mother lived only by prayer. We also are to live by prayer and die to all the rest. We can live to God only by a continual death to self.

⤳ 48
TRUE FREEDOM

When we are no longer embarrassed by the restless reflections of self, we begin to enjoy true freedom.

False wisdom, on the other hand—always on the watch, ever occupied with self, constantly jealous of its own perfection—suffers severely whenever it is permitted to perceive the smallest speck of imperfection. Those who are single-minded and detached from self labor toward the attainment of perfection, and are more successful in proportion to how much they forget themselves and never dream of virtue in any other light than as something that accomplishes the will of God.

The source of all our defects is the love of self. Everything points to that instead of to the love of God. Whoever, then, works strenuously to get rid of self, to deny him-*self* according to the instructions of Christ, strikes at once at the root of every evil, and finds, in this simple abandonment of self, the seed of every good.

Then we hear and understand those words of Scripture, "Where the Spirit of the Lord is, there is freedom."[53] We neglect nothing that will cause the kingdom of God to come both within us and outside of us, but in the midst of our weaknesses we are at peace. We would rather die than commit the slightest voluntary sin, but we have no fear for our reputation from the judgment of others. We welcome sharing the reproach of Christ Jesus and dwell in peace even though we are surrounded by uncertainties. The judgments of God do not frighten us, for we have abandoned ourselves to them, praying earnestly for his mercy according to how much we have attained confidence, sacrifice, and absolute surrender. The greater the abandonment, the more flowing is the peace. It sets us in such a spacious place that we are prepared for everything. We will *everything* and we will *nothing*. We are as free from deceitful cunning as babies are.

Our illumination from God uncovers the slightest transgressions, but never discourages us. We walk before him, but if we stumble, we hasten to resume our way, and have no motto but *Onward!*

If we want to find God, we must destroy the remains of the old Adam within. The Lord held a little child in his arms and declared, "The kingdom of heaven belongs to such as these."[54]

The principal directions for attaining true freedom without neglecting our duties can be summed up like this: Do not reason too much. Always have a just and honest purpose in the smallest matters. Pay no attention to the thousand reflections by which we wrap and busy ourselves in self under the pretense of correcting our faults.

49
DEALING WITH A HAUGHTY SPIRIT

A proud or disdainful manner, one that relishes ridiculing or criticizing others, indicates a self-satisfied mind that is not conscious of its own weak points. It is a prey to its hard-to-please tastes and finds pleasure in the troubles of others. There is nothing more humbling than this sort of pride that is so easily wounded, disdainful, contemptuous, haughty, jealous of its own rights, and averse to forgiving others. It is a proof that we are very imperfect indeed when we are so impatient with the imperfections of others.

There is no remedy for all this except hoping in God, who is as good and powerful as you are weak and bad. Yet he will probably let you grovel on at length without uprooting your natural disposition and your long-formed habits. That is because it is far better for you to be crushed by your own weakness and frailty and by the proof of your inability to escape from it, than to enjoy a sudden advance toward perfection.

Only strive to bear with others and turn your eyes away from people who cannot uplift and enlighten you, in the same way that you would turn those people from temptation. They really are a very dangerous temptation to you. Pray, read, and humble yourself by cultivating lowly things. Soften your heart by uniting it to Jesus in his patience and humiliation. Seek strength in silence.

⤸ 50
THINKING OF DEATH

There comes an age when the thought of death puts itself forward and forces itself upon our consideration much more often and much more strongly than before. Furthermore, there comes a time of retirement in which we have fewer distractions with regard to this great subject. God even makes use of this severe trial to take away our self-deceptions about our courage, to make us feel our weakness, and to keep us very humble in his hands.

Nothing is more humiliating than a troubled imagination in which we can no longer find our former trust in God. It is the crucible of humiliation in which our heart is purified by the conviction of its weakness and unworthiness. The Holy Spirit says, "No one living is righteous before you."[55] It is also written that the heavens are not pure in the eyes of our Judge.[56] It is certain that "we all stumble in many ways."[57] We see our faults and we do not see our virtues. It would be very dangerous for us to see our virtues even if they were real!

What we have to do is walk honestly and justly and without laxness in the midst of this trouble, just as we tried to walk in the ways of God before trouble came upon us. If this trouble shows us something in ourselves that needs correcting, we must first be faithful to this light. However, we must do so under the guidance of a good counselor, so that we may not fall into legalistic scruples. Afterward, when we have seen our faults, we must remain in peace and pay no attention to the self-love that tries to make us feel sorry for ourselves at the thought of our own death. We must detach ourselves from this life, make a sacrifice of it to God, and abandon ourselves to him with confidence.

When St. Ambrose was dying, he was asked if he was not troubled with fear of the judgments of God. He replied, "We have a good Master." This is the answer that we must give to ourselves. It is necessary for us to die in an uncertainty that is inaccessible to knowledge or reason, not only about the judgments of God upon us, but also about our own dispositions. As St. Augustine says, we must be reduced so low that we can offer to God only "our misery and his mercy." Our misery is the proper object of his mercy, and his mercy is our only claim. While you are in this state of sadness, read all that can encourage your confidence and comfort your heart. "Surely God is good to Israel, to those who are pure in heart!"[58] Ask him for the uprightness of heart that pleases him so much and makes him so compassionate to our weakness.

51
THE CROSS AS A TREASURE

We must carry the cross as a treasure. It is through the cross that we are made worthy of God and conformed to the likeness of his Son. Crosses are a part of our daily bread. God regulates the measure of them according to the things we really lack and require. He knows what we need, even if we are ignorant of it. Let him do as he wills, and let us resign ourselves into his hands.

Be a child of divine providence. Leave it to your relatives and friends to reason about things. Do not think about the future as if it were a long distance away. The manna became spoiled when, out of cautious foresight, people wanted to provide sufficient supply for more than one day. Do not say, What will we do tomorrow? "Tomorrow will worry about itself."[59] Confine yourself today to your present needs. God will give you each day the help that is apportioned to that day. "Those who seek the LORD lack no good thing."[60] Providence would like to do miracles for us, but we hinder these miracles by trying to anticipate them. Through our restless efforts we make for ourselves a providence that is as defective as the providence of God should be certain.

Be faithful and teachable. By an endless distrust of yourself, make your weaknesses profitable. And in a childlike manner, bending freely, allow yourself to be corrected. Humility will be your strength, even in the midst of weakness.

I have no doubt that our Lord will always treat you as one of his friends. That is, he will send you crosses, sufferings, and humiliations. These ways and means that God makes use of to draw souls to himself do this work so much better and more quickly than the creature's own efforts. That is because the very fact that it is God's action alone at work is destructive to self-love and tears up the roots that we cannot even uncover without great difficulty. But God, who knows all the secret lurking places of self-love, immediately proceeds to attack it in its stronghold, and on its own ground.

If we were strong enough and faithful enough to trust ourselves entirely to God, and to follow him simply wherever he wished to lead us, we would have no need of great application of mind to labor in the work of our perfection. But because we are so weak in faith that we wish to know where we are going, without trusting in God, our way becomes much longer and spoils our spiritual affairs.

Abandon yourself as much as you can to God, until your last breath, and he will never forsake you.

PART THREE

Meditations
on the Heart of God

INTRODUCTION TO PART THREE
Meditations on the Heart of God

Why has Fénelon—a man who lost his job, his fame, his money, and many of his friends—had such a wide readership for three centuries? Perhaps it is because surrounded by the splendor and decadence of the most powerful court in Europe, he chose a different path, one that took him through enormous inner suffering and into a relationship with God that few have known. His life reflected the truth of these words penned by Thomas à Kempis two centuries before him:

> *All those, then, who with a single heart direct their intention to God and keep themselves clear of all inordinate love or hatred of any created thing, will be most fit to receive grace and will be ready for the gift of devotion.*
>
> *For the Lord bestows his blessing where he finds the vessel empty.*[1]

Having chosen this way, "the royal way of the cross," Fénelon became a shining example to men and women who sought his counsel. In English translation he is best known for the letters he wrote to his spiritual children. Though some of the original letters were lost, excerpts and copies of excerpts from many of them were handed around by the faithful for inspiration and eventually published. The present volume presents a number of these excerpts and short writings, all originally published in French in the early 1700s.

The word "heart" is used in this book to translate two words with different meanings. The one encountered most often is *le cœur*—the physical heart, used figuratively as the seat of the emotions. This is man's heart; it is that part of us that reaches out to God. The other is *le sein (de Dieu)*—God's bosom or heart. This word has a deeper meaning than any one English word can convey. In the high Middle Ages this expression was often used to mean "heaven." But in Fénelon's time it took on the additional meaning of "womb," the place where life begins and is nurtured. Thus the heart of God is the place the human heart seeks and longs for, the only place where our hearts will find rest.

Come with us now and sit at the feet of this beloved shepherd, and hear the words of a wise master whose gentle teachings were forged in the crucible of suffering. Let his words lead you through your places of suffering and brokenheartedness, into the heart of God.

ABOUT PART THREE

Meditations on the Heart of God is composed of excerpts taken from *Holy Reflections For Each Day Of the Month, Meditations On Various Subjects Taken From the Holy Scriptures,* and *Meditations For One Who Is Ill,* all published in the early 1700s.

Scripture references in this translation were taken for the most part from standard English versions. In some cases, the French translation of the Latin Vulgate used by Fénelon differed enough from that of modern translations that a paraphrase of the Scripture reference is given to make his commentary clear. Some excerpts lacked Scripture verses, so where possible, Scriptures used within the text were placed at the beginning of the meditation. In a few cases, Scripture references suggested by the text were added.

Where excerpts had titles they were retained; titles suggested by the text were given to excerpts lacking them. Where the context indicated the need for emphasis, words were set in italics.

Finally, where concepts were used that would have been familiar in the eighteenth century but perhaps not in our time, or where Scripture verses or other quotations were used without a reference, explanatory notes were provided.

1
WHERE IS OUR FAITH?

When the Son of Man comes, will he find faith on earth?
(Luke 18:8, RSV)

If the Son of Man were to come at this very moment, would he find faith in us? Where is our faith? Where is the evidence of it? Do we really believe that this life is only a short transition to a better one? Do we believe that we have to suffer with Jesus Christ before we spend eternity with him? Do we regard the world as a passing illusion, and death as the entrance into the treasures of real value?

Do we live by faith? Does it stir us to life? Do we cherish the timeless truths it presents us? Do we nourish our souls with faith, taking the same care to feed our souls that we take to nourish our bodies with proper food? Do we make it our practice to look at everything through the eyes of faith? Do we use our faith to correct all our thoughts and judgments?

What a pity it is that far from living by faith, we often cause faith to die in our minds and in our hearts! We think as if we were pagans, and we behave in the same way. If someone wanted to believe what one ought to believe, would that person do what we do?

2
THE KINGDOM WITHIN

Unless one is born of water and the Spirit, he cannot enter the kingdom of God. (John 3:5b, RSV)

To see the kingdom of God that is inside us, we need to be born a second time and take on a new nature. Happy are those who have eyes to see that kingdom. Flesh and blood are not capable of seeing it, because mere animal instinct is blind, and is content to be so.

To our fleshly nature, what God is doing inside us is only a dream. For us to see the wonders of that inner kingdom, we have to be reborn. And to be reborn, we have to die. Though the world may scorn, condemn, and mock us, to us it is given to believe, to accept, and to become fully alive.

When we take time for one simple moment of inner recollection and yielding ourselves to God, we see and hear more than the intellectual reasoning of all humanity put together. When we hush our desires and thoughts and turn our attention away from outward things, we enter into the light. And then it is that we discover God reigning on the throne of his kingdom—inside us.

3
THE NARROW DOOR

Strive to enter by the narrow door. (Luke 13:24, RSV)

We can enter the kingdom of God only through hard struggle. We have to assault it as if we were laying siege to it. It has a narrow door. To get through that door, we have to put our sinful frames through discomfort by taking a low place, by submitting, by crawling, by making ourselves small.

The large, wide-open door that the crowd is passing through leads to destruction. All the wide roads that join together and lead to that wide-open door should make us feel afraid. In fact, when the world is laughing with us and our path seems sweet, we ought to realize how unfortunate we are! We will never be good for the life of eternity unless we feel ill at ease in this one.

So let us be careful not to follow the crowd that limits itself to following the broad and comfortable road. We must walk in the footsteps of that small band of saints, climbing up the steep-sloped path of repentance, clambering over the rocks with sweat on our faces. And we must expect that the last step in our lives will be yet one more violent effort to pass through the narrow door of eternity.

⇒ 4
MOLDED INTO JESUS' IMAGE

I have been crucified with Christ. (Saint Paul, in Galatians 2:20a, RSV)

Saint Paul is content to be crucified with Christ, because he knows that we have been predestined by God for one reason alone—to be molded into the image of his Son, being crucified with him on the cross. Just as he did, we must abandon every earthly pleasure. Just as he was, we must remain constant in the midst of suffering.

How wretched we are—we want to tear ourselves away from that cross that joins us to our Master. We cannot abandon the cross without abandoning the crucified Jesus Christ. The cross and Jesus Christ cannot be separated.

So let us live and die with him. Let us not be afraid of anything except failing to complete our sacrifice in patience and in love. How pitiful it is that all the efforts we make in this life serve only to bind us to the world and to tear us away from the cross!

5
DEVOTION TO GOD (I)

If anyone thinks he is religious, and does not bridle his tongue but deceives his heart, this man's religion is vain. (James 1:26, RSV)

There are so many abuses that go under the name of religious piety! Some people's piety consists only in their many prayers. For others, piety consists in a great number of outward works done for the glory of God and the relief of their neighbors. Some consider piety to be a continual desire to gain their own salvation. Others think it consists in practicing great austerity.

All these things might be considered good. They are even necessary to a degree. But we would be wrong to think that true devotion to God consists merely in devout practices.

The devotion that makes us holy and devotes us entirely to God consists in doing all that God wants, and in accomplishing everything he desires from us, in every place and in every circumstance he places us.

Do as many kind gestures as you wish, do as many dazzling works as you please—but you will be rewarded only for doing the will of the sovereign Master. If the domestic who serves you did marvelous things in your home, but did not do the things you have asked him to do, you would not congratulate him for all those marvelous things he has done: you would be justified in complaining that he was serving you badly.

Perfect devotion requires us not only to do the will of God, but also to do it with love. God loves for us to give to him joyfully. In everything he tells us to do, he always asks for our heart. Such a Master is worthy of our joyful service.

⌐ 6
DEVOTION TO GOD (2)

And you, my son Solomon, acknowledge the God of your father, and serve him with wholehearted devotion and with a willing mind, for the LORD searches every heart and understands every motive behind the thoughts. (1 Chronicles 28:9, NIV)

Our devotion to God must never stop. We must put it into practice everywhere—in things we do not like, in things that disturb us, in things that go against our point of view, our inclinations, our plans. True devotion holds us ready to give God everything—our well-being, our fortune, our time, our freedom, our life, and our reputation. To be willing to give of ourselves in this way, and to accept the consequences, is to be truly devout.

But since the will of God is often hidden from us, there is still one more step of renunciation and of death to self to be taken. It consists in accomplishing God's will through obedience—yes, blind obedience, but wise in its blindness. This is a condition that is required of every person. The most enlightened man or woman, the person who is the most gifted in calling others to God and the most capable of leading others to him, must also be led.

⁊ 7
GOD'S WISDOM

The heavenly Father [will] give the Holy Spirit to those who ask him!
(Luke 11:13b, RSV)

There is no "holy spirit," no holy mind,* other than the mind and Spirit of God. Any mind or spirit that takes away from the only real treasure—no matter how penetrating, pleasant, and capable that mind or spirit may be in gaining us corruptible treasures—is only a spirit of illusion that leads us astray. Would we want to ride in a magnificent and beautiful carriage that was only going to carry us over the edge of a cliff?

The mind and spirit are made for the sole purpose of leading to the truth and to sovereign good. Therefore there is no holy spirit, no holy mind, other than the Spirit of God—because it is only his Spirit that leads us to him. So let us renounce our own minds, our own spirits, if we want to have God's. Happy are those who cast off their soiled clothing in order to put on the spotless garments that come from God. Happy are those who trample their empty wisdom under foot in order to embrace the wisdom that comes from the mind and Spirit of God!

---

* In French, the concepts rendered in English as "spirit" and "mind" are the same word: *esprit*. Here Fénelon moves freely from one concept to the other. To make the subtleties implied by the French text more understandable, both English words are placed here where appropriate.

8
A HOLY MIND

Have this mind among yourselves, which is yours in Christ Jesus.
(Philippians 2:5, RSV)

There is a great difference between a clever mind, a great mind, and a holy mind. The clever mind is pleasing because of its charm. The great mind excites our admiration because of its depth. But only a good and virtuous spirit can save and make us happy through its constancy and uprightness. Do not conform your ideas to those of the world. Distrust the mind as much as the world esteems it.

What we call "mind" is a certain facility for producing brilliant thoughts. But nothing is more vain. We make an idol of our minds, just as a woman who thinks herself beautiful makes an idol of her face. Our thoughts reflect who we are.

We must reject not only this false glitter of the mind, but also every trace of human wisdom, no matter how sincere and useful it may seem. Like little children, we must enter into simplicity of faith, into forthrightness and innocence, into dread of sin, into humiliation—and into the sacred folly of the cross.

9
PATIENT ACCEPTANCE

In your patience possess ye your souls. (Luke 21:19, KJV)

The soul deserts its very nature when it becomes impatient. When it submits without complaint, it takes possession of itself in peace and comes into possession of God. To become impatient is to want what we do not have, and not to want what we do have. In so doing, the soul is handed over to its passions, and neither reasoning nor faith can hold it back, so troubled is it. Such weakness! Such swerving away from the right path!

As long as we desire the soul-sickness that brings us suffering—to us it is not sickness—why would we make our sickness a reality by ceasing to desire it?

Inner peace exists not in the flesh but in the will. We can hold on to peace in the midst of the most violent suffering, as long as the will remains firm and submissive to God despite its abhorrence of the situation. Peace on this earth consists in accepting the things that are contrary to our desires, not in being exempted from suffering them, nor in being delivered from all temptations.

⤳ 10
WHAT GOD SENDS IS RIGHT

Father, I have sinned against heaven and before you; I am no longer worthy to be called your son. (Luke 15:21, RSV)

To hear you bluster and complain, it would seem that you are the most innocent soul in the world, and that a crying injustice is being done to you not to let you back into the garden of Eden! Remember everything you have done against God, and acknowledge that he is right.

What you ought to do is tell God, with the same humility as the prodigal son, "'Father, I have sinned against heaven and before you.' I know what your justice demands of me, but I lack the courage to submit to it. If you were to place your confidence in me and spare me, I would become flattered, I would spare myself, and I would betray myself through that self-flattery. But your merciful hand performs what I would evidently never have had the courage to do. It strikes me out of kindness. Let me patiently bear those healing blows."

The least a sinner can do, if he is truly upset with himself, is willingly to bear the suffering that comes his way—suffering he would never have had the strength to choose.

⤳ 11
LOVE GOD'S WILL

Thy will be done, on earth as it is in heaven. (Matthew 6:10b, RSV)

Nothing happens here on earth, just as nothing is done in heaven, except by God's will. But we do not always love the will of God. If we love God's will, and only God's will, we will turn earth into heaven. We will thank God for all he sends our way, the evil with the good. When he sends us afflictions, they become treasures.

We must not trouble ourselves about the past, because there is no evil that God has not allowed to befall a city,[2] that is, that he has not permitted and brought about in the order of his divine providence. And we must have no fear for the future, since nothing will happen to us unless God sends it or allows it.

Dear God, what do I see on every side, but your will that is being accomplished? Let it also be accomplished in me. Let me love it. Let it make everything sweet. Let me bring my own will down to nothing. Dear God, may you be blessed for everything. Accomplish your will, Lord. It is yours to will, and mine to give myself over completely.

⤳ 12
JESUS OUR MODEL

I always do what is pleasing to him [the Father]. (John 8:29, RSV)

Dear Jesus, help us understand where this example ought to be leading us. Here is our model: you acted only according to the good pleasure of your Father—who is willing to be named our Father as well. Act in us as you yourself did—according to the Father's good pleasure. Let us be united inseparably to you, consulting only your plans and purposes.

It is not enough for us to pray, to teach others, to suffer, and to edify others. No, we must eat, sleep, and carry on conversations, having in mind only obedience to God's will. Then we will be in a state of continual sacrifice, uninterrupted love, unceasing prayer.

When, dear Lord, will we reach that point? But it is up to you to apportion your gifts, and it is up to us to bring ourselves to nothing in your sight. Lord, do with us, not only outwardly, but deep within us, as it seems good to you. It is not for us to take the measure of your mercies.

13
PRAY FAITHFULLY

But let him ask in faith, with no doubting, for he who doubts is like a wave of the sea that is driven and tossed by the wind. (James 1:6, RSV)

We are so dependent on God that not only *should* we do everything for him, but also we are *unable* do anything except by him and for him. Therefore, we ought to be asking God to give us the means to please him. And this happy necessity to run to him for all our needs, far from being a source of bother to us, ought to be the source of our complete consolation. What a blessing it is to speak to him in trust, to open our hearts to him, and by means of prayer to be united with him as much as it is possible to be in this life!

As Saint Cyprian said,[3] let us consider whether he will grant us the good things he invites us to ask him for.[4] So let us pray faithfully, never losing the fruit of our prayers by wavering or hesitating in our faith, as Saint James says. Happy is the soul that gains comfort in prayer through the presence of its Beloved!

But how unhappy we are when all we feel is weariness at the heavenly pursuit we call "prayer." The lukewarmness of our prayers is the source of all our other unfaithfulnesses. So let us remember the words of Saint James—if anyone among us is in trouble, he should pray to obtain comfort.[5]

⤝ 14
NEVER STOP KNOCKING

Ask, and it will be given you; seek, and you will find; knock, and it will be opened to you. (Luke 11:9, RSV)

If all we had to do to obtain worldly riches was ask for them, we would be so eager, untiring, and persevering in our asking! If all we had to do to find treasure was dig for it, how much earth would we not move! If all we had to do to enter the king's private council and assume the highest position of honor was knock, such redoubled knocking would be heard!

But what do we not do to find blessing and happiness where they cannot be found? How many rebuffs, how many setbacks are we willing to endure for the phantom of worldly glory! How much suffering for vain pleasures of which nothing remains but remorse!

The treasures of God's grace are the only true riches—yet they are the only riches we balk at asking for and expecting.

However, we must never stop knocking! The promises of Jesus Christ are always faithful—it is we who are unfaithful in asking for them.

⤝ 15
LISTEN TO THE RIGHT VOICE

Lord, to whom shall we go? You have the words of eternal life. (Saint Peter, in John 6:68, RSV)

Jesus Christ is the One we must listen to. As far as people are concerned, we ought to listen to them and believe them only insomuch as they are full of Jesus Christ's truth and authority. Books are good only to the extent that they teach us the good news of the gospel. Therefore, let us go straight to that sacred source.[6]

Jesus Christ spoke and acted only so that we might listen to him and attentively study the details of his life. But how foolish we are! We run after our own thoughts, which are only vain and fruitless, and we neglect the truth himself, whose words are able to make us live forever.

Speak, divine Word, uncreated Word who took on human flesh for me! Let my soul hear you. Say everything you desire—I want everything that is pleasing to you.

⌒ 16
DOING GOD'S WILL

Do this, and you will live. (Jesus, in Luke 10:28b, RSV)

We often say we would like to know what to do to advance in virtue—but when the Spirit of God shows us what to do, we often lack the courage to carry it out.

We have a strong feeling that we are not what we ought to be. We see how our burdens grow day by day. Yet we feel we are doing a lot just by *saying* we want to be delivered out of ourselves. Let us count it as nothing if we say we are willing to follow God, and then do not go as far as *sacrificing* the things that stop us from walking in God's ways. Let us not hold the truth captive through our unrighteous halfheartedness.

So let us listen to what God inspires in us. Let us test the spirit that is moving in us, to see if it comes from God. And after we have recognized God, let us stop at nothing to make him happy. The psalmist does not simply ask God to teach him *what* his will is—he asks God to teach him to *do* it.[7]

⇌ 17
THE RIGHT USE OF CROSSES

Those who go out weeping, bearing the seed for sowing, shall come home with shouts of joy, carrying their sheaves. (Psalm 126:6, NRSV)

The more we are afraid of crosses, the more we have to conclude that we need them. And the heavier our crosses are, the more we have to believe that God loves us. We ought to judge the seriousness of our illnesses by the strength of the treatment the spiritual Physician applies to them.

We must be very corrupt, and God must be very merciful, since he takes great pains to heal us—even though the process of healing may be difficult. So let us turn our crosses themselves into a source of love, comfort, and faith, saying with Saint Paul, "For this slight momentary affliction is preparing us for an eternal weight of glory beyond all measure."[8]

Happy are those who go forth weeping, bearing the seed for sowing, for they will bring in an indescribably joyful harvest of eternal life!

⇌ 18
THE BLESSING OF SUFFERING

I have been crucified with Christ. (Saint Paul, in Galatians 2:20a, RSV)

With the Savior we are bound to the cross, and it is he who binds us to it through his grace. It is because of Jesus that we do not want to leave the cross, because he cannot be separated from it. Holy and suffering body of Jesus, with which our bodies become united and form but one single living sacrifice, as you give me your cross, give me your spirit of death to self and abandonment.

Cause me to think less about my suffering than about the blessing of suffering with you. What am I suffering that you have not suffered? Or rather, how much have I suffered, if I dare compare myself to you?

Cowardly nature of mine, be silent. Look at your Master and blush with shame.

Lord, make me love and I will no longer be afraid of suffering. And then, if I do suffer difficult things that are painful to my nature, at least I will not be suffering any more than I am willing to suffer.

19
BE MERCIFUL

Be merciful, even as your Father is merciful. (Luke 6:36, RSV)

Just because other people are weak, is that a good reason to speak more harshly to them? You who complain that others are making you suffer, do you think you are not making anyone else suffer? You who are so shocked by your neighbor's faults, do you imagine you are perfect yourself?

How dumbfounded you would be if all the people on whom you keep pressing so hard were suddenly to turn around and start pressing hard on you! But when you find your justification on earth, could not God, who knows everything, and who has many things he could reproach you for—could he not silence you with a single word and stop you? Does it not ever enter your mind to be afraid that he will ask why you do not show your brother a little of that mercy that he, who is your Master, showers so abundantly on you?

🜺 20
ONE THING IS NEEDFUL

Martha, Martha! You are anxious and troubled about many things; one thing is needful. (Luke 10:41–42, RSV)

We think there are a thousand things we should be concerned with, but there is actually only one. If we take care of that one thing, all the others will find themselves done. And if we fail to take care of the one thing that is needful, all the others—no matter how success-fully we may seem to do them—will fall into ruin. So why are we so torn between matters of the heart and our worldly cares?

From this day forward I resolve to give my total attention to the only thing on earth I ought to be concerned with. Illumined by God's holy light, I resolve to stop worrying and to do every moment, with all the strength of my mind and body, whatever God in his providence places in my path. I will not be grieved about turning everything else over to God, because it is not my work I am doing, but God's. And I ought to want to do only what God gives me to do.

I resolve not to become keenly excited about anything, because it is dangerous to want to appropriate God's work to ourselves. If we do that, then we do God's work in our own strength; we turn good into bad and we allow pride to take over. And then we become flushed with the pursuit of success. We conceal our illusion by using the pretext of seeking God's glory.

Dear God, give me the grace to be faithful in my actions, but indifferent to success. The only thing I ought to be concerned with is to desire your will and to quietly meditate on you—even in the midst of busy times. It is up to you to crown my feeble actions with such fruit as is pleasing to you—and none at all, if that is what you find best for me.

⇒ 21
BE READY

You must also be ready; for the Son of man is coming at an unexpected hour.
(Luke 12:40, RSV)

These words of Jesus were said to every person, without exception. They are accomplished in every person of good will, even though we may have made preparation for death. We make plans that presuppose we will live a long life, whereas life is going to end. The time people do not think will be their last often actually is. Perhaps death will come at this time in our lives. If people who are nearing the end of an incurable illness still hold onto hope for healing, how much more hope do we hold on to when we are in the fullness of health!

But where does this stubborn hope in life come from? It comes from the fact that we love life with a passion. And where does our strong desire to keep death away come from? It comes from the fact that we do not love the kingdom of God or the splendor and majesty of the life to come.

Men and women who are slow of heart, who cannot rise above this earth where we are so wretched and desolate! The true way to hold ourselves at the ready for our last moment is to care little for all other moments, and always to live in expectation of our life's end.

⪜ 22
STEADFASTNESS IN HOPE

Eye hath not seen, nor ear heard, neither have entered into the heart of man,
the things which God hath prepared for them that love him.
(1 Corinthians 2:9, KJV)

What relationship is there between what we do here on earth, and what we hope for in heaven? The first Christians never stopped rejoicing at the sight of what they were hoping for—for at every moment, they believed they were seeing heaven open before them. Suffering, disrepute, torture, cruel deaths—none of these things had the power to dishearten them. They were intimately acquainted with God's infinite generosity in rewarding such sufferings—and they never thought they suffered enough. They were transported by joy when they were judged worthy of some deep humiliation.

And what about us? Fainthearted souls that we are, we know nothing about suffering, because we do not know how to hope. We become overwhelmed by the slightest crosses—often even those we bring on ourselves because of our own pride, rashness, and weakness!

⪜ 23
A HARVEST OF JOY

May those who sow in tears reap with shouts of joy! (Psalm 126:5, TEV)

We have to sow seed in order to gather a harvest. This life is intended for sowing. In the next life we will enjoy the fruits of our labors. But we earthbound men and women are so fainthearted and impatient—we want to reap before we sow. We want God to comfort us and make the way smooth in order to lead us to himself. We express a desire to serve him, provided that our service to God costs us little. Our arrogance leads us to hope for a great many things, but we want to suffer very few things.

How blind we are! Will we never see that the kingdom of heaven is taken by violent attacks, and that only souls who violently and courageously gain victory over themselves are worthy of winning heaven?[9]

So let us weep here on earth. For happy are those who weep now,[10] but how terrible it will be for those who laugh now.[11] How terrible for those who have their consolation in this world! The time will come when those vain joys will be put to confusion. Then the world will have its turn to weep. And God himself will wipe away all tears from our eyes.[12]

⤳ 24
OUR DAILY BREAD

Give us each day our daily bread. (Luke 11:3, RSV)

Dear God, what is this bread? It is not only the physical sustenance that in your providence you give us for the necessities of life, but it is also the nourishment of *truth* that you give daily to our souls. That kind of bread nourishes us unto eternal life. It makes our souls grow and become robust when our faith is tested. Every day, you renew this bread. Both inwardly and outwardly, you give our souls precisely what we need to continue in our life of faith and self-denial.

All I have to do is to eat this bread, and in a spirit of sacrifice to receive all the bitter-tasting things that you send my way—both in outward matters and in the depths of my heart.

Indeed, *what happens to me in the course of each day is my daily bread*— provided I do not refuse to take it from your hand and feed on it.

⌒ 25
HUNGER FOR
RIGHTEOUSNESS

Blessed are those who hunger and thirst for righteousness, for they shall be
satisfied. (Matthew 5:6, RSV)

Why do we not have this hunger and thirst? Why are our souls not as
hungry and thirsty as our bodies are? Bodies that have no desire for
food are sick. In the same way, our souls suffer from sickness when we
do not seek after the things that satisfy them, nor the food and drink
that come from God.

The soul's food is truth and righteousness. To know good, to be filled
with it, to strengthen ourselves with it—this is the spiritual food, the
food from heaven, that we need to eat. So let us reach out and eat it.
Let us be hungry for it. Let us stand before God as poor beggars who
wait hopefully and expectantly for a little bread. Let us be aware of our
weakness and our failure. How terrible for us if we forget how weak
we are!

Let us read, let us pray, with that hunger to nourish our souls and
that burning desire to quench our thirst. Only a continual great desire
to be taught by God can make us worthy of discovering the wonders
of his law.

Each of us receives this sacred bread to the extent that we desire it.

26
TRUE PEACE

Peace I leave with you; my peace I give to you; not as the world gives do I give to you. (John 14:27, RSV)

Every one of us is searching for peace, but we do not always search for it where it can be found. The peace that the world hopes for is as different and as removed from the peace that comes from God, as God himself is different and removed from the world. To put it another way, the world promises peace, but it never gives it. The world does offer a few passing pleasures—but those pleasures cost far more than they are worth.

Jesus alone can give peace to mankind. He brings us into harmony with himself. He brings our passions into submission. He sets limits to our desires. He comforts us through the hope of riches that will never perish. He gives us the joy of the Holy Spirit and causes us to taste that inner joy even when we are suffering. The spring that produces peace cannot run dry, and the depths of the soul in which it resides cannot be reached by all of humanity's evil. Therefore for the righteous person it becomes a treasure that no one can take away.

True peace can be found only in possessing God. And possessing God here in this life can be found only in submission to faith and obedience to God's law. Both of these things reflect a pure and unalloyed love in the depths of the heart.

Therefore, thrust away all forbidden things. Cut out all unlawful desires. Dismiss all your bustling about and your worrying. Desire only God, seek only God, and you will enjoy peace—in spite of the world. What is troubling you? Poverty? Ridicule? Failure? Inward and outward crosses? Look on all these things as genuine favors from the hand of God, distributed to his friends, favors that he allows you to share. Then the world will change complexion, and nothing will take away your peace.

27
TRUE JOY

I looked upon laughter as a dream, and I said to joy, "Why do you deceive me?" (Ecclesiastes 2:2, after the VULGATE).

The world rejoices as do sick persons who are in the throes of delirium or as do sleepers who have pleasant dreams. People thrash about, but only in vain—because they are committed to a hollow image, a passing figure, a fleeting shadow. When we are in that state we rejoice, but only because we are deceiving ourselves into believing we possess many things—when actually we do not possess anything at all.

If we have sought after the world's joy, when we awake from death we will find ourselves empty-handed. And then how ashamed we will be of our joy! How terrible therefore for people who find false comfort in this world that will exclude them from true comfort! So let us never stop saying to the vain and fleeting joy inspired by this world, "Why do you deceive me so rudely?"

Nothing is worthy of giving us joy except our blessed hope. Everything else, because it is not founded on that hope, is only a dream.

28
SEEK THE WATER THAT SATISFIES

Everyone who drinks of this water will thirst again. (John 4:13, RSV)

The more we drink the impure and poisoned waters of this age, the thirstier we are for them, and the more we plunge into the world. Desires come to life in our hearts. The possessions that come through riches only excite our greed, for ambition is more unhappy because of what it does not have, than satisfied with all it does possess.

Enjoying the world's pleasures only makes the soul thirsty and weak. The soul becomes corrupted. It can never be satisfied. The more a soul lets itself go, the more it wants to succumb.

It is easier to keep our heart in a state of repentance and burning desire for God than to bring it back to him once it has gone down the slope of pleasure and laxity.

So let us keep watch over ourselves. Let us stay away from drinking water that only increases our thirst. Let us keep careful watch over our hearts, for fear that the world and its vain comforts will come in and trouble our peace.

⫷ 29
HAPPY TEARS

Blessed are those who mourn, for they shall he comforted.
(Matthew 5:4, RSV)

Such a new kind of tears, said Saint Augustine—they make the people who shed them become happy. Their happiness comes from being afflicted and grieving over the corruption of the world around us, the world's pitfalls that surround and try to trap us, and the wickedness we see within our own hearts.

It is a great gift from God to be afraid of losing his love and to be afraid of straying from the narrow path. It is the one good possession in this life. When we are in danger of losing everything we have and of losing even our own selves, we should not be full of joy. When all we see in ourselves is vanity, backsliding, scandal, forgetfulness of and defiance toward God whom we love, we grieve.

So let us weep when we see others and ourselves in God's holy light. Let us weep—our sadness will gladden God's heart. He himself is the One who inspires that sadness in us. It is his love that makes our tears flow. Then we will become happy—because God himself will come and wipe away our tears.

🖎 30
ETERNAL RICHES

Then [Jesus] looked up at his disciples and said: "Blessed are you who are poor, for yours is the kingdom of God. Blessed are you who are hungry now, for you will be filled. Blessed are you who weep now, for you will laugh. Blessed are you when people hate you, and when they exclude you, revile you, and defame you on account of the Son of Man. Rejoice on that day and leap for joy, for surely your reward is great in heaven; for that is what their ancestors did to the prophets.

"But woe to you who are rich, for you have received your consolation. Woe to you who are full now, for you will be hungry. Woe to you who are laughing now, for you will mourn and weep." (Luke 6:20–25, NRSV)

We hear Jesus say, "Woe to you who are laughing now"—and yet we want to laugh. We hear him say, "Woe to you who are rich, for you have received your consolation"—and yet we are constantly seeking after earthly riches. He says, "Blessed are you who weep now"—and yet the thing we are most afraid of is to weep.

Here on this earth it is true that we ought to be weeping, not only for the dangers of our sinful condition, but also for everything around us that is vain and dissolute. Let us weep for ourselves, and for those around us. Everything we see both inside ourselves and outside ourselves is only affliction of spirit, temptation and sin. Everywhere we find cause for tears. How truly terrible it is to love the things that are so unworthy of being loved. Now *that* is a reason for weeping! Shedding tears is the best thing we can do.

Happy are the tears that are brought about by grace, causing us to lose our desire for things that will pass away, and giving birth within us to the desire for riches that will never perish!

ᔐ 31
EARTHLY WISDOM

To set the mind on the flesh is death. (Rom. 8:6a, RSV)

Worldly people have shrewd and wise minds, as Jesus tells us in the Gospel—and their wisdom is often greater than that of godly people. But in spite of its dazzling, deceptively beautiful appearance, worldly wisdom has a fearsome flaw—it brings death to all who take it as the rule by which they live. Tortuous in its logic and abounding with subtleties, worldly wisdom is the enemy of God's wisdom, for God always walks in uprightness and simplicity. What good are all their talents to those who are worldly-wise, since they find themselves caught in their own traps?

Saint James the apostle says such wisdom is earthly, unspiritual, and devilish.[13] It is earthly because it limits its concern to acquiring and owning earthly goods. It is unspiritual because it aspires only to furnish others with what fires their passions and to plunge them into sensual pleasures. It is devilish because, in addition to having the mind, spirit, and shrewdness of the devil, it has all his evil intent.

With earthly wisdom, we imagine we are deceiving others—when actually we are deceiving only ourselves.

ᔐ 32
TRUST GOD

It is better to take refuge in the Lord than to put confidence in man.
(Psalm 118:8, RSV)

Every day you put your trust in friends who are weak, in people who are unknown to you, in unfaithful household servants. And yet you are afraid of trusting God! The signature of a public official puts your mind at ease about your possessions, yet the everlasting good news of Jesus Christ does not give you any reassurance at all! The world makes you every sort of promise, and you believe it. But God swears his promises to you, and you find it hard to believe him. How shameful this is for him! What a terrible thing this is for you!

Let us put things back in their proper order. With temperance and moderation let us do the things that depend on us. Let us faithfully await the things that depend on God. Let us control any unchecked emotions, any anxiety disguised as right thinking or zeal.

Those who live in such a way establish their foundation on God, and become immovable like Mount Zion.

⌒ 33
STRENGTH THROUGH WEAKNESS

When I am weak, then I am strong. (2 Corinthians 12:10, RSV)

Lord, when I thought I could do everything, I could do nothing. And now that it seems to me I can no longer do anything, I am beginning to be able to do everything in you who strengthen me.[14] How blessed is my lack of ability, because it makes me find in you everything that is lacking in me! I rejoice in my weakness, because it opens my eyes to what the world is—and to what I really am in myself. I count it a blessing to be laid low by your hand, because it is in your making me into nothing that I will be covered by your almighty power.

Some people feel pity for me because I have been brought low. You are blind, my friends! Do not feel sorry for this person who is loved by God, and on whom he brings suffering only out of love. It was in the past that I was to be pitied, when corrupt prosperity was poisoning my heart, and I was so far from God.

34
GOD'S MERCY

The Lord is gracious and merciful, slow to anger and abounding in steadfast love. (Psalm 145:8, RSV)

As you stand before God, think about the mercy he has shown you, the enlightenment he has given you, the good thoughts he has inspired in you, the pitfalls of this world from which he has kept you safe, and the way he has helped you inwardly. Allow yourself to be moved to tears as you remember all the precious signs of his goodness.

Think about the crosses he has entrusted to you so that you may become a living sacrifice, because they are the clear signs of his love. Let your gratefulness for the past inspire you with trust for the future. Be persuaded that he has loved you too much not to love you still.

Do not mistrust God—no, you must mistrust yourself. Remember that he is, as Saint Paul put it, "the Father of mercies and the God of all consolation."[15] Ask him, with King David, "Lord, where is your steadfast love of old?"[16]

God has taken away the soft and comfortable things from your life. Why? Because you need to be humbled and to come to know yourself; because in vain you have sought elsewhere for help and comfort.

35
BECOME MATURE

Lord, what wilt thou have me to do? (St. Paul, in Acts 9:6, KJV)

Saint Paul was miraculously turned around and changed by the grace of the Savior he was persecuting. What an unhappy thought: how much have *we* persecuted the Savior through our unfaithfulness, our petulance, our untamed emotions that have disturbed the work he is doing? He has had to bring us low through trials. He has had to crush our pride. He has had to baffle our fleshly wisdom. He has had to dismay our vaunted self-worth.

Therefore let us say to him, "Lord, what wilt thou have me to do?—I am ready to do anything you ask." We must make this offer complete, holding nothing back. We must not make vague promises we will not actually put into practice when it comes to details. Saint Augustine tells us that for too long we have been dragging around with weak wills, longing after good but not putting forth the effort to bring it about.

It does not cost us anything to *want* to become mature, if we do not put forth any *effort* to become mature. We need to want God's maturity and perfection in our lives more than anything else.

So let us each probe our hearts and ask ourselves—am I determined to sacrifice to God my strongest friendships, my most deeply rooted habits, my foremost inclinations, my most gratifying pleasures?

⤳ 36
TIME IS PRECIOUS

Let us do good while we still have time. (Galatians 6:10, after the VULGATE*)*
Night comes when no one can work. (John 9:4b, RSV*)*

Time is precious, but we do not know yet how precious it really is. We will know only when we are no longer able to take advantage of it. Our friends ask for our time as if it were nothing, and we give it as if it were nothing. Often our time is our own responsibility: we do not know what to do with it, and we become overwhelmed as a result. The day will come when a quarter-hour will seem more valuable and desirable than all the fortunes in the universe.

Liberal and generous in every way, God in the wise economy of his providence teaches us how we should be prudent about the proper use of time. He never gives us two moments at the same time. He never gives us a second moment without taking away the first. And he never grants us that second moment without holding the third one in his hand, leaving us completely uncertain as to whether we will have it. Time is given to us to prepare for eternity. Eternity will not be long enough for us to ever stop regretting it if on this earth we have wasted time.

⥈ 37
REDEEM THE TIME

See, then, that ye walk circumspectly, not as fools but as wise, redeeming the time, because the days are evil. (Ephesians 5:15-16, KJV)

All our heart and all our time are not too much to give to God. He gave them to us only to serve and love him. So let us not hold anything back from him. We cannot be doing great things all the time, but we *can* do the things that are suitable to our condition in life. We are already doing a great deal if we hold our tongues, suffer, and pray when we cannot do something outwardly.

To offer up to God each mishap, setback, complaint, or confusion; to comfort a sick person, encourage a downcast soul, prevent suffering at its onset, teach a person who needs instruction, or soften the heart of someone who is bitter—all these things serve to redeem eternity through the good use of time.

But to truly gain eternity, we must redeem the time itself, as Saint Paul says. This means we must renounce engaging in excessive amusements and unnecessary exchanges with other people. We need to renounce pouring out our hearts to others in order to flatter our self-esteem and carrying on conversations that divert the mind, so we can be free to go about God's work more diligently. Promise him that you will be faithful to your disciplines of prayer and worship.

38
THE RADIANT PATH OF FAITH

Walk before me, and be thou perfect. (Genesis 17:1b, KJV)

Lord, this is what you said to faithful Abraham, and in fact everyone who walks in your presence has true perfection. We lose our perfection only when we lose sight of you. When we keep our eyes unceasingly turned toward you, we have everything. Yet, what a deep pity! Where am I going when I do not see you at all? Where is my purpose? What is it? Where is my light? If we keep our eyes fixed on you with every step we take, we will never stray for a moment. How wonderful it is to remain on the radiant path of faith!

Shining faith! Admiring gaze that brings humanity to maturity and completion! Dear God!—wherever I look, it is you alone that I see in everything that my eyes seem to see. Your providence is what holds my attention. My heart keeps watch only for you in the midst of the multitude of business affairs, duties, and even thoughts that you oblige me to have. I center all my concentration on you, the sovereign and sole object of my attention.

To divide my thoughts in order to obey you is to reunite them with your will. What could I see in unworthy created things if you stopped asking me to apply myself to them, and if I stopped seeing you through them?

39
GOD'S KINDLY HAND (1)

Yea, I have loved thee with an everlasting love; therefore, with loving-kindness have I drawn thee. (Jeremiah 31:3b, KJV)

God did not wait for us to become something before he would love us. No, before the worlds came into being, and even before we had our very existence, he was thinking about us. And his desires for us were only to do us good.

What he once meditated on in eternity, he has carried out in time. His kindly hand has showered us with every sort of good thing. And even though our expressions of unfaithfulness and ingratitude almost equal the instances of his favors toward us, they have never been able to stop the flow of his gifts or dam up the flood of his graces.

Love without measure, you have made me what I am, you have given me what I have, and you promise me infinitely more besides! Love that has no beginning, you have loved me for infinite ages, even when I could neither feel nor recognize your love! Love that knows no interruption or inconstancy, love that all the bitter waters of my wickedness have never been able to extinguish! Have I a heart, dear God, if I am not completely filled with gratitude and tenderness toward you?

40
GOD'S KINDLY HAND (2)

If anyone does not love the Lord, let him be outcast. Maranatha—Come, O Lord! (1 Corinthians 16:22, NEB)

What do I see? A God who, even after having given absolutely everything, gives himself. A God who comes to search for me even in the darkest depths because my sin has made me descend that far. A

God who takes the form of a slave in order to deliver me from being enslaved by my enemies. A God who makes himself poor in order to make me rich. A God who calls me and runs after me when I flee from him. A God who dies in torment to snatch me from the arms of death and to give me back a life of blessing. And yet how often do I want neither him nor the life he is offering me!

What kind of person could love another person as God loves us? Of how much would we be worthy of being outcast if after all God has done, we did not love the Lord Jesus!

☞ 41
TRUE LOVE FOR GOD

Whom have I in heaven but thee? And there is nothing upon earth that I desire besides thee. (Psalm 73:25, RSV)

When we tell God we love him with all our heart, often we are just using words, making a speech that has no reality. From our childhood on, many of us have been taught to speak in such a way, and so we continue to do so when we have grown up—often without knowing what we are saying.

But to love God means to have no will other than his. It means faithfully to observe his holy law. It means to have a painful and intense fear and dread of sin. To love God means to love what Jesus loved—poverty, humiliation, suffering. It means to hate what Jesus hated—the world, our pride, our passions.

Could we think we love someone we would not want to be like? To love God means to willingly have fellowship with him. It means to want to go to him in prayer. It means to sigh after and long for him. How false is a love that takes no pains to go and see One it loves!

∼ 42
DIVINE FIRE

I came to cast fire upon the earth, and would that it were already kindled!
(Jesus, in Luke 12:49, RSV)

The fire that Jesus came to cast upon the earth is the fire of divine love. Jesus brought this fire to us in his heart, and now his only desire is to inflame our hearts with it as well. But humanity lives in deadly coldness. We love a bit of money. We love land and houses. We love a reputation, a name, titles and credentials. We love to seek after changing, deadly things—such as conversations and pleasures that leave us empty afterward. God is the only one for whom we have no more room for love. Instead, we exhaust ourselves running after the most wretched of his creations.

Jesus came to earth wanting nothing greater than to light his divine fire in our hearts and make us feel the happiness and blessing of divine love. Yet we prefer the unhappiness of loving the lowest and most harmful things.

Dear God, reign over us in spite of our passions! How could we find anything to love outside of you? May the fire of your love extinguish any other fire! Give us the grace to love you, and we will love you and no other. And we will continue to love you throughout eternity.

∼ 43
SET ME APART

Though heart and body fail, yet God is my possession forever. (Psalm 73:26, NEB)

Is it possible to know you, dear God, and not love you? Your beauty, strength, grandeur, power, and goodness; your generosity, magnificence, and perfection of every kind—these are far beyond what any created being could understand. And what touches me in the depths of my heart is that you love *me*. It might seem that the reverence I owe you and the vast inequality that exists between me and you ought to stop me from daring to love you. But you allow me—no, that is saying too little—you *command* me to love you. And so, Lord, I give up trying to know or own myself.

Sacred Love, you have wounded my heart, and yet you of your own free will were yourself wounded for me. So come now and heal me—or rather, come, take the wound you have given me and make it deeper and sharper. Set me apart from everything created. No longer can I be content with created things. They hinder me, they disturb me. You alone are sufficient for me. No longer do I desire anything but you.

ᔧ 44
SET ME AFLAME

The Lord does not see as mortals see; they look on the outward appearance, but the Lord looks on the heart. (1 Samuel 16:7, NRSV)

What a wonder! Earthly lovers carry their foolish passions to extremes of fervent love—yet we who claim to love you do so weakly and faintheartedly. No, no, dear God, worldly love must not be stronger than divine love. Show what you can do with a heart that is completely given over to you.

My heart is open to you. You know its innermost recesses. You know what your grace has the power to stir up in it. You are only waiting for me to consent and give you my free will. This I do most ardently, a thousand times over!

Take possession of everything in me. Show yourself to be God. Set me aflame. Consume me. Weak and powerless creature that I am, all that I have to give you is my love. Increase it, Lord, and make it more worthy of you. Oh, if only I were capable of doing great things for you! Oh, if only I had much to sacrifice for you! But all that I am capable of is so little. From this moment on all I want to do is sigh after you, long for you, and die to myself so that I may love you more.

45
THE WORDS OF ETERNAL LIFE

Lord, to whom shall we go? You have the words of eternal life.
(John 6:68, RSV)

We do not know the gospel well enough—and what prevents us from learning that Good News is that we think we already know it. But we are not acquainted enough with its teachings and we do not enter into its spirit.

With great curiosity we search out the thoughts of mortals, and yet we neglect the thoughts of God. One word of the good news of the gospel is more precious than all the other books in the world put together—it is the source of all truth.

We ought to listen with such love, such faith, such adoration, to the words of Jesus Christ in the gospel! From this moment forward let us say to him, along with Saint Peter, "Lord, to whom shall we go? You have the words of eternal life."

46
LET THE LIGHT
SHINE THROUGH

See to it, then, that the light within you is not darkness.
(Luke 11:35, NIV)

It is not surprising that our *faults* cause us to appear flawed in God's eyes. But the fact that even our *virtues* are often only imperfections is what really ought to make us tremble.

Often our great spiritual wisdom is merely fleshly and worldly behavior. Our modesty is often only a composed—and hypocritical—outward appearance designed to observe social conventions and attract praise to ourselves. Our fervor can be just a mask for fierce moodiness or pride. Our frankness and openness with others can hide impatient brusqueness. And so on.

But in offering a sacrifice to God by making solemn promises to him, are we not promising to allow his dazzling light to show through us, as through the purest Christian virgin? But sometimes the sacrifice itself is executed with such great cowardliness that the light changes into darkness.

Therefore let us see to it that the light within us is not darkness.

⤳ 47
THE BLIND WORLD'S FATE

Woe to the world because of the things that cause people to sin!
(Matthew 18:7, NIV)

Lord, let me be willing to repeat this awful saying by Jesus Christ, your Son and my Savior! These words are terrible for the world, which is forever rebuked, but they are sweet and comforting for those who love you and despise the world. For me these words would resound as terrifyingly as a clap of thunder if I ever turned my back on you and entered once again into slavery to this age.

Blind world, what an unjust tyrant you are! You flatter so that you can betray, you amuse and entertain so that you can strike a deathblow. You laugh and you entice people to laugh. But you despise people who weep. All you want to do is enchant the senses with a vain joy that turns into poison.

But you, vain world—you will weep forever, while God's children will be comforted. Oh, how I despise your contempt, and how afraid I am of falling into your complacency and self-satisfaction!

⤳ 48
LOVE NOT THE WORLD (1)

Do not love the world or the things in the world. (1 John 2:15, RSV)

How far-reaching these words of Jesus are! "The world" is the blind and corrupt multitude that Jesus Christ condemns in the Gospel, and for whom he does not pray even as he is about to die.[17] All of us speak against the world—and yet each of us carries the world in our hearts.

"The world" is nothing other than all people who love themselves, and who love things without regard to God. Therefore, since all that people have to do to be classified as "the world" is to love themselves and to try to find in created things that which is found only in God, *we ourselves are the world.*

So let us own up to the fact that we belong to the world, and that we do not have the spirit of Jesus Christ. What a pity it is to give the outward appearance of renouncing the world, but all the while inwardly sustaining the world's thoughts and feelings!

⤳ 49
LOVE NOT THE WORLD (2)

But far be it for me to glory except in the cross of Jesus Christ, by which the world has been crucified to me, and I to the world. (Galatians 6:14, RSV)

When do we show that we love the world? When we are jealous of authority. When we love a reputation that we are not worthy of. When we spend idle time in the company of others. When we look for comforts that magnify the flesh. When we are weak and fainthearted in our Christian practices. When we do not take care to study the truths of the gospel.

So the world lives in us. But the truth is that we *desire* to live in it, since we so strongly desire for others to love us, and we are so afraid that others might forget us. How blessed and happy was Saint Paul, who was able to say, "The world has been crucified to me, and I to the world."

What a blessed thing it is to know how worthy of contempt the world is! It is making a very small sacrifice to God to sacrifice the world's fleeting illusions. How weak people are when they do not despise the world as it deserves! And how much people are to be pitied if they believe they have given up a great deal by taking leave of the world. Clergy, religious, or laymen seeking retirement from the world are only following that commitment more cautiously than the rest.

Indeed *all* of us Christians, through our baptism, have renounced the world. We are in search of the safe harbor if we turn and flee the raging storm.

⟿ 50
BREAK MY BONDS

I am not praying for the world, but for those you have given me, for they are yours. (John 17:9b, NIV)

As he was facing his life's end, Jesus Christ prayed for those who were about to torture him and put him to death—but he refused to pray for the world. So what should I think of those persons who are known as decent and honest folk, and whom I have called my friends? Yet those who persecuted and murdered Jesus Christ were less hateful to him than those persons to whom I once opened my heart in friendship.

What could I expect, seeing my weakness in the presence of those friends—people who take pride in forgetting God, in treating religious devotion as weakness, and in neglecting all their Christian duties? Can I really think that I love God and that I am not ashamed of his gospel, if I love the company of his enemies so much and am afraid of displeasing them by showing that I fear God?

Lord! Bear me up against the swirling current of the world. Break my bonds. Keep me far away from the tents of wickedness.[18] Join me in close union with those who love you.

⟿ 51
DANGEROUS FRIENDS

Do you not know that friendship with the world is enmity with God? Therefore whoever wishes to be a friend of the world becomes an enemy of God. (James 4:4, NRSV)

The world already bears God's condemnation on its forehead, and yet it dares to set itself up as a judge to hand down decisions on every subject. We say we want to love God, and yet we cringe in fear of displeasing the world, God's irreconcilable enemy! Adulterous soul, unfaithful to the holy Bridegroom, do you not know that friendship with the world makes you an enemy of God? Therefore, woe to those who try to please the world—that blind, corrupt judge!

But what is "the world"? Is the world nothing but a mirage, an empty phrase? No! It is that crowd of worldly friends who carry on conversations with me every day, people who pass for moral folk, people who have their honor, people whom I love and by whom I am loved—but who do not love me for God's sake. Those are my most dangerous friends! An avowed enemy could only kill my body—but those people have killed my soul.

So that is what I mean by "the world"—and I must flee from it in horror, if my desire is to follow Jesus Christ.

⌇ 52
FLEEING FROM THE WORLD

But far be it from me to glory except in the cross of our Lord Jesus Christ,
by which the world has been crucified to me, and I to the world.
(Galatians 6:14, RSV)

We think we are far away from the world when we are in a place of
quiet religious retreat. But we still speak the world's language. We have
its feelings and curiosities. We still want a reputation and friendships.
We want to be entertained. We still have high-minded opinions of ourselves. We still suffer the slightest humiliations with great indignation.

We *say* we want to forget the world, but in the depths of our hearts
we do not want to be forgotten by it. We are searching to no avail when we
try to find a halfway point between Jesus Christ and the world. As the
apostle Paul said, it is not enough for the world to be dead to us. We
must also be dead to it.

⌇ 53
THE LAST WILL BE FIRST

And behold, some are last who will be first, and some are first who will be
last. (Luke 13:30, RSV)

Many people live common, ordinary lives, but reach maturity in
Christ. Yet many people who have taken vows to become Christ's
chosen brides have been showered with God's graces and invited to
taste the heavenly manna, but still they languish in faintheartedness and
immaturity!

Many sinners, who have spent years wandering far from God and
paying no heed to the gospel, all at once turn away from their former
life in earnest and fervent repentance. And often they surpass people

who have tasted the gifts of the Holy Spirit from their earliest youth, and on whom God has granted his sweetest blessings! How beautiful it will be when those who are last win the garland of victory in this way, and by their example become the condemnation of those who were first!

But how painful it will be for those who were first when they become last, and find themselves behind people for whom they were once models. How painful it will be to lose their garlands, and to lose them for a few diversions that slowed them down!

I cannot help looking at the quiet, worshipful spirits of certain people who live in the world, and see how detached from the world and humble they are, without blushing with shame when I see how often we, who ought to be doing nothing but God's business, are dissolute, vain, and attached to our worldly goods.

So let us hurry up and run, for fear of being left behind.

⇒ 54
ATTENTION TO LOVE

Love one another earnestly from the heart. (1 Peter 1:22b, RSV)

Through these words the apostle Peter asks us to express our love by always being careful not to hurt our neighbor. Without careful attention, love—which is so fragile in this life—is quickly lost. One word said curtly or irritably or with a haughty or disdainful look can affect those who are weak.

We need to take great care with others, as they are so dear to God and are such precious members of the body of Jesus Christ. If you are lacking in this care, then you are also lacking in love—because we cannot love without giving our attention to the object of our love. This attention to love ought to fill our whole beings—our minds and our hearts.

It seems to me that I hear Jesus Christ saying to you, as he said to Saint Peter, "If you love me, feed my sheep."[19]

55
SERVICE TO OTHERS

For the Son of man also came not to be served but to serve.
(Mark 10:45a, RSV)

Jesus Christ came not to be served, but to serve. And this is what everyone who has any authority over other people ought to be saying. This is what pure ministry is. Those whom we appear to command, we should in reality be serving. We must suffer their imperfections, lift them up gently and patiently when they fall, and wait for them to follow along God's path. We must become all things to everyone and think of ourselves as having been made for them.

We need to humble ourselves in order to gently speak the most needed corrections. We must never give up in discouragement. Instead, we need to ask God to change their heart—something we cannot do ourselves.

So examine yourself with respect to the people who have been given to you to care for, and for whom you bear responsibility in the sight of God.

56
A HUMBLE HEART

Learn of me; for I am meek and lowly in heart. (Matthew 11:29, KJV)

The Son of God was the only one who could teach us this divine lesson. As Saint Paul told us, Jesus is the One who "always had the nature of God, but he did not think that by force he should try to become equal with God."[20] What has he not done out of love for us?

What has he not suffered at our hands, and what does he suffer still? As Isaiah said, "Like a lamb about to be slaughtered, like a sheep about to be sheared, he never said a word [of complaint]."[21]

But look at us—we grumble about the smallest problems. We are vain, fragile, and overly sensitive. There is no true or constant gentleness without humility. As long as we are full of ourselves, everything in us will be shocked by faults in other people.

If we are convinced that nothing is our rightful due, then *nothing will make us bitter.* If we think often of how destitute we are, we will become merciful toward weaknesses in other people.

As Saint Augustine tells us, there is not a single page in the Scriptures where God does not thunder forth these great and loving words, "Learn of me; for I am meek and lowly in heart."

57
TRUE GLORY

For everyone who exalts himself will be humbled, and he who humbles himself will be exalted. (Luke 14:11, RSV)

Since we so love a lofty place, let us seek loftiness where it can be found: let us look for the high place that will last forever. What an admirable ambition—to want to reign for all ages with the Son of God and to be seated forever on the same throne with him!

But such ambition it is—such childish jealousy—to be eager to have a name among people! If we do so we will achieve a reputation that is even less solid than smoke that turns into the plaything of the wind! Is it worth all the trouble we put ourselves through to have a few people say they are our friends without really being so, and to keep up vain appearances?

Let us aspire to real greatness. True greatness can be found only by making ourselves humble here on earth. God opposes proud people, starting in this life. He brings envy, criticism, and slander on them and causes them to suffer untold setbacks. And finally he will humble them in eternity.

But one who is humble, who remains hidden, who desires to be forgotten, and is afraid of being sought out by the world, will *already in this life* be respected for not wanting to be sought out. And eternal glory will be the reward for that one's disregard for false and contemptible glory.

ᔰ 58
OUR DELIVERER IS COMING

Rejoice in the Lord always; again I will say, Rejoice. Let your gentleness be known to everyone. The Lord is near. (Philippians 4:4–5, NRSV)

Our distaste for our uncontrolled emotions and for the world's hollow vanities ought to be the spring from which our joy flows. The only foundation of our joy should be our hope, and we can hope only to the extent that we are dissatisfied with the world.

Our anticipation of Jesus' coming ought to make us modest, self-disciplined, and faithful. One day he will come and give us a garland of honor—and we need to hold ourselves at the ready to receive him. We should be glad that he is coming, because although he will be the world's Judge, he will be our comforter.

It is so sweet to be at peace, waiting expectantly for Jesus Christ, while the children of this age are afraid of his appearing! They will tremble and shudder. And we? We will see our beloved rescuer coming. What a happy, enviable state to be in!

So you have not yet reached that state? Then aspire to it! The only things that keep us from being in that state of trust and consolation are our faintheartedness and our desire for pleasure.

⌐ 59
THE FLESH AND THE WORD

He who eats me will live because of me. (John 6:57b, RSV)

We eat the body of Jesus Christ, but his Spirit is what gives us life. As he himself said, the flesh is of no avail.[22] The flesh is united to the Word in such a way that Saint John was not afraid to say, "the Word became flesh."[23]

Yet God joined the flesh and the Word for the sole purpose of communicating his Spirit to us in a way that we are better able to touch and feel. By so doing he reaches down and becomes one with us in the flesh. He gives us his flesh to eat only to make us one body with him, and to bring our souls to life with his divine life.

So why is it that we, who so often obtain life *from* him, refuse to live *for* him? What becomes of that bread from heaven, that completely divine flesh? What purpose does our receiving communion serve? Does Jesus Christ live inside us? Do his thoughts and actions show forth in our human flesh? Are we growing in Jesus Christ because of our feeding on him?

How shameful it is that we are always searching for pleasure, always grumbling at the slightest suffering, always crawling around searching for comfort in the most miserable of places, always hiding our faults without correcting them—while at the same time we have been joined into one flesh with Jesus Christ himself!

⟿ 60
CHRIST LIVES—IN ME

He who eats me will live because of me. (John 6:57b, RSV)
It is no longer I who live, but Christ who lives in me. (Galatians 2:20, RSV)

Jesus Christ is our whole life—that is the eternal truth that ought to nourish, teach, and sustain us. So why is it that we can feed on such a divine source of nourishment and yet continue to waste away? How can we fail to grow in virtue, resist growing in spiritual health and strength, live in falsehood, harbor dangerous desires in our hearts, and fail to take pleasure in the only source of true good? Is that the life of a Christian who eats the bread from heaven?

Jesus Christ wants only to unite himself with us and join with us in body and in spirit. Why? So he can live deep within our hearts. He must be manifested in our mortal bodies. He must radiate from us, since he and we have become one flesh. I live, yet "it is no longer I who live, but Christ who lives in me"—his created child who has died already to the things of the world.

⇒ 61
REST IN GOD'S HEART

I slept, but my heart was awake. (Song of Solomon 5:2, RSV)

Our sleep will be peaceful when we rest in God's heart, abandoning ourselves to his providence and ever maintaining a sweet awareness of his mercy. When we do this, we are no longer seeking anything for ourselves, and our entire being rests in him.

What we leave behind are our faltering and troubled rationalizations, our desires for ourselves, our impatience to gain a higher place. Then we find ourselves resting in the heart of God*—for God is the one who has put us there with his own hands, and he cradles us there in his arms.

Can we be in danger where God places us—a place where we are as a little child who is rocked and hugged by its mother? Let us let go and give him the freedom to act. Let us rest on him and in him.

This confident, trusting rest, which quells every movement of our limited human reasoning, comes as we maintain true vigilance over our hearts. To place ourselves in God's hands without leaning on any person or any thing—this is what it is to keep our hearts awake even as we sleep.

In this way love will always jealously keep its eyes open. It will always reach out to its Beloved. And when we do that, we will not fall into the deadly sleep of our souls.

---

* *Le sein de Dieu*: the heart, the bosom, the womb. (See the preface to Part Three for further exploration of this term.)

⪜ 62
TEACH US TO PRAY

Lord, teach us to pray. (Luke 11:1, RSV)

Lord, I do not know what I ought to be asking of you. You are the only One who knows what I need. You love me better than I know how to love myself. Father!—give your child what I do not know how to ask for myself. I do not dare ask for crosses or for consolation. All I can do is present myself to you.

Lord, I open up my heart to you. Observe my needs—the ones that I am not even aware of. Look at them, and act according to your mercy. Bring suffering on me or heal me, cast me down or raise me up—I adore your will for me even when I do not know what it is.

I will remain silent, offering myself up and giving myself over completely to you. I no longer have any desire other than to accomplish your will. Teach me to pray. May you yourself pray in me and through me.

⪜ 63
WHERE IS OUR LOVE?

Lord, you know everything; you know that I love you.
(Saint Peter, in John 21:17, RSV)

Do we dare to say this to our Lord as Saint Peter did? Are we loving God even when we are not thinking about him? What better friend is there with whom we would like to speak if not him? Where do we become more bored and restless than right in front of the church altar?

What are we doing to please our Master and to make ourselves as he wants us to be? What are we doing for his glory? What have we sacrificed for him in order to accomplish his will? Do we prefer his will over our slightest interests, over our smallest sources of pleasure? Where is that love we think we have?

Saint Paul warned: "Let anyone be accursed who has no love for the Lord."[24] Woe to those who do not love the Lord Jesus, who has loved us so much. Will he give his eternal kingdom to those who do not love him? If we loved him, could we be unresponsive to his blessings, to his inspirations, to his graces?

"For I am persuaded that neither death, nor life, nor angels, nor principalities, nor powers, nor things present, nor things to come, nor height, nor depth, nor any other creature, shall be able to separate us from the love of God, which is in Christ Jesus, our Lord."[25]

⤚ 64
BEHOLD MY LOVE

"Yes, Lord; you know that I love you." (Saint Peter, in John 21:1, 5 RSV)

Dear God, dear Father, my all in all, you know better than I do how much I love you. You know it, but I do not know it myself—because nothing is more hidden to me than the depths of my heart.

I want to love you. I am afraid of not loving you enough. What I am asking you for is an abundance of pure love. You see my desire—and indeed you are the one who is creating it within me. So look inside the heart of this mortal that you have created, and behold the love you have placed within me.

Dear God, you who love me enough to inspire me to love you to the utmost, please do not look any longer on the torrent of unconfessed sin that once engulfed me. Look within me and see only your mercy—and my love.

⮑ 65
STRIVE FIRST FOR GOD'S KINGDOM

But strive first for the kingdom of God and his righteousness, and all these things will be given to you as well. (Jesus, in Matthew 6:33, NRSV)

Are we not ashamed to strive for *things* at the same time we are striving for the kingdom of God? We have the very source of every good thing, yet we think we are still poor.

Even in their religious devotion, some seek a source of worldly comfort and consolation. They look at religious devotion as a way to lighten the pains they are suffering and not as a state of turning away from themselves and making sacrifices. That mistake is the source of every discouragement.

Let us begin by placing ourselves in God's hands. As we serve him, let us never become anxious and troubled about what he will do for us.

Life is so short—if we suffer a little less or a little more, that is no great thing, when we keep our sight on the kingdom that will last forever.

⮑ 66
I SHALL NOT WANT

The Lord is my shepherd; I shall not want. (Psalm 23:1, KJV)

When I have God, what else could I want? Truly, God himself is the only good there is—and his goodness is never-ending. And so I say to all the falsely "good" things of the earth, "Get away from me! You are unworthy of bearing the name 'good.' The only thing you are good for is to make people bad!" Nothing is good except God. He is in my heart, and I will always carry him within me.

It does not matter if God takes away my pleasures, my riches, my honors, my authority, my friends, my health, and even my life. As long as he does not hide himself from my heart, I will always be rich. I will not have lost anything at all. No, I will have held on to the One who is of everything.

The Lord has been searching for me in all my wanderings away from him. He has loved me when I have not loved him. He has looked on me with gentle tenderness in spite of my ingratitude. I am in his hands. He is leading me according to his wishes.

I feel how weak I am—and how strong God is. And if I keep my trust in his power, I will never lack for anything.

⮥ 67
HUNGER FOR GOD

Whom have I in heaven but you? And there is nothing on earth that I desire other than you. My flesh and my heart may fail, but God is the strength of my heart and my portion for ever. (Psalm 73:25–26, NRSV)

Lord, you are the God of all nature, and everything obeys your voice. You are the soul of every living thing and even of every nonliving thing. You are my soul even more than this very soul that you gave to my body. You are closer to me than myself. All things belong to you. Should my heart not also belong to you—this heart that you made and to which you give life? It is yours, not mine.

But you, dear God, you also belong to me, because I love you. You are everything for me. I have no other possession, you who are my eternal inheritance! What I long for is not earthly consolations, pleasant feelings inside, brilliant enlightenment, or even extraordinary inner graces. I am not asking for any of those gifts that come from you but that are still not you yourself.

I hunger and thirst for you and you alone. I want to forget myself, to lose sight of myself. Do with me according to your will. Nothing else matters. I love you.

⟲ 68
UNSHAKABLE DESIRE
FOR GOD

Glory to God in the highest, and on earth peace, good will toward men.
(Luke 2:14, KJV)

When we seek only the glory of God, we will find our peace again. But God's glory is not to be found in all the thoughts and actions of humanity. God wants to be glorified only through our bringing our human nature down to nothing and giving ourselves completely over to his Spirit. We must not want his glory more than he wants it himself. So let us give ourselves over as quiet instruments for carrying out his divine plan.

Many things will have to be rooted out: our bustling urgency, our movements based on self, our restless agitation that comes disguised as zeal. When these are gone—that is true peace and good will.

The way to have a good will that conforms to God's is to give up our desires and fears and to leave ourselves completely in his hands. Those who do so are as unshakable as Mount Zion.[26] They can never be moved, because their only desire is for God. And it is God who brings everything to pass.

⟲ 69
LEARNING FROM THE MASTER (I)

Learn from me, for I am gentle and humble in heart, and you will find rest
for your souls. (Matthew 11:29b, NIV)

Dear God, I am coming to sit at your feet to be taught and examined by you. You are present here. You are drawing me here by your grace. I am listening only to you. I believe only in you.

Lord, I worship you. My heart loves only you. It longs for you alone. It is with joy that I bring myself low before you, who are eternal

Majesty. I come to receive everything from your hand, and to renounce myself without reservation.

Dear God, send your Holy Spirit. Let your Spirit become mine, and let my own mind and spirit be forever brought to nothing! I give myself over to that Spirit of love and truth. Let him illumine me today and teach me to be gentle and lowly in heart!

Dear Jesus, you are the One who is teaching me this lesson in gentleness and lowliness. Anyone else who might want to teach it to me would only repel me. Everywhere I would see only imperfection and pride. So you are the One who must teach me.

Speak, Lord, for your servant is listening.

⇒ 70
LEARNING FROM THE MASTER (2)

Jesus taught them as one who had authority. (from Matthew 7:29, RSV)

Good teacher, you reach down to teach me through your example. What authority! All I have to do is to fall silent, to worship, to merge myself with you, to pattern myself after you.

The Son of God came down from heaven to dwell among mortals, took on a body made of dust, and died on the cross. All this to make me deeply ashamed of my pride. The One who was everything brought himself down to nothing. And I who am nothing, I want to be—or at least I want people to believe me to be—everything that I am not. Such lies! Such foolishness! Such impudent vanity! Such devilish presumption!

What kind of person could claim to be excused from following your example? Could the lowliest person? Could the sinner who has so often shown such terrible ingratitude that he or she is worthy only to be struck down by your justice?

But Lord, you did not just tell me, "Be gentle and humble." No, *you* said that you are gentle and humble. It is enough to know that this is who you are to conclude that we want to be like you.

71
LEARNING FROM THE MASTER (3)

Learn from me; for I am gentle and lowly in heart, and you will find rest for your souls. (Matthew 11:29b, RSV)

Dear God, you are both *gentle* and *lowly*, because lowliness—humility—is the source of true gentleness. Pride is always haughty, impatient, ready to become bitter. But people who in good faith make light of themselves are willing to be made light of by others. People who believe that nothing is owed to them never believe they are being mistreated.

Acting according to our nature, we cannot produce true gentleness. We can only produce lifelessness, indifference, or artful deception. To be gentle toward another person, we have to let go of ourselves.

And then, dear Lord, you add, "... gentle and *lowly in heart*." Lowliness is not putting ourselves down only in our minds. Humility comes through a heartfelt desire: our wills consent to it and grow to love it so we may glorify God. It comes through taking pleasure in seeing our wretched condition, bringing ourselves low before God, so that we may owe our healing to him alone. Merely to see how wretched we are and to fall into despair over what we see is not being humble. On the contrary, to do that is to have a fit of pride that cannot consent to being brought low.

Finally, dear Savior, you promise me that in humility I will find rest for my soul. What dismay!—how far astray I have gone from that kind of peace! I have searched for it in foolish and turbulent passions, and in the vain imaginations of my pride. But pride cannot coexist with peace. Pride always wants what it cannot have. It always wants to pass itself off as something it is not. It constantly rears its head, and constantly God resists it. He brings our pride low through the envy or contradiction of other people or through our own faults that we cannot help being aware of.

Cursed pride, you will never enjoy the peace of God's children who are simple and small in their own eyes!

⤳ 72
MAKE ME WORTHY OF YOUR PEACE

And the peace of God, which surpasses all understanding, will guard your hearts and your minds in Christ Jesus. (Philippians 4:7, NRSV)

Dear God, how good you are to make me love your peace![27] But it is not enough for me to love and desire it. Make me worthy of it—by crushing my pride. Bring down my mind as well as my body. Let my pride be able to breathe no longer. Complete the work you have begun in taking me out of worldly fellowship with those who neither know you nor love you. Quench in me even the last vestiges of my fierce shame. Break the bonds that keep me a prisoner, and forge new ones that attach me to you alone.

What have I done to you, dear God, to be worthy of such undeserved mercy! The grace you showed me in the past, I trampled under foot. I have repaid with ingratitude all your former goodness toward me. So the only merit that I have in your sight is this: *I am in such a wretched condition that you are moved to show mercy.*

Knowing that, will I still hesitate between the world, which wants me to be lost, and you, who want to save me? Will I push away the cross you offer me with such love, to deliver me from the sickness of my soul—a sickness more terrible than illnesses of the body?

Lord, I throw myself on your mercy. I am worthy only to be handed over to your eternal justice. Chasten me, Lord, strike me down. Do with me according to your good pleasure. I want no other will than yours. I will praise you in all my sufferings. I will kiss the hand that strikes me. I believe that I will yet be spared.

Lord, I stand ready for anything you send me—whether that means living separated from the world, confessing aloud the good news of your gospel, or dying on the cross with you. Jesus, you are my love and my life.

⫷ 73
SEE GOD'S MERCY

I will keep quiet, I will not say a word, for you are the One who made me
suffer like this. (Psalm 39:9, TEV)

Is it my place to complain when God afflicts me, knowing that it is
out of love that he makes me suffer in order to heal me?* Therefore,
Lord, correct me—I give you my permission.

And yet, how gentle are your hardest blows, since they hide such
mercy! Indeed, if you had not afflicted my body, my soul would never
have stopped administering its own deathblow. It was covered with
the most horrible sores. You saw my soul, you had mercy on it. Now
you are bringing down this body full of sin. You are reversing my
ambitious plans. You are giving me back the desire for your eternal
truth, which I had lost so long ago.

Dear Lord, may you be forever blessed! I bend over to kiss the
hand that is correcting me. I worship the arm that is reaching out to
chastise me.

*This meditation and those that follow are taken from *Meditations For One Who
Is Ill*. They are the cry of the heart to God in a time of physical and emotional
suffering.

⫷ 74
LIFE-GIVING PAIN

Be gracious to me, O Lord, for I am languishing. (Psalm 6:2a, NRSV)

Dear God, I cannot offer anything that could cause you to have mercy
on me—except my unworthiness. Look and see how much I need
your help, and reach out to help me. I am aware of my need. And

Lord, I am happy to be aware of it, if that awareness helps me keep mistrusting myself! You have afflicted my flesh in order to purify it. You have broken my body in order to heal my soul. With life-giving pain, you are tearing me away from corrupt pleasures.

My physical suffering afflicts me deeply. Yet I was blithely untroubled by the illness of my soul, which had fallen prey to vain ambition, to the burning fever of raging passions. I was sick, and I did not believe I was. My sickness was so great that I was not even aware of it. I was like a person with a high fever who mistakes the burning of that fever for the flush of good health. How blessed is my sickness, because it is opening my eyes and changing my heart!

↝ 75
THE PRECIOUS GIFT OF SUFFERING

For he has graciously granted you the privilege not only of believing in Christ, but of suffering for him as well. (Philippians 1:29, NRSV)

What a precious gift suffering is, and we do not recognize it! Suffering is no less precious than the faith poured out in our souls by the Holy Spirit. It is a blessed sign of mercy when God makes us suffer!

But is our suffering to be forced and full of impatience? No, that is the way the demons suffer. Those who suffer without being willing to suffer will find in their affliction the mere beginning of eternal sorrow. Those who submit to God in their suffering transform their anguish into infinite good. Therefore, dear God, I long to suffer in peace and with love. It is not enough to believe your holy truths—we must follow them. They condemn us to suffering, but they reveal its value.

Lord, bring new life to my languishing faith. Let others see the faith and patience of your saints shining once again in me! And if some impatient word escapes my lips, at least let me immediately humble myself and offer reparation for it through my suffering!

⤳ 76
SUSTAIN MY HEART

Do not forsake me, O Lord; O my God, do not be far from me; make haste to help me, O Lord, my salvation. (Psalm 38:22, NRSV)

You see all these painful things that are afflicting me. My body is complaining—what shall I reply to it? The world is trying to gain my attention and flatter me: how must I push it away? What shall I say, Lord? I am grieved. I have only enough strength to suffer and remain silent.

Answer me yourself through your almighty Word. Thrust aside the deceitful world that has already seduced me once. Sustain my heart, despite the weakness of my nature. I am suffering intensely because of the troubles with which you are afflicting me, and because of my strong passions that have not yet been extinguished.

Lord, I am suffering—make haste, come quickly to help me! Deliver me from the world and from myself. Deliver me from my troubles by giving me the patience to suffer them.

⤳ 77
GIVE ME YOURSELF

The Lord gave, and the Lord has taken away; blessed be the name of the Lord. (Job 1:21, NRSV)

Lord, these are the words you gave your servant Job to say as his troubles multiplied. How good you are to once again put those words in the mouth and in the heart of such a sinner as I! You once gave me health, and I forgot you. You have taken it away, and now I am coming back to you. Precious mercy, you are wrenching away God's gifts that were separating me from God, in order to give me God himself!

Lord, take away anything in me that is not you, provided only that you give me yourself. Everything belongs to you. You are the Lord.

Take charge of everything: worldly goods, honors, health, life. Tear away—down to the roots—everything that would take your place within me.

⤸ 78
BE MY PATIENCE

Come to me, all you that are weary and are carrying heavy burdens, and I will give you rest. (Matthew 11:28, NRSV)

What a sweet and gentle word this is from Jesus Christ, who takes on himself all the burdens, all the weariness, and all the sufferings of mankind! Dearest Savior, do you truly want to carry all my troubles? Yes, you are inviting me to lay them on your shoulders. All that I suffer is meant to find relief in you.

So, Lord, I join my cross to yours. Carry it for me. I am falling down in exhaustion—just as you once were when another person was made to carry your cross. Lord, I am walking after you toward Calvary, to be crucified there. And when it is your will, I want to die in your arms.

But the weight of my cross is crushing me. I do not have enough patience: be my patience yourself. I beg of you to do as you have promised. I am coming to you. I cannot go on any longer.

And this is enough to be worthy of your compassion and your help.

⇒ 79
YOUR SERVANT IS LISTENING

Speak, Lord, your servant is listening. (1 Samuel 3:9, TEV)

Lord, I am keeping silent in my affliction. I am keeping silent, but I am listening to you with the silence of a contrite, humble soul to whom there is nothing left to say in its suffering.

Dear God, you see my wounds. You are the One who made them. You are the One who is bringing them on me. I am keeping silent. I am suffering. And I am adoring you in the midst of my silence. But you hear my sighs of grief, and the groans of my heart are not hidden from you.

Lord, I do not want to listen to myself. All I want to do is listen to you and follow you.

⇒ 80
DELIVER ME FROM MYSELF

"Now my soul is troubled. And what should I say—'Father, save me from this hour'? No, it is for this reason that I have come to this hour. Father, glorify your name." (John 12:27–28, NRSV)

Dear God, even though you are placing me in peril and afflicting me, you are my Father, and you always will be. Deliver me from this terrible hour I am going through, this time of bitterness and despondency!

Let me breathe on your breast and die in your arms. Save me—either by diminishing my troubles or by increasing my patience. Cut to the quick, burn the chaff. But have mercy, take pity on my weakness.

And if it is not your will to deliver me from my suffering, then deliver me from myself, from my weakness, from my sensitiveness, from my impatience.

⇍ 81
FLOODED WITH GRACE

Against you, you alone, have I sinned. (Psalm 51:4, NRSV)

I have sinned against all your laws. In my pride, my slackness, and my bad example, there is nothing holy in religion that I have not violated. I have even caused offense against your Holy Spirit. I have trampled on the blood of the covenant. I have rejected the former mercies that once penetrated my heart. Lord, I have done every evil thing.

I have exhausted every wickedness, but I have not exhausted your mercy. On the contrary, your mercy takes pleasure in overcoming my unworthiness. It rises like a flood over a dike. In return for so much evil, you give me back everything good. And since you are giving yourself, dear God, to one who has sinned so much, and you are flooding me with grace, shall I refuse to carry my cross along with your Son, who is righteousness and holiness itself?

⇍ 82
MY STRENGTH FAILS ME

My strength fails me. (Psalm 38:10, RSV)

My strength fails me. I feel nothing but weakness, impatience, the affliction of a feeble nature, and the temptation to murmur and despair. What has become of the courage of which I was so proud, and which inspired in me so much confidence in myself? How grieved I am that together with all my troubles, I also have to endure the shame of my weakness and my impatience.

Lord, you are attacking my pride on every side. You are leaving it no resources at all. I am all too happy to endure these things, provided that through these terrible lessons you teach me that I am nothing, that I am capable of nothing, and that you alone are everything!

≈ 83
JOIN ME TO YOURSELF

And I, when I am lifted up from the earth, will draw all people to myself.
(John 12:32, NRSV)

Lord, you promised that when you were lifted up on the cross, you would draw all people to yourself. The nations have come to worship the Man of Sorrows. Even Jews in great numbers have recognized the crucified One as Savior. So your promise has indeed been carried out in the sight of the whole world. But from high up on your cross your almighty power and virtue are still continuing to draw souls to you.

Suffering God! You are taking me out of the deceitful world. You are tearing me away from myself and my vain desires, so that you may cause me to suffer with you on the cross.

It is on the cross that we belong to you. It is on the cross that we come to know you. It is on the cross that we love you. It is on the cross that we are fed with your truth. Without the cross, everything else is nothing but religious sentimentalism. Jesus, join me to yourself! Let me become one of the members of the body of the crucified Jesus Christ!

≈ 84
SET ME FREE

Woe to the world because of the things that cause people to sin!
(Matthew 18:7, NIV)

The world says, "How terrible for those who suffer!" But from the depths of my heart faith replies, "How terrible for the world when it does *not* suffer!" The world sows the entire earth with evil traps to cause souls to go astray. For a long time my own soul was lost in the world. How grievous this was!

Dear God, how good you are to use my infirmity to hold me far away from that corrupt world.

Strengthen me through suffering and complete your work of setting me free from everything, before you allow me to become exposed to those enemies of yours who cause people to sin. Let my infirmity teach me to know that the world's delights are full of poison.

≈ 85
THE SACRIFICE OF MY DAYS

If we live, we live to the Lord; and if we die, we die to the Lord. So, whether we live or die, we belong to the Lord. (Romans 14:8, NIV)

Dear God, what does it matter to me whether I live or die? Life is nothing. It is even dangerous once we start loving it. All death can do is destroy a body made of clay. But it delivers the soul from sickness of the body and from its own pride. Death takes the soul away from the devil's traps and makes it pass for all eternity into the kingdom of truth.

Therefore, dear God, I am not asking you for health or life. I am offering you a sacrifice of my days. You have numbered them. I am not asking for any extension of them. What I *am* asking is to die rather than to live as I have lived. If you want me to die, I will die in patience and love.

Dear God, you hold in your hands the keys to the grave; you can open it or shut it. Do not give me life, if I cannot become detached from it. But whether I live or whether I die, from this moment on I want to be entirely yours.

PART FOUR

God of My Heart
Meditations on Feasts and Fasts

INTRODUCTION TO PART FOUR
God of My Heart:
Meditations on Feasts and Fasts

Fénelon's letters reveal his wise, uncompromising words of counsel to his spiritual children. His meditations on themes from Scripture show his deep love for God and his utter reliance on God. The following meditations on important days in the church year help complete the picture of this man who lost fame and honor, and yet carried no trace of bitterness. Instead, he pressed forward, like the apostle whom he admired so much, Saint Paul, who was able to say,

> Yet whatever gains I had, these I have come to regard as loss because of Christ. More than that, I regard everything as loss because of the surpassing value of knowing Christ Jesus my Lord. For his sake I have suffered the loss of all things, and I regard them as rubbish, in order that I may gain Christ and be found in him, not having a righteousness of my own that comes from the law, but one that comes through faith in Christ, the righteousness from God based on faith. I want to know Christ and the power of his resurrection and the sharing of his sufferings by becoming like him in his death, if somehow I may attain the resurrection from the dead.
>
> Not that I have already obtained this or have already reached the goal; but I press on to make it my own, because Christ Jesus has made me his own. Beloved, I do not consider that I have made it my own; but this one thing I do: forgetting what lies behind and straining forward to what lies ahead, I press on toward the goal for the prize of the heavenly call of God in Christ Jesus.[1]

Following his exile from the French court, Fénelon devoted himself to his diocese in Cambrai, which had recently been annexed as part of northern France. His task as the first French archbishop was immense: he devoted himself unswervingly to the people of his diocese, and in particular to his seminarians, the future priests who would minister to the faithful. But always, Fénelon devoted himself foremost to his personal relationship with God.

The early 1700s saw the publication of twenty-one meditations by Fénelon entitled *Entretiens affectifs sur les principales fêtes de l'année.* These writings are available in several public-domain sources in French, including a fine series of Fénelon's works published in 1823 in Paris by L'Imprimerie de J.-A. Lebel. Those twenty-one meditations are the material of this book.

The title of this work reveals much about the writer. *Entretiens* are *conversations* or *talks. Affectifs* means the same in French as *affective* in English: *expressing emotions or feelings.* Taken together, *entretiens affectifs* could best be thought of as *personal conversations.*

With whom, we might wonder, was Fénelon carrying on this conversation? As we will see in these pages, his primary conversation was an intimate, ongoing dialogue with God.

THE CHURCH YEAR

The church year consists of two types of celebrations, called *feasts,*[2] a word that in a secular context refers to large meals. In religious use, the word *feast* means a religious observance commemorating an event or honoring a person or several persons.

One cycle of feasts remembers events in the life of Christ. That part of the church calendar, called the *temporal cycle,* includes Advent, Lent, Eastertide, Ascension, Pentecost, and other feasts. The other part of the church calendar, called the *sanctoral cycle,* remembers important saints on days set aside for special commemorations dedicated to those saints.

With the abundance of celebrations about which Fénelon could write, we might wonder why he chose these particular twenty-one feast days and not others. As we will see, these meditations include highlights of the entire church year. Their intention was not to be comprehensive,[3] but to reveal Fénelon's personal conversations with God.

The translation in Part Four

Like nearly all scholars of his day, Fénelon read and wrote freely in Latin. Since Fénelon's use of French was strongly influenced by Latin, the modern translator needs to take this into account when rendering his French into English. As in Part 3, this translation has undertaken to render Fénelon's words *thought by thought* rather than word by word. Here are three examples that demonstrate this approach:

annihilation—In English, this word brings to mind images of bombs utterly destroying a city. However, when Fénelon wrote of the *annihilation* of self, his meaning was that of the Latin *annihilare*, meaning *reducing to nothing*. This translation renders this word as *bringing low*, or *bringing down to nothing*, or *humbling*.

répugnance—In English, this word usually refers to a strong dislike or antagonism. However, when Fénelon uses this word, he is using it in its alternative meaning of "the quality of being contradictory or inconsistent." This translation uses the second meaning.

sagesse—This word is usually translated as *wisdom*. Sometimes it is best rendered that way, as in the expression "Eternal Wisdom of God." But when Fénelon refers to a person's *sagesse*, he is referring to head knowledge as contrasted with heart knowledge. In those cases, the word has been rendered as *learning* or *intellect*.

Walking with God Through the Church Year

For more than thirty years, Fénelon served as a wise mentor to many members of the king's court. His letters of counsel have inspired generations of Christians ever since.

These meditations give us another side of Fénelon: a glimpse of his personal conversations with God. As he walks with God through the church year, we are privileged to travel alongside him. It is our prayer that as you read his words, you will find yourself challenged to follow Fénelon on his journey, traveling the Royal Way of the Cross.

⟿ 1
ADVENT

Advent is the Christian season that begins the church year in the West.
Beginning on the Sunday nearest to November 30, it includes four
Sundays. While Advent is a period of expectant waiting and preparation
for the celebration of the birth of Jesus, it also looks beyond Jesus' birth to
his Second Coming.

In this meditation, Fénelon expresses his longing for Christ to come again
into this perishing world. "Lord," he writes, "take away my sin. Come reign
within me. . . . I do not want to love myself at all. My only desire is to love
your coming."

During this season of Advent, dear God, I wish to withdraw from
external and earthly affairs, so that I may silently worship the mysteries of your Son and await his birth in the inner recesses of my heart.
Come, Lord Jesus. Come, Spirit of truth and love, who formed him in
the womb of the Holy Virgin.

I am waiting for you, divine Jesus, as the prophets and patriarchs
waited for you. I eagerly say with them, "Shower, O heavens, from
above, and let the skies rain down righteousness; let the earth open,
that salvation may spring up."[4] You came once already. The righteous
of ancient times saw the Desire of all nations,[5] yet the world did
not know him.[6] "The light shines in the darkness, and the darkness
did not overcome it."[7] Why are you waiting to come? Return, Lord.
Return to strike the thoughtless world and to judge those who do
not see.[8]

King of whom the princes of this world are only a flimsy image, *your*
kingdom come.[9] When will this reign of justice, righteousness, peace,
and truth come down from on high upon us? Your Father gave you all
the nations. He gave you all authority in heaven and on earth.[10] And
yet you are unrecognized, despised, offended, and betrayed. Therefore,
when will the judgment of this hard-hearted world come? When will
the day of your triumph come? Arise, arise, God! Be the judge of your

own cause. Strike the foolish with the breath of your mouth. Deliver your children. Vindicate yourself in that great day in the sight of all the peoples: it is your glory and not ours that we seek.

Dear God, I love you for yourself, and not for my own self. I am suffering. I am dried up with sadness as I see wickedness gaining the advantage on earth and your good news being trampled under foot. I am suffering as I feel myself, in spite of myself, subjected to emptiness and futility. How long, Lord, will you leave your inheritance desolate? Return, Lord Jesus. Let the light of your face shine on us.[11]

I do not want to hold on to any of the things that surround me here on earth. All of them threaten instant ruin. The immense vaults of heaven will crumble into the abyss; this earth that is so covered with sin will be consumed and renewed by the refining fire. The stars will fall from heaven; their light will be extinguished. The burning elements will be consumed; all of nature will be shaken.[12] Let the foolish tremble at that sight!

I cry out with love and confidence, "Strike, Lord; glorify yourself at the expense of all who injure your holiness. Strike me. Do not spare me, so that I may be purified and made worthy of you."

This foolish world is concerned only with the present, fleeting moment. All of this is going to perish, and they want to enjoy it as if it were going to last forever. Heaven and earth will pass away like smoke; only your word will endure for all eternity.[13]

Humanity does not know truth. Lies are worshiped, and they fill the hearts of mankind. Everything is false and deceitful. Everything that is seen, touched, felt, and measured by time is nothing. Must it be that this vain apparition should be considered so solid, and that the unchangeable truth must be considered a dream? Lord, why do you allow the world to be bewitched?[14] The whole earth is plunged into the sleep of death: awaken it by your light.

I want only you. I await only you. I look on the thunderbolt that is ready in your hands to crush the proud mortals and to avenge your scorned patience—and far from being afraid of death, I look at it as the deliverance of your children. Yes, Lord, we will die, and the deadly spell will suddenly be broken. You will no longer be offended. I will love you. I will love only you. I will no longer love myself.

How I love your coming! Already, according to your teaching, I lift up my eyes[15] and my head to come before you. Transported by my love, I will come toward you, as the chief of your apostles taught me.[16] I am weak, miserable, and fragile, it is true. I have everything to fear if you judge me in the strictness of your justice. But the more fragile I am, the more I conclude that life is danger, and that death is grace.

Lord, take away my sin. Come reign within me. Tear me away from myself, and I will be fully yours. What do I have to do on earth? What can I desire in this valley of tears, in which evil seems to triumph and in which good is so imperfect? Nothing but your will can keep me in it. I love nothing that I see. I do not want to love myself at all. My only desire is to love your coming.

2
SAINT THOMAS
(DECEMBER 21)

Saint Thomas the apostle is best known to us for his doubt that Jesus had risen from the dead. John recounts the story of Thomas' demand to feel Jesus' wounds before being convinced that his Lord was alive. When Jesus appeared to him, he cried out, "My Lord and my God!" Jesus said to him, "Have you believed because you have seen me? Blessed are those who have not seen and yet have come to believe."[17]

Though having revealed his human weakness and often maligned as "doubting Thomas," this apostle was transformed by his encounter with the risen Christ. According to tradition he went on to become a great missionary, taking the message of Jesus Christ to India and, some say, possibly even China and Japan.

In this meditation, Fénelon dwells on the theme of bringing the self down to nothing in order to allow God to accomplish his work through us. In this way, he joins Saint Paul, who said, "I will boast all the more gladly of my weaknesses, so that the power of Christ may dwell in me . . . for whenever I am weak, then I am strong."[18]

Dear God, open my eyes and enlarge my heart so that I may understand and feel the gifts that you placed in this apostle. Spirit who sent him, who led him, and who filled him: fill me, inspire me, transform me into a new creation. Father of light and mercy, you do with mortals what you will. They seem no longer to be mortals the moment you speak. Therefore what is that weak, lowly, timid man, who in the eyes of the world is poor, coarse, and ignorant? Where does he go? What does he aspire to do? He aspires to change the face of the farthest nations, using truth alone to conquer peoples that conquering kings were unable to overcome with their weapons. He aspires to discover a new world in order to take to it a new faith.

To undertake such things in the world is to be completely dead to our own learning and insight. It is to be impassioned by the foolishness of the cross. This is how, vanquishing Spirit, in your children you bring to nothing all learning, all insight, all self-regard, all human rules, all means of reasoning. You call that which is not, in order to confound that which is.

You take pleasure in choosing what is the lowliest thing in the eyes of the world, in order to do in the eyes of the world what is the greatest and most impossible thing. You are jealous of the glory of your work, and you want to found it only on nothingness. You dig until you reach nothingness in order to establish it, just as wise men when building dig down to solid rock. Therefore, dig in me, dear God, until you bring my self down to nothing. Neutralizing Spirit, I invite you to overturn, to put everything in disorder. Do not spare any human ordering of things. Undo everything in order to redo everything. Let your creature be completely new. Let no trace remain of former things. Then, having erased and defaced everything, and having reduced everything to pure nothingness, I will become all things in you, because I will no longer be anything in myself.

I will no longer have any consistency, but in your hand I will take on all the forms that suit your purposes. It is by bringing my limited self down to nothing that I will enter into your divine immensity. Who will understand this? Who will give me souls that seek and desire to be humbled? As long as we hold onto the slightest thing, we will remain bound.

As good as it may seem to exercise restraint in our words and actions, when it comes to holding back with regard to God, we are guilty of stealing. That is because we owe God everything, since everything comes from him. The purer the gifts are, the more God is jealous of not letting us possess them in ourselves. Therefore, it is only by being brought down to absolutely nothing that we are turned into his true instruments.

Do with me, Lord, as you did to your apostle Thomas. He was one of those who were reduced to nothing, people about whom it is said that they were given over to your grace. He was nothing due to riches, or reputation, or talents, or even virtue. He was weakness itself. But

234 | The Complete Fénelon

you took pleasure in making your strength shine through him. He took your name to the far reaches of the East, to those peoples who lived in darkness and the shadow dark as death,[19] and who did not even have eyes to see the light.[20]

The world, completely worldly as it is—critical, wicked, full of scandal, unteachable, hard-hearted, so false and deceitful that it even deceives itself, having no appetite for the truth, which it hates, mad lover of flattering lies—this world was unable to resist the one who was nothing in himself. That one, through his nothingness, was everything in God. God speaks through his puny creature, and God's spoken word, which made the world, renews it.

Dear God! I hear this word, and as I understand it, I leap with joy in the Holy Spirit. You have hidden your word from the great and the learned—they will never understand it—but you reveal it to those who are little and simple.[21]

Everything consists in making ourselves small and in making ourselves as nothing. As long as we are still something, we are nothing, and we are not good for anything. What remains, even the thing that is the most hidden and the thing that appears to be the best, resists everything that God wishes to do, and stops his all-powerful hand.

But this truth has such a small outreach! What a pity! Where is there a courageous soul who wants to be nothing, who lets go of everything and shakes off everything—talents, mind, friendship, reputation, honor, virtue? Where are those faithful souls? Instead, we do as Saint Thomas did when he did not believe: we want to see, we want to touch, we want to assure ourselves of the gifts of Jesus Christ, and we want to procure our advancement.

But "blessed are those who have not seen and yet have come to believe,"[22] and who worship God in spirit and truth through the sacrifice of burnt offering, which is the total loss of everything that is in us! This is what makes the life of an apostle, a life that is transformed in Jesus Christ.

⇒ 3
CHRISTMAS DAY
(DECEMBER 25)

*In a stable, from the womb of a humble maiden, God entered the world
as a helpless baby. Christmas reminds us that the creator of the universe
humbled himself and took human form, in order that the world might be
saved through him. Why? "So that everyone who believes in him may not
perish but have eternal life."[23]*

*In this meditation, Fénelon expresses his desire to be humble and little,
like a child. As Jesus said, "Let the little children come to me, and do not
stop them; for it is to such as these that the kingdom of heaven belongs."[24]*

I worship you, baby Jesus, as you lie exposed in the manger. I love
nothing more than your being a baby born in poverty. Oh, who will
give me the gift of being as poor and as childlike as you? Eternal
Wisdom, brought down to the form of a baby, take away my vain and
presumptuous knowledge and make me a child with you. Be silent,
those of you who are the wise in this world. I do not want to be
anything, I do not want to know anything. I want to believe everything, I want to suffer everything, I want to set aside everything, even
including my own judgment!

Blessed are the poor—not just any poor, but the poor in spirit[25]—
whom Jesus made like him in his manger, and from whom he took
away even their very power of reasoning! You mortals who are wise
in your own thoughts, farsighted in your plans, and composed in your
speech, I fear you: your greatness intimidates me, in the way that children are afraid of grown-ups. I need nothing more than the children
of a holy childhood.

The Word made flesh, the all-powerful word of the Father, falls silent,
stumbles over words, cries, and gives out childish utterances—and what
do I do? I take pride in the arrangements that my mind makes, and
I am afraid that the world does not have a high enough opinion of

my abilities! No! I will be one of those blessed children who give up everything in order to gain everything. They are not concerned about anything concerning themselves: they count themselves as nothing. Let people go ahead and look down on them and not condescend to trust their discernment. The world will be great as long as it pleases.

Even good people, people who have good intentions and a zeal for good works, will grow every day in prudence, in foresight, in ability, in intensity of virtue. But all my pleasure will lie in growing smaller, in becoming despicable and obscure, in keeping silent, in consenting to be physically and morally weak and to be seen as weak. My pleasure will be in taking the shame of Jesus the crucified one, and joining to it the powerlessness and the speaking with broken words of Jesus the little child.

Most of us would prefer to die with Jesus in his agony than to see ourselves lying in swaddling clothes alongside him in the cradle. Being little horrifies us more than dying, because death can be suffered through a standard of courage and greatness. But it is torture to no longer be counted as anything, like children. It is torture to no longer be able to count ourselves as anything. It is torture to fall back into childhood, as do some older people who are victims of dementia, people whom hard-hearted children make fun of. It is torture to see, with clear and penetrating vision, how worthy of disdain is this state. All these things are the most intolerable kind of torture for a great and generous soul, one that would take comfort from every other kind of hardship by making use of its courage and its learning.

Knowledge, courage, intellect, virtue itself: these are the last things that the soul that is dying to itself has the most difficulty in letting go of. Nothing else that we leave behind has the same hold on us. With those other things, it is as if we are using our fingertips to remove a garment that does not cling to us. But to deprive ourselves of our very knowledge and judgment, which constitute the most intimate life of the soul, is to skin us alive; it is to tear us apart right down to the depths of our bones.

I hear my intellect telling me, "Come, now! Do we have to stop being reasonable? Do we have to become like insane people who have to be locked up? Is not God wisdom and knowledge itself? Does our knowledge and understanding not come from his, and consequently, are we not required to follow it?" But there is an extreme difference between being a reasoning person and being reasonable. We will never be as reasonable as when we stop our reasoning.

By giving ourselves over to God's pure reason, which our weak and vain intellect is incapable of understanding, we will be delivered from our knowledge and understanding—which went astray when sin entered the world. We will be delivered from our carelessness about what we say and do, and from our pigheadedness. The more we are dead to ourselves by the Spirit of God, the more careful we are about what we say and do—and yet without thinking about it. Indeed, the only way that we fall into carelessness about what we say and do is through continuing to live by our own thinking, our own views, our own natural inclinations. We continue to desire, we continue to think, we continue to speak according to our own ways. Dying totally to our own intellect would create in us the true, consuming knowledge and understanding of the Word of God.

It is not through an effort of reasoning within that we will rise above ourselves. On the contrary, it is through bringing the self down to nothing, through bringing down our very reasoning powers, which are the most essential part of ourselves, that we will enter into a new being. In that new being, as Saint Paul says, Jesus Christ will be our life, our righteousness, and our wisdom.[26] We will go astray only if we choose to do so. Therefore we will be sheltered from going astray only by letting ourselves be led, by being little, teachable, simple, given over to the Spirit of God, flexible and ready for every kind of movement. In that state we will have no stability within ourselves, we will not resist anything, we will no longer have any will of our own or any judgment, and in a simple and unaffected manner we will say what comes to us and love only to give up after having said it.

This is the way little children let themselves be carried, picked up, and put to bed; they leave nothing hidden, and keep nothing to themselves. In this way, we will no longer be wise, but God will be wise within us and for us. Jesus Christ will speak within us, while we will think that we are just stammering out words. Jesus, little child: little children are the only ones who are able to reign with you.

⇐ 4
ST. JOHN THE EVANGELIST
(DECEMBER 27)

The apostle John is known as "the beloved disciple," in part because the Gospel of John points to John himself as being "the disciple whom Jesus loved,"[27] and in part because in his letters, John wrote often about love: "God is love, and those who abide in love abide in God, and God abides in them."[28] One of the most beautiful images of John's love for Jesus is that of the young disciple's placing his head on Jesus' breast at the Last Supper.[29] Many years after the Resurrection, in his letters the aged John often wrote of love to his Christian friends. He called his friends "my little children," a reminder of Jesus' words to his disciples, "Truly I tell you, unless you change and become like children, you will never enter the kingdom of heaven."[30]

In this meditation, Fénelon expresses his desire to be filled with love for Jesus.

Jesus, I desire to lean with John on your breast and feed on love by placing my heart on yours.[31] Like the beloved disciple, I want to be taught by your love. After having experienced your love, this disciple said that "his anointing teaches you about all things."[32] This inner anointing of your Spirit teaches in silence. We love, and we know what we must know; we taste, and we have no need to hear anything. Every human word is excess and only distracts us, because inside, we have the abundant word that nourishes the deepest part of the soul. In it, we find all truth. We no longer see anything except one thing, which is the simple and universal truth: and this truth is God. In the sight of God, created things—those deceitful nothings—disappear and leave no trace of their lies.

Love is the true teacher of souls, but we do not want to listen to it. We listen to beautiful speeches, and we listen to our own intellect. But the true Teacher, who teaches without reasoning and without words, is not listened to. We are afraid to open our hearts to him. We make offers to him and yet we hold back. We are afraid he will speak and ask for too much. We would like to let him speak, but on the condition that we will take what he says only as far as following our learning will allow. Therefore, our learning judges the one who ought to judge it.

Love desires souls who are completely given over to its transports, souls who are not afraid, no more than were the apostles, to be fools in the eyes of the world.[33] Divine Spirit, it is not enough to be filled with you. No, we must be absolutely impassioned by you. What would we not learn without resorting to intellect or knowledge, if we consulted nothing else but pure love! Pure love wants everything for God. Pure love leaves nothing to the creature, and puts only the truth of the kingdom of God in the depths of the soul! Love is the deciding factor in every case. Love is never wrong, because it puts no stock in mortals and brings everything back to God alone. It is a consuming fire[34] that burns up everything, that devours everything, that brings everything down to nothing. Pure love makes its victim into the perfect sacrifice.[35]

Love reveals God so well! For pure love no longer lets anything be seen except God himself, but with a very different aim from that of humans, who consider him only with cold, dry speculation. Pure love lets us love everything that we see, and it is love that gives piercing eyes to see him. A moment of peace and silence reveals more wonders than the deep reflections of all knowledgeable humanity put together.

But yet, how is it that love teaches all things, since love can allow only one thing and closes its eyes to everything else, in order to keep them fixed on one single object? I understand this secret, which is that the true means of knowing everything else well, *during this life*, is not to know it, because we hold it in contempt.

Therefore this is "all-knowingness." The learned of this world do not know it, for it is reserved for those who are poor in spirit, those who are taught by the anointing of pure love. These are the ones who penetrate to the depths everything that has been created, and yet do not stoop even to pay attention to it, or to open their eyes to see it. What does it matter that they do not know how to reason about God? They know how to love him, and that is enough. Blessed knowledge this is, which extinguishes all curiosity and satisfies the soul with pure truth. This blessed knowledge not only shows the soul all truth by satisfying the soul's thirst by occupying it with God, but it also transports that simple, unique truth into the depths of that soul, in order to no longer be anything but one and the same thing with it!

How grievous it is that there are so many great teachers who see nothing at all, while thinking that they know everything! They want to know everything. They want to know about the nature of the several states of being, about the properties of those states, about the order of the universe, about the history of the human race, about the works made by men and women, about the arts that humans have invented, about the various languages of the world, about the rules of conduct that humans practice among themselves. How disgusted they would be with all this curious research if they knew mortals really well! Does one take interest in an earthworm? And is nothingness not even more unworthy of our spending time on it? Well, what can we learn from something that is nothing? There is only one everlasting truth, and this truth absorbs everything and leaves no curiosity outside of itself: everything else is only nothingness, and consequently is a lie.

If a person becomes knowledgeable due to a need brought about by conditions in that person's life, that is well and good. But if we believe that we know something when the only thing we know is *nothing*, if we hope to embellish our minds with that knowledge, if we seek to feed our minds and satisfy them by concerning ourselves with vain, hollow, created things—what foolishness this is! What ignorance this is on the part of those who want to know everything!

Jesus, I no longer have any teacher but you, no other book than your breast. There, I will learn everything by knowing nothing and by bringing myself down to nothing. There, I live the same life that you live in the bosom of your Father. I live on love. Love does everything within me. It is only out of love that I was created. And it is only inasmuch as I love, that I do what God intended for me to do by creating me. Therefore, I perceive everything, and I no longer want to perceive anything except you.

Keep silence, curious world, world that holds itself as wise. On Jesus' breast, I have found the ignorance and the foolishness of his cross, in comparison with which all your talents are only so much rubbish. Go ahead and hold me in contempt as much as I disregard you.

🍃 5
THE CIRCUMCISION
(JANUARY 1)

The Feast of the Circumcision of Our Lord[36] celebrates the eighth day after
Jesus' birth, when, following the tradition of the descendants of Abraham, he
was circumcised and given the name Jesus, which means "Savior." The One
who created the law, and who at his transfiguration would be seen talking with
Moses, the lawgiver, and Elijah, the most important prophet, submitted as a
child to the Jewish law. Later, he would say, "Do not think that I have come to
abolish the law or the prophets; I have come not to abolish but to fulfill."[37]

The spilling of Jesus' blood at his circumcision was the first time his blood
was shed for humankind.

In this meditation, Fénelon explores the theme of suffering, admitting
freely that suffering horrifies his human nature. But he speaks to his soul
as a parent would to a wayward child, reminding it that it has promised to
follow Jesus—all the way to the cross.

Jesus, I adore you as you undergo the knife of circumcision. How I
love you in this moment of abjection and weakness! I see you covered
with shame, ranked with sinners, subjected to a humiliating law. I see
you suffering from sharp pain and already, in the first days of your
infancy, shedding the first fruits of that blood that on the cross will be
the recompense of the whole world.

Therefore, you come into the world only to suffer. First, you take
the name *Jesus*, which means "Savior," and it is to save sinners that you
place yourself among the suffering sinners. With such comfort and
consolation, child Jesus, do I see your tears and your blood flow! Right
here is the beginning of the mystery of pain, deep personal humiliation, and disgrace. Precious victim, living sacrifice! You will grow up.
But you will grow up only to make the signs of your love grow as well.
You hold back your sacrifice only to make it greater and more severe.

But Jesus, what do I see in your pains? Is this something that ought
to arouse tender compassion within me? No, because it is for myself,

not you, that I ought to weep. I cannot reflect on your humiliation and suffering without becoming immediately aware that you
humble yourself and you suffer only because of my needs. You do
this to atone for my sins of pride and slackness. You do this to teach
me to suffer and to bear the shame that I deserve. Vain and cowardly
human nature shudders at the sight of its Savior who is brought
low and suffers. It feels itself being crushed by the authority of this
example.

So we must prepare our hearts for shame and bitterness. Yes, I want
this, Jesus! I am taking up my cross to follow after you.[38] If people
look down on me, they will be right. The disregard that I have for
myself is sincere only inasmuch as it makes me agree to be disregarded
by others. What an injustice it is to take what to us seems lowly and
unworthy, and to want to dazzle our neighbor with it!

Therefore, Jesus, I give myself over to every sort of disgrace that you
send my way. I do not refuse any of it, and there is not a single one
that I do not deserve. Is honor due to an earthworm? Sinful soul, what
do you deserve, if not to be the rubbish of the world?[39] Can I ever be
brought too low, I who by my nature am only nothing, and by my own
will am only sin? To my soul that is so vain and ungrateful toward God
I say, "Soul, I tell you to bear without complaining the shame that is
your portion. No more honor, no more propriety, no more reputation.
All those beautiful names must be sacrificed to a Savior who is covered
with reproach. What is there in you that does not ask for humiliation?
Is it your pride? Well, it is your very pride that makes you even more
afflicted and more unworthy of any honor."

But what a pity it is, Jesus, that there is a vast difference between
general feelings of humiliation, and the practice of it! From afar we
hail the cross, but up close we are horrified by it. I promise you now
to walk in the bloody footprints that you have left for me so that I can
follow you, bearing the cross after you. But when the reproach and the
pain of the cross appear, all my courage will abandon me. Then what
vain pretexts of propriety I will have! What shameful scrupulousness!
What diabolical jealousies!

Dear God, I talk magnificently about the cross, and all I want to know is the name! I am afraid of it. I run away from it. The very sight of it devastates me. What is the matter with you, soul of mine? Where does your grumbling come from, your falling into discouragement, your going around to all your friends begging for a little comfort? "Well, it's because God is humiliating me and loading me with crosses." So! Is this not what you promised him to love? What is the matter with you, then? What is troubling you? Must Christians be driven to distraction when they get what they have wanted, and when they are made to be like the suffering Jesus?

Child Jesus! Give me the simplicity of your childhood so full of pain. If I cry, if I moan, at least may I never resist your crucifying hand. Cut to the quick. Go ahead and burn. The more I am afraid of suffering, the more I need it.

6
EPIPHANY (JANUARY 6)

The Feast of Epiphany commemorates the arrival of the wise men[40] from the East who came to Jerusalem, asking, "Where is the child who has been born king of the Jews? For we observed his star at its rising, and have come to pay him homage."[41] The Magi were sent to Bethlehem, where the star that had been leading them stopped over the place where Jesus was. There, they worshiped the child.

In contrast to both the secular and the religious leaders of Jerusalem, the Magi recognized the kingship of this lowly child. Later, when Jesus was presented in the temple, the aged, righteous Simeon also recognized that Jesus was the Savior—and not only of God's chosen people, Israel, but of the whole world: "My eyes have seen your salvation, which you have prepared in the presence of all peoples, a light for revelation to the Gentiles and for glory to your people Israel."[42]

In this meditation, Fénelon expresses his desire to follow in the footsteps of the Magi, those wise men who set out on a journey that others thought foolish and fanatical. But in the end, the Magi found the world's greatest treasure.

Dear God, I am coming to you, and I never tire of coming. I have nothing in myself, and I find everything in you alone. How poor I am! How rich you are! But what need do I have to be rich, since you are rich for me? I adore your eternal riches. I love my poorness. I take pleasure in being nothing before you. Today, give me your Spirit so that I may contemplate your holy Son, Jesus, who is worshiped by the Magi. I worship him alongside them.

Those Magi followed the star without reasoning everything out. Those who were so wise ceased to be wise in order to submit themselves to a light that surpassed their own. Their riches, their affairs, people's talk—they counted these as nothing. What could people think of them? They set forth without knowing where they were going. "What has become of the learning of these men who used to govern others?

Such willingness to believe on uncertain evidence! Such imprudence! Such blind, fanatical zeal!"—this is how people must have talked about them as they watched them set out on their journey.

But the Magi counted as nothing the contempt that was heaped on them, their reputation that was trampled under foot, and even the witness of their own learning that failed them. They were willing to pass for fools, and to not even catch sight of the means to justify what they were doing. They undertook a long and difficult journey without knowing what they would find.

It is true that the Magi saw an extraordinary star. But how many other people who were taught in the movements of the stars found nothing supernatural in that star! The Magi were the only ones who were illumined and touched to the bottom of their hearts. An inner light of pure faith led them more surely than the light of the star. After all that, we must not be surprised that they had no trouble worshiping a poor baby in a manger. How little did these men become, men who were great in the world! How their learning was confounded and humbled!

Magi, was this what you came from the far reaches of the East to worship? What! A child who feeds at his mother's breast and cries? It seems to me that I hear them answer, "The wisdom and knowledge of God dazzle our own. The more the object seems worthy of disregard, the more worthy of God it is for us to bring ourselves down low to worship him." Magi, you had to have become very much like children yourselves in order for you to find the true God in the child Jesus!

But who will give me that holy, childlike quality, that divine foolishness of the Magi? Get away from me, irreverent and cursed learning and knowledge of Herod and the city of Jerusalem! They reason, they take pleasure in their learning, they make themselves judge of God's counsel, they are even afraid of seeing what cannot be known. I fear that haughty and profane learning. I abhor it. I do not want to listen to it anymore. I no longer aim to follow anything except the childhood of Jesus. Let the harebrained world say all that it will, let it even be scandalized: *Woe to the world because of stumbling-blocks!*[43] It is the reproach and the foolishness of the Savior that I love.

I no longer value anything: I place no value in human respect. I give no value to any fear of the reviling, harsh, and abusive language and the condemnation of the falsely wise. Even people who are considered good Christians, who are still too set on their own understanding, will not stop me. When I see the star, I will tell them, as did Saint Paul to the Corinthian Christians, who were still too attached to worldly propriety and to their intellects, "We are fools for the sake of Christ, but you are wise in Christ."[44]

This is a blessed ambition! But how can I accomplish it! Lord, you are inspiring it: make it possible for me to follow it. You are giving me the desire for it: give me also the courage to carry it out. Let there be no other light than the one from on high. Let there be no other intellect than that of sacrificing all my use of reason. Keep silence, presumptuous intellect. I can no longer tolerate you.

Dear God, eternal truth, sovereign and pure reason, pure intelligence: come and be the only power of reason that enlightens me in the darkness of faith.

7
THE CONVERSION OF ST. PAUL (1) (JANUARY 25)

The Feast of the Conversion of Saint Paul celebrates one of the most important events in the early Christian church. The Pharisee Saul of Tarsus was attempting to brutally suppress this sect that he deemed heretical, even standing by and approving the stoning of the martyr Stephen. As he approached Damascus with letters from the high priest calling for the arrest of Christians in that city, suddenly a blinding light from heaven flashed around him. Stricken blind, Saul fell to the ground and heard the voice of Jesus asking Saul why he was persecuting him. The voice then told Saul to enter the city, where he came under the care of a Christian disciple named Ananias.

Completely converted, Saul took the name by which he is known to us today—Paul—and dedicated the rest of his life to spreading the message of Jesus Christ. Paul's missionary journeys, documented in the book of Acts, spread the Christian message across Asia Minor, to other lands in the Mediterranean basin, and into Europe.

In this meditation, Fénelon asks God to cast him down as God cast down Saul, so that he might become pliable in God's hand, as ready to do God's will as was Saul when he became Paul, which means little.

I am coming to you, Lord Jesus, more downhearted than Saul was at the gates of Damascus. It is your hand that casts me down. I adore that hand—it performs everything. All-powerful hand, my joy lies in seeing myself as being at your disposal. Strike me. Cast me down. Dear God, I am coming under that terrible, merciful hand. As you cast me down, enlighten me, touch me, convert me as you converted Saul.

As I fall, my first cry is to say, "Lord, what do you want me to do?"[45] How I love that cry! It contains everything. All by itself it includes all the most perfect prayers and all of the highest virtues. With the master, there are no conditions and no limits: I am ready to do everything and to do nothing, to desire everything and to desire nothing, to suffer without comfort and to enjoy the sweetest comfort.

I do not say to you, "Dear God, I will undergo the greatest hardships, give up the most difficult things, and demonstrate amazing changes in my behavior." It is not up to me to decide what I will do. What I will do is to listen to you and to await your word.

It is no longer a question of my will: my will is lost in yours. Just tell me what you desire, because I want everything that it is your desire for me to want. Not just bodily deprivations, but also humiliations of mind, and sacrifices of health, inner tranquility, friendship, reputation, inner consolation, feelings of peace, earthly life, and even that inner support that is a foretaste of eternity: all those things are in your hands. Give, take away—what does it matter? Do as you will, Lord, and never consult me. Just show me your commands, and just let me obey.

In whatever bitter and painful trial in which you may put me, let there remain in me just one word: "What do you want me to do?" Cast me down, like Saul, in the dust, in the sight of all of humanity. But cast me down in such a way that I may be able to rise back up. Blind me as you blinded him. Reproach me for my acts of unfaithfulness. I want those acts to be known, and I will willingly say, like Saul, in the sight of the whole church, "I was irreverent, an unbeliever, a blasphemer, a persecutor of Jesus Christ. He converted me in order to revive the hope of the most hardened sinners, and to give a touching example of the patience with which he waits for the souls who have wandered the farthest away."

Come and look at me, all of you who forget God, who violate his law, who insult virtue. Come and look at that loving hand that blinds me in order to give me light, that casts me down in order to raise me up. Come and admire with me that mercy that takes pleasure in blazing forth its light in the bottomless pit of my distress. Lord, far from complaining about my fall, I kiss and worship the hand that is striking me. Do you want me to fall still lower? I want this if it is your will: "What do you want me to do?"

Dear God, I feel the truth and the strength of those words, "It is hard for you to kick against the goads."[46] How hard it is to resist the inner drawing and attraction of your grace! "Who has resisted him, and succeeded?"[47] Unbelieving and worldly people are not the only ones who do not enjoy any peace until they turn to you. This is also true of the soul that you have delivered from the bonds of sin: it cannot enjoy any peace if it continues to resist, to hold back, or to delay that piercing goad of your Spirit that pushes it to strip itself bare, to become childlike, to die to itself.

Prudence resists the goad. It gathers a thousand reasons to resist. It looks at the blessed foolishness of the cross as if it were a path leading it astray. It would prefer the most horrendous ascetic practices to the simplicity and the littleness of God's children, who prefer to sit trustingly on God's lap than to be great and wise within themselves.

How grievous this battle is! How it agitates the soul! How much it costs the soul to sacrifice its intellect and the beautiful assumed appearance that conceals its real intentions! But also, without this sacrifice, the soul finds no peace, no moving forward. On the contrary, it finds the trouble of a soul pressed by God, a soul that is afraid to see how far God wants to take it in order to tear out any roots of support of its own self-esteem.

Dear God, I no longer want to resist you. I will not hesitate any longer. I will be more and more afraid not to do enough than to do too much. I want to be Saul when he was converted. After what you did for that persecutor, there is nothing that you cannot do with a sinful soul. It is because I am unworthy of anything that you will take pleasure in doing the greatest things in me. But, whether those things are great or small, it is all the same to me, as long as I fulfill your underlying purposes and intentions. I am pliable for everything in the hands of your divine guidance and care.

I will end in the way I began: "What do you want me to do?" I must have no other will. God of Israel, keep watch over this will that you are forming in me.

8
THE CONVERSION OF ST. PAUL (2) (JANUARY 25)

Having explored the importance of Saul's conversion by Jesus and Saul's new life as the apostle Paul, Fénelon now allows Jesus' gaze to fall squarely on Fénelon himself. Freely exposing his inner failings, and hearing Jesus' call to love him and him alone, Fénelon asks, "How can I do this, Lord?" Jesus gives his comforting reply: the same hand that converted Saul into Paul—"the little one"—will make Fénelon what he ought to be.

Dear God, I thank you a thousand times for having placed before my eyes Saul, the persecutor whom you converted and who became the apostle to the Gentiles. It was for the glory of your grace that you did that. You owed yourself such a great example in order to bring comfort to all sinners.

What an unhappy situation I face! What punishments have I not deserved from your justice! I have forgotten you—you who made me and to whom I owe all that I am. To my ingratitude, I have joined the hardening of my heart. I have disregarded your grace. I have been insensitive to your promises. I have abused your mercies. I have saddened your Holy Spirit and resisted his beneficial activities. I have said in my rebellious heart, "No, I will not take the Lord's yoke upon me."[48] I have run away when you have pursued me. I have looked for ways to assume a false appearance in order to conceal the real state of my soul, so that I might distance myself from you. I have been afraid of seeing too clearly and of becoming acquainted with certain truths that I did not wish to pursue. I have become irritated against the crosses that serve to detach me from life. I have criticized virtue, bearing it impatiently as being my condemnation. I have been ashamed of appearing to be good, and I have gloried in being ungrateful and unproductive. I have walked in my own ways, at the mercy of my passions and of my pride.

Dear God, what would I have left at the sight of so many acts of unfaithfulness, if not to be gripped with horror for myself? No, I could not continue to stand myself or to hope in you, if I did not see the unbelieving Saul—blasphemer, persecutor of your holy ones—out of whom you made a chosen instrument.[49] He fell to the ground an unbeliever, and he got back up a man of God. Father of mercies, how good you are! The human desire to cause pain and distress cannot have the same value as your fatherly goodness. Therefore, it is true that you still have treasures of grace and patience for me, a poor sinner, I who have so many times trampled under foot the blood of your Son.

You have not yet grown tired of waiting for me, dear, patient God, God who fears to punish too soon, God who cannot bring yourself to strike this clay jar formed by your hands.[50] I am moved by that patience that gradually turned my impatience and my baseness in a different direction.

I am dismayed: will I continue to be evil because you are good? Is it because you love me so much that I would think that I am excused from loving you? No, no, Lord. Your patience energizes me. I can no longer see myself for a single moment opposing the one who gives me good for evil. I denounce the slightest imperfections. I hold nothing back. May everything perish that delays my sacrifice! There must be no *tomorrow* of the careless soul who keeps running away from its conversion. It must be *today, today.*[51] What I have left of life is not too long a time to mourn so many wasted years. Like Saul, I say, "Lord, what do you want me to do?"

It seems to me that I hear you answer:

"I want you to love me, and for you to be happy and blessed in loving me. *Love, and do what you will.*[52] For, by truly loving, you will do only what pure love makes souls do that are detached from themselves. You will love me. You will bring others to love me. You will have no other will but mine. Out of this, my reign will be accomplished. Out of this, I will be worshiped in spirit and truth. Out of this, you will sacrifice the pleasures of corrupt flesh and the pride of the mind that is agitated by vain illusions. The whole world will no longer be anything for you. You will no longer want to be anything, so that I alone may be everything. That is what I want you to do."

"But how can I do this, Lord? This work is above human capability."

"Well!" you answer me in the depths of my heart, "*you of little faith*,[53] look at Saul and have no doubt about anything. He will say to you, *I can do all things through him who strengthens me.*[54] This man, who was breathing threats and murder against the churches,[55] no longer breathes anything but the love of Jesus Christ. It is Jesus Christ who lives triumphant in his apostle, who has died to every human thing. Look at him as God has made him. The same hand will make you what you ought to be. Your pride that is hidden in the innermost recesses of your heart uses every subtlety to escape notice and dodge pursuit. Vain self-satisfaction corrupts the best of actions. The headstrong, self-willed flesh revolts. The mind seems to fade away. Evil shame binds you. Habits exercise their tyranny. Temper and temperament bring the best of resolutions to nothing. But God can do everything, and he *wants* to do everything in order to bring you back to him."

So, Lord, bring about Saul's conversion inside of me.

⁀ 9
THE PRESENTATION
IN THE TEMPLE (FEBRUARY 2)

The Feast of the Presentation in the Temple celebrates the fortieth day after Jesus' birth, when Mary and Joseph presented the infant Jesus to God in the temple and ceremonially redeemed him—bought him back—by present-ing an offering. This ancient practice commemorates God's preserving the firstborn children of the Hebrew slaves in Egypt, while God's angel struck down the firstborn of the Egyptians.[56] God then told Moses to consecrate all the firstborn to him.[57] This practice of offering the firstborn to God and then redeeming them by presenting an offering continued throughout the succeeding generations. The offering was to be a sheep or a goat, but if a family was poor, they could bring two doves or two pigeons.[58] Mary and Joseph brought two doves, the offering of the poor.[59]

In this meditation, Fénelon offers himself alongside Jesus. He is fully aware that unlike Jesus, the child of poverty who was the spotless Son of God, he is impure, unworthy, and full of self. Yet, he comes to God in the full knowledge that he no longer belongs to himself, but to God alone.

Moses, in order to preserve the memory of God's blessings, ordained that the Israelites should offer their firstborn sons and then redeem them afterward, because God had miraculously preserved all the firstborn of Israel while the angel struck down the firstborn of Egypt. In obedience to that law, Jesus, today you are offered in the temple. And the law, which was made only for the children of mortals, is accomplished by the Son of God.

Divine child, allow me to present myself with you. I want to be, like you, held in the pure hands of Mary and Joseph. I want to be no longer anything but one same child with you, one same living being offered in sacrifice to God. But what do I see? You are being redeemed, just as the children of the poor are redeemed: two doves are the price paid for Jesus.

Immortal king of all the ages! Soon you will not even have a place to lay your head.[60] You will make the world rich with your poverty, and already you appear in the temple as one of the poor. Happy and blessed are those who make themselves poor with you! Happy and blessed are those who no longer have anything, and no longer want to have anything! Happy and blessed are those who in you and at the foot of your cross have lost every possession, who no longer own even their very hearts, who, far from having anything, are no longer their own. What a rich and blessed poverty! What a treasure that is unknown to those who are falsely wise! What bareness that is above all the most dazzling possessions! Thanks to you, child Jesus, I want to give up and lose everything, even my own heart, even the slightest desire of my own, even the last remnants of my will. I am running after you, as stripped and childlike as you are yourself.

I understand well enough, through the painful distaste that I have for myself, how much I am an impure and unworthy sacrifice in the sight of your Father. Therefore, I dare to offer myself only insomuch as I am no longer myself and no longer anything but one same thing with you. Who can understand this? Yet it is nonetheless true that we are worthy of God only inasmuch as we are outside of self and lost within him.

So, tear me away from myself. No more returning to my sense of self-worth, no more troubled desires, no more fear or hope for my own interest. The *self*, in terms of which I used to view everything, must be blotted out once and for all. Let me be put in a high place, let me be put in a low place, let me be remembered, let me be forgotten, let me be praised, let me be blamed, let me be trusted, let me be considered suspect even if unjustly, let me be left in peace or thwarted—what does it matter? That is no longer my business. I no longer belong to myself, and therefore I have no stake in everything that is done to me. I belong to the one who brings about all these things according to his good pleasure. His will is done, and that is enough. If there still remained a vestige of the self that might complain and grumble, my sacrifice would not be perfect. Burning up the living being offered as a sacrifice ought to wipe out any remains of self, but instead it brings out all the rebellion of our nature:

"This treatment that I am receiving is not fair. That accusation is false and wicked. This loss of possessions is overwhelming to me. That deprival of any sense of comfort is too bitter a loss. This trial in which God is putting me is too violent. Good people, whose help I was waiting for, just treat me with coldness and indifference. God himself is rejecting me and withdrawing from me."

Well, weak soul, base and undisciplined soul, soul of little faith, do you not want everything that God wants? Do you belong to him or to yourself? If you still belong to yourself, you have reason to complain and to seek what is pleasing to you. But if you no longer wish to be your own, then why are you still listening to yourself? What is there left for you to say in favor of this unhappy *self* that you have renounced forever, without holding anything back? If self is vanquished, if every one of its resources is torn away from it by the roots, so much the better. This is the sacrifice of truth. Everything else is just shades of darkness. This is how the living being offered in sacrifice is burned up and God is worthily adored. Jesus, I am offering myself along with you. Give me the courage to no longer count myself as anything, and to leave nothing of myself inside me!

You were redeemed by two doves. But that price paid to redeem you did not deliver you from the sacrifice of the cross on which you were going to die. On the contrary, your presentation was the beginning of the firstfruits of your offering on Calvary. Therefore, Lord, since all the outward things that I am giving you cannot redeem me, I have to give myself wholly and completely, and I have to die on the cross. To give up tranquility of mind, reputation, possessions, life—this is still nothing. We have to give up our *selves*. We have to love ourselves no longer. We have to give ourselves over without pity to your justice. We have to become strangers and outsiders to ourselves, and no longer have any stake or interest in anything but God, to whom we belong.

⬟ 10
LENT

The Christian season of Lent remembers Jesus' fasting for forty days in the wilderness.[61] The purpose of Lent is to prepare the believer for the remembrance of Jesus' crucifixion and death, and to await the joyful remembrance at Easter of Jesus' resurrection. For many Christians, Lent is a time of abstinence from certain kinds of food.

In this meditation, Fénelon shies away from a fearful, self-absorbed fast that focuses on morsels of food. Instead, he desires a joyful privation of the senses that turns its focus on the divine Bridegroom, a soul that joins the psalmist in crying out, "My soul longs, indeed it faints for the courts of the LORD; my heart and my flesh sing for joy to the living God."[62]

Dear God, I have now entered a time of privation and abstinence. But it serves no purpose to fast from food, which nourishes the body, if we do not also fast from everything that serves to nourish the love of self. Divine spouse of souls, give me the inner chasteness, the purity of heart, the separation from every created thing, the soberness that your apostle spoke of [63]—soberness that consists not only of the sparing use of food and drink, but also the cultivation of an earnestly thoughtful character marked by temperance, moderation, and seriousness.[64] When practicing soberness, we use created things only out of necessity. It is a blessed fast when the soul holds all the senses in a state of being deprived of anything that exceeds what is sufficient and necessary. It is a holy abstinence when the soul's hunger is filled by God's will and never feeds on its own will. Like Jesus, it has another food on which it feeds. Lord, give me that bread that is above every substance, the bread that will satisfy the hunger of my heart forever. Give me that bread that puts out the fires of every desire, the bread that is the true manna and that takes the place of everything else.[65]

Dear God, let all created things keep silence before me, and let me keep silence before them in this holy season of Lent. Let my soul be fed in silence by fasting from all vain conversation. Let me feed on you alone and on the cross of your son, Jesus.

But must I be in continual fear of breaking this inner fast through consolations that I might enjoy on the outside? No, dear God, you do not want that kind of anguish and worry. Your Spirit is a spirit of love and freedom, not a spirit of fear and servitude.[66] Therefore, I will renounce everything that is not in your order of things for me. I will renounce everything that I experience that diverts me too much from my true purpose. I will renounce everything that people who are leading me to you deem that I must set aside. Finally, I will renounce everything that you yourself will take away from me through the events of your divine providence.

I will peacefully bear all these privations. And here is what I will add to them: in every innocent and necessary conversation, I will cut out what you cause me to feel inwardly to be nothing other than seeking myself. When I feel myself brought to make some kind of sacrifice over and above that, I will do it cheerfully. Furthermore, dear God, I know that you desire that hearts that love you should keep a wide berth from things of the world.

I will behave with confidence and trust, like a child that plays in its mother's arms. I will rejoice before the Lord. I will do my best to give joy to others. I will pour out my heart without fear in the company of God's children. All I want is forthrightness, freedom from guile, and the joy of the Holy Spirit.

Therefore, dear God, keep far away from me that sad and fearful understanding that is always gnawing on itself, that is always holding scales in its hands to weigh the tiniest thing, out of fear of breaking that inner fast! It does you an injustice not to behave simply with you, like a child. That kind of harsh inflexibility is unworthy of your fatherly compassion. You want us to love you alone—that is what is meant by your being a "jealous God."[67] But when we love you, you allow love to behave freely, and you see quite well what truly comes from love.

Therefore, dear God, I will fast from every movement of the will that is not yours. But I will fast out of love, in the freedom and in the abundance of my heart. How unhappy is the soul that is shrunken and dried up upon itself, that is afraid of everything, and that, because of its fear, has no time to love and to run generously after the divine Bridegroom! How strict is the fast that you cause the soul to undergo, yet without torturing it. Nothing remains in the heart except the beloved, leaving the soul only fainting and ready to expire with love.[68]

This is the great fast, when mortals see their poverty completely exposed, when the slightest vestige of their life in themselves is torn out by the roots. Who can understand that great fast of pure faith? Where is there a soul that has enough courage to accomplish it? What limitless privation that is! What renouncing of ourselves as well as of the most vain things outside ourselves! What faithfulness of a soul that leaves itself behind in order to follow you out of a jealous love, without shrinking back, allowing everything to be taken away from it!

Lord, this is the sacrifice of those who worship you in spirit and truth.[69] It is out of these trials that we become worthy of you.

Go ahead, Lord: make my soul empty, hungry, and fainting. Do with me according to your good pleasure. I will keep silence, I will worship you, and I will keep saying, "Your will be done,"[70] and not mine. You are the only thing that I desire, dear God.

11
HOLY THURSDAY

Holy Thursday commemorates the Last Supper, when Jesus ate the Passover meal with his disciples and gave them his last teachings before his arrest and crucifixion. This day is sometimes called "Maundy Thursday" from the Latin mandatum, meaning command, in honor of Jesus' new commandment that the disciples love one another[71] It was at the Last Supper that Jesus instituted the sacrament of the Eucharist, or Holy Communion, when he declared the bread to be his body and the wine his blood, and he told his disciples, "Do this in remembrance of me."[72]

In this meditation, Fénelon dwells on the holy sacrament of Jesus' body, which is given for us. As Fénelon meditates on the full meaning of this sacrament, in which divine wisdom has decreed that Jesus himself should be hidden beneath the veil of common bread, he asks but one thing of God: "Word of God made flesh, be hidden within this weak creature that I am, just as you are hidden within the element of the sacramental bread."

Jesus, eternal wisdom, you are hidden in this sacrament, and it is there that I worship you today. How I love this day on which you gave yourself completely to the apostles! What am I saying?—just to the apostles? No, you gave yourself no less to us as to them. What a precious gift, a gift that has been renewed every day for so many centuries, a gift that will endure without interruption as long as the world exists! What a token of the goodness of the Father of mercies! What a sacrament of love is this bread that is above all substance! Just as my body is nourished with coarse and corruptible bread, so my soul ought to be nourished every day with eternal truth, which not only became flesh in order to be life, but also became bread in order to be eaten and to feed the children of God.

Where then is the deep wisdom that formed the universe?[73] Who could believe that you could be underneath this common-looking appearance? All we see is a little bread, and as we receive the life-giving flesh of the Savior, we also receive all the treasures of divinity. Such wisdom, such infinite love! For whom do you do such great things?

For ungrateful mortals, we who are coarse, blind, brutish, insensitive, incapable of enjoying your gift. Where are there souls who feed on your pure truth, who live on you alone, who let you live in them and who transform themselves into you?

I understand: it is your will to act in such a way that, through this sacrament, we may have no other wisdom and understanding than yours, and no other will than your will, which must become ours. That divine wisdom must be hidden within us, as it is under the veil of the sacrament.

The outside must be simple, weak, and contemptuous in the sight of the proud learning and understanding of mortals. The inside must be completely dead to self, completely transformed, completely divine.

Up till now, dear Savior, I have not fed on your truth. I have fed on the ceremonies of religion, on the display of certain virtues that cultivate courage, good manners, regularity in outward actions, the victory over my character that I needed to win in order not to show anything that might not be perfect.

Look, there is the common veil—the outward appearance—of the sacrament. But where is the very heart of the sacrament? Where is that real, essential truth that is above every substance that is limited to what we can grasp? What a deep pity it is that I have not sought after it. I have attempted to put the outside in order, without changing what is inside me.

The business of worshiping in spirit and truth,[74] which consists of vanquishing every movement of my own will in order to let God's will alone reign in me, is almost unknown to me. My mouth has eaten what can be seen and tasted outwardly in the sacrament, but my heart has not been fed with the substance of that truth. I serve you, dear God—but in my own way, and according to the outlook of my own learning and understanding, which are pure foolishness. I love you—but for my own good rather than for your glory. I desire to bring glory to you—but with a fervor that does not abandon itself unreservedly to the full extent of your purposes for me. I want to live for you—but closed in upon myself—and I am afraid to die to myself.

Sometimes I think I am ready for the greatest sacrifices, and then the tiniest giving up of something that you require of me a moment later troubles me and discourages me. Such love you show, that my wretchedness and my unworthiness do not cause you to reject me. It is under this veil, this veil that mortals disdain and hold in contempt, that you desire to conceal the strength and the grandeur of your mystery. Just as mortals look on the sacrament and see only common bread, you desire to make me into a sacrament that tests the faith of others and even of myself. In that state of weakness, I give myself over to you. I can do nothing, but you can do everything. And I am not at all afraid of my weakness, since I feel your all-powerfulness so close to me.

Word of God made flesh, be hidden within this weak creature that I am, just as you are hidden within the element of the sacramental bread. Sovereign and life-giving word, speak in the silence of my soul. Let everything become silent that is not you. Make my soul itself become silent. Let it no longer talk to itself interiorly, so that it may listen only to you. Bread of life, I no longer wish to feed on anything other than you alone. Any other food would make me live to myself, would give me my own strength, and would fill me up on the outside.

Let my soul die the death of the upright.[75] Let me die that happy death that must precede the death of the body. Let me die that inner death that divides the soul from itself,[76] that makes it so that it no longer encounters or owns itself. Give me this death that puts out the fires of restless and transitory warmth of feeling, the death that neutralizes all self-interest, that brings down to nothing all return to the self. This love brings about a marvelous agony. The bread from heaven puts to death and the same time it brings to life. It tears the soul away from itself and at the same time it puts the soul in a state of peace. It takes everything away from the soul and at the same time it gives the soul everything. It takes away everything within the soul and at the same time it gives the soul everything in God, in whom alone all things are pure.

My love, my life, my all! I no longer have anything but you. I will eat this divine bread every day, and I will have no greater fear than the fear of being without that heavenly food.

12
GOOD FRIDAY

Good Friday follows Jesus through his passion and death on the cross. In this meditation, Fénelon considers how foolish the mystery of the crucified Jesus appears to the world. Even for Christians, it is all too easy to say we will follow Jesus, as long as it is easy and "reasonable" to do so. But those who heed Jesus' call to follow him must take up their cross daily and follow the Savior through suffering and contempt, all the way to Calvary. "My dear Savior," Fénelon writes, "let those who will, drink your bitter cup. As for me, I want to drink it right to the bitterest last dregs."

We mortals cannot understand the mystery of Jesus' passion. It was "a stumbling-block to Jews and foolishness to Gentiles."[77] The Jews were fervent partisans of the glory of their religion. They could not tolerate the public disgrace and ill fame that marked Jesus. The Gentiles were learned and full of their philosophy, and their learning was repulsed at the sight of a crucified God: it was to turn human intellect upside down to preach this God on the cross.

Nevertheless, that cross, preached throughout the world, surpasses the proud fervor of the Jews and the haughty learning of the Gentiles. Here is what the mystery of Jesus' passion leads up to: it confounds the unhallowed learning of those who are learned in the ways of the world, people who, like the Gentiles, regard devoutness in religion as foolishness, if it is not always endowed with a certain outward display. And it confounds the proud fervor of certain devout persons, who want to see nothing in religion except what conforms to their false ideas.

Dear God, I count myself among those scandalized Jews. It is true, Jesus, that I worship you on the cross. But that worship is only in ceremony, and not at all in truth. True worship of the crucified Jesus Christ consists in sacrificing ourselves with him. It consists in losing our reasoning power in the foolishness of the cross. It consists in taking within ourselves all its reproach and contempt. It consists in being, if God wills it to be so, a spectacle of horror—of intense fear and dread—to all those who are wise in this world. It consists in consenting to appear as if we have gone out of our minds, like Jesus.[78]

We can say this, giving the consent of our mouths. But our hearts do not say this at all. We offer excuses, hollowly cloaking our real intentions. We shudder. Cowards, we shrink back as soon as we have to appear exposed and heaped with contempt along with the man of suffering.[79] Dear God, my love, we love you in order to take comfort, but we do not love you as far as following you right up to death on the cross.

Everyone flees from you, everyone abandons you, everyone refuses to admit knowing you, everyone denies you. As long as our intellect finds it to be to our credit and our welfare to follow you, we hurry after you. Like Saint Peter, we boast,[80] but all we need is one question from a servant and we turn everything upside down.[81] We want to limit religion to the small measure of our minds, and as soon as it goes beyond our weak intellects, it turns into an offense to our sense of propriety.

However, religion ought to be in practice what it is in speculation. That is, it has to actually go as far as knocking our intellect off its feet and surrendering us up to the foolishness of the crucified Savior. How easy it is to be a Christian on the condition that we are wise, masters of ourselves, full of courage, great, punctual in fulfilling our duties, and marvelous in every way! But to be a Christian in order to be little, weak, worthy of contempt, and out of our minds in the eyes of the world—we cannot hear this without being filled with intense fear and dread of it.

So we are only half-Christians. Not only do we give ourselves up to our vain intellect, like the Gentiles, but also we go on to take pride in following our religious fervor, like the Jews. "That would be to degrade religion, to make it of little value," people say. "That would be to turn it into small-mindedness—why, we need to show how great religion is!" What a deep pity this is. Religion will be great in us only insofar as it makes us humble, teachable, little, and unconcerned about ourselves.

We would like a Savior who comes to make us perfect, who fills us with our own excellence, and who fulfills all the most flattering views we have of our knowledge and understanding. On the contrary, God has given us a Savior who turns our knowledge and understanding on its head, who places us, with himself, bare and exposed on a disgraceful cross.

Jesus, this is where everyone abandons you. "We must not take things so far," we say. "That would be to carry the truths of Christianity too far and to make them odious and distasteful in the sight of the world." Well, do we not know that ungodly, irreverent people will be scandalized, since even good, religious people are?

How could the mystery of the cross not seem excessive to the learned Gentiles, since it scandalizes reverent and fervently religious Jews? My dear Savior, let those who will, drink your bitter cup. As for me, I want to drink it right to the bitterest last dregs. I am ready to suffer pain and suffering, deep personal humiliation and disgrace, ridicule and scorn, and people's insults on the outside—and on the inside, temptation and being forsaken by the heavenly Father. I will say, as you taught me, "Remove this cup from me; yet"—in spite of all my intense fear and dread—"not my will but yours be done."[82]

These truths are too strong for worldly people who know you only halfway and who can follow you only in the comforting moments of the Transfiguration.[83] As for me, I would fail in responding to your love if I pulled back.

Let us go to Jesus. Let us go to Calvary. My soul is deeply grieved, even to death.[84] But what does that matter, provided that I die pierced with the same nails and on the same cross as you, my dear Savior!

⤳ 13
HOLY SATURDAY

Holy Saturday remembers the period between Jesus' death and his resurrection, when his body lay in the darkness of the tomb. In this meditation, Fénelon expresses his desire to be united to Jesus in his death by asking God to tear out his own self-life by its roots. When we allow God to do this work in us, he writes, "Infinite love will love within us, and our love will bear the character of God himself."

What comes to my mind's eye today is Jesus between the death that he suffered and the life that he is going to take up again. His resurrection will be no less real than his death, and his death is only a passage from a life of suffering to a life of happiness and blessing. Savior, I worship you, I love you in the tomb, I enclose myself inside it with you. I no longer want the world to see me. I no longer want to see myself. I descend into darkness and dust. I am no longer counted among the living. Let mortals forget me, tread me under foot! I am dead, and the life that is prepared for me will be hidden with Christ in God.[85]

These are astonishing truths. Those who live good, religious lives can hardly bear them. So, what do these words of the apostle mean, "Therefore we have been buried with him by baptism into death"?[86] Where is this death that our stamp as Christians ought to be working within us? Where is that burial place?

How pitiful it is that I want to be noticed, to be approved of, loved, distinguished. I want to give my neighbor something to think about, possess my neighbor's heart, make myself an idol in reputation and in friendship. To steal from God the trifling incense that burns on the altars is nothing in comparison with the sacrilegious grand theft of a soul that desires to take away what is due to God and make itself the idol of other created beings.

Dear God, when will I stop loving myself, to the point of no longer wanting people to love me and hold me in their esteem? Glory belongs to you alone. Love belongs to you alone. I ought no longer to love anything but in you, for you, and out of pure love for you. I ought to love myself no longer except out of pure Christian charity, like a stranger. Therefore shouldn't I be ashamed to want others to love me?

My vain sensitiveness is not satisfied with a love that comes from Christian charity. It is wounded and hurt that it only has what has been granted to it because of God. "How unfair this is! I will revolt against it!" says my blind and detestable pride. Punish my pride, dear God. I am for you and against myself. I take the side of your glory and your justice against my vanity. Foolish creature, idolatrous with yourself! So, what do you have, independently from God, that is worthy of that tenderness, that attachment, that love that does not depend on Christian charity? How we need Christian charity in order to stand firm when we face this sense of unfairness, when we want others to do for us what God forbids us to do for ourselves!

God imprints love into the hearts of his created ones: is this the use of love that he desires for us to make of it? Has he not made us capable of love, only so that we might turn each other away from the sole aim and goal of pure love? No, dear God, I no longer want people to love me. People scarcely need to tolerate me out of love for you. The more sensitive and aware I am concerning my neighbor's love for me, the more unworthy I am of it, and the more I need to have it taken away from me.

The same is true, Lord, of reputation as well as friendship. Give, take away, according to your purposes. Let reputation, which is dearer than life to me, become like a filthy cloth,[87] if this brings you glory. If people pass over me and over me again like the dead who are in the tomb, if people count me as nothing, if people hate me, if people spare me from nothing—this is well and good. If there still remains within me any voluntary attachment to things, some secret design on having a reputation, I have not died with Christ and I am not in a state of entering into his risen life.[88]

It is only after the complete destruction of the evil and corrupt life of the old self that we pass into the life of the new self.[89] Everything

has to die: comforts, consolations, tranquility of mind, tender friendships, honor, reputation. Everything will be given back to us a hundred
times over,[90] but everything has to die. Everything has to be sacrificed.
When we have lost everything in ourselves, we will get everything
back in God. What we used to have in ourselves with the lack of
purity of the old self will be given back to us with the purity of the
renewed self, just as metals that are placed in a fire do not lose their
pure substance, but are refined of the dross they contain.[91]

Therefore, therefore, dear God, the same Spirit who groans and
prays in us[92] will love more perfectly in us. How much greater our
hearts will be, how much more tender and more generous! We will
no longer love as feeble creatures with hearts confined to narrow
boundaries. Infinite love will love within us, and our love will bear
the character of God himself.

Let us have as our only thought, that of uniting ourselves with Jesus
Christ in his agony, in his death, and in his tomb. Let us bury ourselves
in the dark night of pure faith. Let us deliver ourselves up to all the
horrors of death. No, I no longer wish to regard myself as being of
this world. Let the world forget me, just as I am forgetting it and as I
want to forget myself! Lord Jesus, you died only to make me die. Tear
my life out by its roots. Do not let me breathe any longer. Do not
allow me to hold anything back. Push my heart to the limit. I put no
bounds on my sacrifice.

14
ASCENSION

Jesus' ascension into heaven is celebrated on a Thursday, forty days after Easter. While there are several accounts of the Ascension in the Bible, Fénelon used this one to begin his meditation: "Then [Jesus] led [the disciples] out as far as Bethany, and, lifting up his hands, he blessed them. While he was blessing them, he withdrew from them and was carried up into heaven. And they worshiped him, and returned to Jerusalem with great joy."[93]

In this meditation, Fénelon tells of his longing to be with Jesus in heaven instead of in exile on earth. But as long as God wills for us to remain here below, we must use our time on earth as a preparation for heaven. Applying St. Paul's words "I beseech you . . . to present your bodies as a living sacrifice,"[94] Fénelon asks God to take away everything within him that stands in the way of God's being his all. "When everything is taken away," he tells God, "it is then that you alone will remain in my soul."

It seems to me that I am accompanying Jesus with the disciples on the road to Bethany. There, he goes up to heaven before my eyes. I worship him, and I can never tire of looking at him. I can never tire of following him with affection. I can never tire of delighting deep within my heart in the words of life that were the last ones to leave his holy lips when he departed from earth.

Lord, you never stop being with me and speaking to me! I sense the truth of this promise: "And remember, I am with you always, to the end of the age."[95] You are with us, and not just on this tangible altar, to which you call all your children to eat the bread that has come down from heaven.[96] No, you are also inside us, on that invisible altar, in that inaccessible church and sanctuary of our souls, where we worship in spirit and in truth. It is there that pure living beings are offered in sacrifice. It is there that are put to death all of our selfish desires, all of our self-interested turning inward upon ourselves, and all of our movements of self-love. It is there that we eat the true bread of life, of which your flesh, worthy as it is of worship, is only the outer surface. It is there that we are fed with the pure substance of everlasting life.

It is there that the Word made flesh gives himself to us as our inner word, as our promise, our wisdom, our life, our being, our all.

If we have come to know him through our flesh and through our senses, seeking something we can touch and feel, even so we do not yet know him. Pure faith and pure love feed on God's pure truth, which is made one and the same with us.

This is how the kingdom of our dear God comes to us even now, in this life of misery. This is how the will of the Father is accomplished on earth as it is in heaven. While it is God's will to keep me outside of heaven in this place of exile, I am not going to look for heaven anywhere else. I am going to find heaven on earth.

I am not acquainted with and I do not want any other heaven than my dear God, and my God is with me in this valley of tears.[97] I carry him, I glorify him in my heart. He lives within me. How blessed is everlasting Zion, where Jesus reigns with all the saints! How many glorious things are spoken of Zion![98] How I love that glorious kingdom that will have no end! To you alone, Lord, be glory, majesty, power, and authority, before all time and now and forever.[99]

Lord Jesus, far from causing me distress on our behalf that you are no longer visible on earth, I rejoice in your triumph. It is your glory alone that I am thinking about. Here on earth I join my feeble voice with the voices of all the blessed ones in singing the hymn of the conquering Lamb.[100] I am all too happy, Jesus, to suffer in this place of exile in order to bring you glory!

It is true that your tangible presence is the sweetest of all perfumes. But it is not for myself that I seek you; it is for yourself. If I were to look at myself, what could bring me comfort in this life of misery, when I do not have you, when I displease you through so many faults, when I see myself constantly at risk of losing you forever? What would be capable of making my troubles more bearable, and of allowing me to remain firm in the face of life? But I love your will better than my own security.

Therefore, I live since you want me to live. This life, which is only a death, will last as long as it is your will. You know, God of my heart, that I want to hold on to nothing in this life except at your command. I am in this foreign land only because you hold me here. I love you more than my happiness and my glory.

It is better to obey you than to rejoice in you. It is better to suffer according to your purposes than to enjoy your delights and see the light of your face. As you deprive me of yourself, take away everything from me. Strip me bare. Tear out my roots without pity. Do not leave anything to my soul. Do not leave it even itself.

If the Savior's presence had to be taken away from us, what must we have left? If God was disposed to take away such a holy comfort from the apostles, with what indignation will he destroy in us so many pleasures that preserve certain secret remnants of our self-life! What consolation can be as pure as that of seeing Jesus? And as a result, can there be any consolation that we would dare refuse to sacrifice?

Dear God, do not listen to my slackness. Strip me bare. Flay me, if you have to. Cut me to the quick. When everything is taken away, it is then that you alone will remain in my soul. Amen—so let it be.

⌁ 15
PENTECOST

Pentecost celebrates the descent of the Holy Spirit upon the disciples as they
were gathered in Jerusalem fifty days after Jesus' resurrection, and ten days
after his ascension. How bereft the disciples must have felt after Jesus had
spent forty days with them and then was taken up into heaven! Yet, before
his passion, as Jesus was foretelling his death, he promised the disciples that
he would not leave them "comfortless" or "orphaned."[101] *Instead, he told*
them, "the Advocate [or Comforter], the Holy Spirit, whom the Father will
send in my name, will teach you everything, and remind you of all that I
have said to you."[102]

That promise was fulfilled in a mighty way at Pentecost when "suddenly
from heaven there came a sound like the rush of a violent wind, and it filled
the entire house where they were sitting. Divided tongues, as of fire, appeared
among them, and a tongue rested on each of them. All of them were filled
with the Holy Spirit and began to speak in other languages, as the Spirit
gave them ability."[103] *This was the birthday of the church. Empowered by*
the Holy Spirit, within a short time the little band of believers began to
spread the good news of Jesus Christ across the known world.

In this meditation, Fénelon puts himself in the disciples' place during
the ten days after the Ascension, when they were deprived of Jesus' physical
presence with them but the Holy Spirit had not yet come. God's way is
not our way, Fénelon says: Jesus had to be taken away in order for the
Holy Spirit to come. "Happy are those from whom Jesus turns away and
withdraws!" he writes. "The comforting Spirit will come upon them. He
will soothe their pain and with great care will wipe away their tears."

Lord, you began by removing from your disciples what seemed the
most excellent means of sustaining them, comforting them, and
bringing them to perfection: the tangible presence of Jesus, your
Son. But you tore away everything in order to establish and bring
about everything. You took away everything in order to return
everything again, with interest. That is your way. You take pleasure
in turning the order of the human mind upside down.

After taking away the tangible presence of Jesus, you gave your Holy Spirit. How precious, how valuable, how powerful this deprivation is, since it brings about more than the presence of the Son of God himself! How lacking in energy, how deprived of moral strength are the souls who think that they are so poor when they are deprived, when that very privation makes them richer than if they possessed the greatest treasure! Blessed and happy are those who lack everything and even God himself—that is, God whom they can see and touch. Happy are those from whom Jesus turns away and withdraws! The comforting Spirit will come upon them. He will soothe their pain and with great care will wipe away their tears.

Unhappy and cursed are those who have their comfort on earth, who find their mental tranquility, their support, and the attachment of their will outside of God. The good Spirit that is promised to all those who ask for him is not sent to them. The Comforter sent from heaven is only for souls who cling neither to the world nor to themselves.

I am very concerned, Lord! Where is that Spirit who ought to be my life? He must be the soul of my soul. But where is he? I do not feel him. I do not find him. In my senses, all I feel is a fragile lack of vigor. In my spirit, all I feel is self-indulgence and lying. In my will, all I feel is instability and dividedness between your love and a multitude of vain pleasures. So I ask, where is your Spirit? Why does he not come and create in me a new heart like yours?[104] Dear God, I understand that it is in this impoverished soul that your Spirit will condescend to dwell, provided that this soul opens itself up to him without holding anything back. It is the tangible absence of the Savior and all his gifts that attracts the Holy Spirit.

Therefore, come, Holy Spirit. You cannot find anything more barren, more stripped, more lacking, more abandoned, more feeble than my heart. Come, bring peace to it—not the peace of abundance that flows like a river,[105] but dry peace, the peace of patience and sacrifice, the peace of severe pain and grief. That true peace is nonetheless even more pure, intimate, deep, and inexhaustible, because it is founded on unreserved denial of self.

Spirit of Love! Truth of my God! Light and love! You teach the soul without using words. You ask nothing of the soul, yet through silence you draw it toward every sacrifice! Love that causes us to lose our appetite for any other kind of love, you make us loathe ourselves, forget ourselves, and abandon ourselves! Love that flows through the heart like a spring of life,[106] who can know you, if not the one in whom you dwell?

Keep silence, blind mortals: love is not found within you. You do not know what you are saying. You see nothing, you hear nothing. The true Teacher has never taught you. He it is who fills the thirsty soul with truth without any distinct knowledge. He it is who brings to life in the depths of the soul the truths that Jesus' spoken words had made known only to the eyes of the mind. Then we taste, then we are fed, then we become one with the truth. We no longer see the truth as an object outside of ourselves. The truth *becomes us*, and we experience it as intimately as the soul experiences itself.

What a powerful comfort this is without our seeking to be comforted! We have everything without having anything. There we find the oneness of the Father, the Son, and the Holy Spirit: We find the Father, the Creator who creates in us everything that he wants to do there in order to make us children like himself. We find the Son, the Word of God, who becomes the intimate creating Word and spoken word of the soul, who falls silent before everything in order to allow only God to speak from this point on. Finally, we find the Spirit, who blows where he will,[107] who loves the Father and the Son within us.

My love, you who are my God, love yourself, glorify yourself in me. My peace, my joy, and my life are in you, who are my all, and I am no longer anything.

⇌ 16
THE BODY AND BLOOD OF CHRIST (CORPUS CHRISTI)

The Feast of the Body and Blood of Christ, or Corpus Christi as it is often known, honors Jesus' institution of the Eucharist at the Last Supper. Because the Last Supper was instituted on Holy Thursday on the night before Jesus' passion and crucifixion, Christians set aside a day after Pentecost as a joyful celebration of Jesus' giving his body and blood to us in the Eucharist. Originally celebrated on the Thursday following Trinity Sunday (the Sunday that follows Pentecost), the Feast of the Body and Blood of Christ is now often held on the Sunday after Trinity Sunday.

In Fénelon's time, it was customary to place the Blessed Sacrament on display for one week, giving the faithful an opportunity to worship the risen Christ who is present in the sacrament.

In this meditation, Fénelon considers the meaning of the presence of Jesus himself hidden in the Eucharist. Speaking to Jesus, he says, "Hidden God, I want to live hidden with you in order to live your divine life. Beneath all my wretchedness, my weakness, my unworthiness, I will hide Jesus. I will become the sacrament of his love."

I worship Jesus in the Blessed Sacrament in which he conceals all the treasures of his love. One week is too short a time to celebrate so many mysteries of the humble Jesus. All I see is love, goodness, and mercy. But Lord, why do you do this? Why conceal your eternal majesty? Why expose it to the ingratitude of human souls, to mortals' lack of profound and adoring, awed respect?

Yes, I see: you do this because you love us, you go in search of us, and you give yourself entirely and completely to us. But yet, in what manner do you make this gift? Under the form of the most familiar kind of food. My bread, my life, my Savior's flesh, come and stimulate my hunger! I no longer want to feed on anything but you.

Creating Word, wisdom, spoken word, eternal truth, you are hidden underneath that flesh, and that sacred flesh is hidden underneath that coarse appearance of bread. Hidden God, I want to live hidden with you in order to live your divine life. Beneath all my wretchedness, my weakness, my unworthiness, I will hide Jesus. I will become the sacrament of his love. On the outside, people will see only the rough, coarse veil of the sacrament, the imperfect and fragile creature. On the inside, the true God of glory[108] will live.

Therefore, God of love, when will you come? When will I love you? When will you be the only food of my heart, and my bread that is above every substance? The outward bread, that fragile creature, will be broken and exposed to all sorts of unforeseen events, but Jesus, immortal and impassible, will be in it, undivided and unchanged.[109] Living on him, I will no longer live except for him, and he alone will live in me.

Divine creating Word, you will speak, and my soul will fall silent in order to hear you. That simple word that created the world will make itself heard by his creature, and it will act in all that it will express. It will form his new creature just as it formed the universe.[110] Therefore, fall silent, my soul. Do not listen to anything ever again here below. Do not listen to yourself any longer in the silence that is the humbling, the bringing down to nothing, of the mind and the spirit. Let the Word made flesh speak. How many things he will say! He is, all by himself, all truth.[111]

What a difference there is between the creature—who says some sort of truth in passing, and who says what is not its own but what is, so to speak, borrowed from God—and the Son of God, who is truth itself![112] He is what he says he is: he is truth in the flesh. Therefore, he does not say the truth in the same way we say it. He does not make it pass before the eyes of our minds successively and through unconnected thoughts. He brings truth itself into the depths of our being. He incorporates it into us—brings it bodily into us—and we into it. We are made the truth of God.

So it is not through the strength of intellect or knowledge, it is through the simplicity of love that we are in the truth. All the rest is only shadows and lies. We no longer need to waste our time talking and convincing ourselves in detail. It is love that imprints all truth. In a single glance, we are gripped with the sight of the humbleness, the nothingness of the creature, and the everythingness of God. That sight decides everything, it brings about everything, it leaves nothing to the mind. We see only one single truth, and all the rest disappears.

Foolish and scandalous world, we can no longer see or hear you. The love of self horrifies us. We endure ourselves patiently, as Jesus endured Judas. Everything is passing before my eyes. But nothing matters to me, nothing is my business except the one single business of doing the will of God in the present moment, and to desire to do his will on earth as it is desired in heaven.

Jesus, this is the true worship that you are looking for.[113] How easy it is to worship through ceremonies and praises! But there are few souls who give you that inner worship. How grievous it is that everywhere we see religion only in outward appearance, religion that consists only of following a set of laws and rules. We desire to possess your truth with our minds. We desire to participate in your sacrifice, and never sacrifice ourselves with you.

Unless we lose ourselves in you, we will never become one with you. Hidden God, how unknown you are to mortals! You who are love, we do not know what it is to love. Teach me to love, and you will have taught me all the truth there is through that one single truth.

17
ST. MARY MAGDALENE
(JULY 22)

Saint Mary Magdalene serves as a model of faith, faithfulness, and love for Jesus. John, the "beloved disciple," who wrote so much about love, tells her story:

> *But Mary stood weeping outside the tomb. As she wept, she bent over to look into the tomb; and she saw two angels in white, sitting where the body of Jesus had been lying, one at the head and the other at the feet. They said to her, "Woman, why are you weeping?" She said to them, "They have taken away my Lord, and I do not know where they have laid him."*
>
> *When she had said this, she turned around and saw Jesus standing there, but she did not know that it was Jesus. Jesus said to her, "Woman, why are you weeping? Whom are you looking for?" Supposing him to be the gardener, she said to him, "Sir, if you have carried him away, tell me where you have laid him, and I will take him away." Jesus said to her, "Mary!" She turned and said to him in Hebrew, "Rabbouni!" (which means Teacher). Jesus said to her, "Do not hold on to me, because I have not yet ascended to the Father. But go to my brothers and say to them, 'I am ascending to my Father and your Father, to my God and your God.'"*
>
> *Mary Magdalene went and announced to the disciples, "I have seen the Lord"; and she told them that he had said these things to her.*[114]

In this meditation, Fénelon describes his desire to follow Mary Magdalene in her search for Jesus. Using imagery from the Song of Solomon, in which the bride goes in search of her lost bridegroom, he tells Jesus, "I run toward the fragrance of your perfumes." "God of love," he writes, "you desire souls who venture everything and promise nothing, who never say, 'I can,' or 'I cannot.' We can do all things through you."

Dear Savior, I would like to follow you, just as Mary Magdalene did, right up to the dust of your tomb. She is the one, Lord, from whom you cast out seven demons.[115] How glad I am to see that the saints that you rescued out of the most dreadful states are the ones who go in search of your mercies with even more courage and tenderness!

Lord, all of your disciples ran away.[116] Only Mary Magdalene, who had been the prey of so many demons, bathed your tomb with her tears. She was inconsolable at not being able to find your body. She asked for it of everyone that she met. Carried away by her deep grief, she did not weigh or measure what she said. She did not even know the words that she spoke. When love speaks, it does not consult the intellect.

In full liberty, like your true children, I run toward the fragrance of your perfumes.[117] I run, dear God, with Mary Magdalene toward your tomb. I run, without stopping, toward the complete death of my entire self. I go down into the dust, into complete darkness, into the painful and intense dread of the tomb. I almost no longer find, dear Savior, any remains of your presence, no trace of your gifts. The bridegroom has disappeared from it. All is lost. Nothing is left—no bridegroom, no love, no light. Jesus has been taken away.

Such deep grief! Such a test of faith through deep suffering! All hope is gone! I have lost even my own love. Jesus, who is hidden and buried in the depths of my heart, is no longer to be found there! Where is he?[118] What has become of him? I ask all of nature about him, and the whole world is silent. All I have left of my love is my affliction at having lost him. Where is he? Give him to me. Take away everything else. I will carry him away.

Poor soul, you have no idea of what you are saying. Yet, you are so blessed and happy that you love, without knowing that it is love that makes you speak!

God of love, you desire souls who venture everything and promise nothing, who never say, "I can," or "I cannot." We can do all things through you.[119] We can do nothing without you. Those who love with a perfect love no longer use themselves as a measuring stick. They are ready for anything and cling to nothing.

⤳ 18
THE ASSUMPTION
(AUGUST 15)

The Feast of the Assumption, or the Feast of the Dormition as it is called by Eastern Christians, celebrates the Virgin Mary's entrance into heaven.

In this meditation, Fénelon focuses on the passage from Acts that gives us a glimpse of Mary's life after Jesus' ascension. The disciples returned to Jerusalem, and there, "They were constantly devoting themselves to prayer, together with certain women, including Mary the mother of Jesus, as well as his brothers." [120]

Fénelon takes Mary as his model, using her example of devoting herself to prayer to show that true worship does not consist in outward, showy religious practices. Instead, it consists in "letting God alone desire and love himself without limit inside us."

Dear God, today I present myself to you with Mary, the mother of your Son. Give me thoughts and give me a heart that corresponds to Mary's thoughts and Mary's heart. Dear Jesus, look at your mother who leaves the earth in order to be reunited forever with you. Mary, I leave the earth along with you. With Mary, my heart rises up to heaven in order to love only God. Dear Holy Spirit, who descended upon this Virgin in order to make her fertile, descend on me in order to make me pure.

What do I see in Mary during the later days of her life? She was "constantly devoting" herself "to prayer, together with certain women," says Saint Luke. That is, she was doing outwardly just what the others were doing. Perfection—which was without doubt within the mother of the Son of God—does not consist in outwardly showy, exceptional actions that go beyond what is usual and customary. We do not see prophecy, or miracles, or instructing people, or religious ecstasy. We see only what is simple and common. Her life was completely interior: she was "constantly devoting" herself to prayer. That was the business to which she limited herself: without making herself specially noticed, she devoted herself to prayer with the other women. How much purer, how much more divine her prayer must have been! But the treasures remained hidden. On the outside, all people saw was tranquility of mind, religious contemplation, simplicity, a common life.

When will mortals have a personal acquaintance with worshiping in spirit and truth?[121] For me, Mary is the model of that kind of worship. Mortals look for worship where it cannot be found, in grandiose schemes, in conduct full of stern ascetic practices. All of these things have their time, and God calls us to them when it is his will. But true worship, pure love, does not depend on all these things: it consists in loving in silence, desiring God alone, clinging to nothing in this world—not even to our own gifts in order to take credit for them out of self-satisfaction. It consists in bearing everything in a spirit of love. It consists in bearing up under life with all the wrongs, all the disorders, all the evil that life is full of, through handing over control of our lives to God and withdrawing inwardly, just as Mary lived in that bitter separation from being with her Son. It consists in counting ourselves no longer as anything in all the things that we have to do or to endure. It consists in not thinking we are capable or incapable of anything, but in letting ourselves be led like little children—or in being like Mary, who let herself be given by her Son to John in order to be attended to by him. It consists in no longer having anything for ourselves, and no longer belonging to ourselves. It consists in living or dying with the same disposition, or rather, in not having a disposition or a will, but letting God alone desire and love himself without limit inside us. This is what pure, simple, and perfect worship is! These are the worshipers that the Father is looking for.

But, what a pity! Where will the Father find such worshipers? We are always afraid of going too far, and of losing ourselves by giving ourselves to God. Pure faith is not enough for self-seeking souls who lack determination and boldness. They desire to see and possess tangible gifts. They want to lean, as the Scripture says, on an arm of flesh[122] or on the strength of their minds. To set out like Abraham,[123] without knowing where we are going, is something that causes the senses and the mistrustful mind to shrink back in dread and dismay.

What a pity it is that we want to serve God, but only on the condition that we regulate and measure all our steps, take care of our business, and make for ourselves a kind of easy and convenient life. We do not want anything, we say. Well! Do we not want the conveniences of life, the comforts of friendship, the success of things we think are good, the preservation of a good reputation? God of truth, make your purest rays of grace shine into those timid and mercenary souls—souls that serve only to get something in return! Show them that they want everything, although they think that they want nothing. Press them, without letting up, from sacrifice to sacrifice. They will recognize, each time they come to something new that they have to sacrifice, that there was not a single thing that they were not holding tightly onto.

What agonies we experience when God takes us at our word, and takes only what we have so many times given up to him! Abandonment—giving up control of our lives: we talk about it without having any knowledge or familiarity with it! We talk about true sacrifice, but the words are on our lips but not in our hearts!

I no longer place my trust in my soul or my reliance on it. I trust in and rely on God alone, who will uproot me from myself.

Mary, mother of Jesus! I want to live and die with you in pure love.

⌇ 19
ST. AUGUSTINE (AUGUST 28)

Saint Augustine (354–430) was a brilliant scholar who lived a wild youth and by the age of thirty rose to a position of power as a professor of rhetoric for the imperial court in Milan. His Confessions *tell his story: disillusioned by the meaninglessness of his life, he underwent a personal crisis after reading an account of the life of Saint Anthony of Egypt and being influenced by the Christian bishop Ambrose. Augustine's deep inner struggle resulted in his embracing the faith of his godly Christian mother, Monica. Abandoning his career, he returned to his native North Africa, sold his family lands, gave the money to the poor, and entered the Christian priesthood.*

At Hippo, in present-day Algeria, Augustine became not only the Christian bishop but also a distinguished preacher and writer, working tirelessly to turn others to the Christian faith. His prolific writings made him a central figure in the history of Western thought and resulted in his being declared a Doctor of the Church.

In this meditation, Fénelon, a distinctive scholar in his own right, takes Augustine as an example to follow: Augustine, he writes, "finds the truth contained within disregard for his entire self, and in the love of God, which is the only good."

What do I see, Lord, in Saint Augustine? Utter affliction and distress, and then a mercy that transcends it. How a weak and afflicted soul is comforted at the sight of such an example! Dear God, this is how you take pleasure in saving what had been lost, in restoring what had gone astray, in placing back into your tender and fatherly breast what had been far off from you and had been given over to its passions.[124]

Beloved saint, you have placed me before your eyes to teach me, in the bottomless pit of my darkness, to hope and never to be discouraged, since the fountain of mercies is never dried up for the hearts of those who repent of sin.[125] And you teach me to put up with myself in all the most humiliating things I see within me.

What did the love of God not do in the heart of Augustine! In him, there was blind love, love gone astray, senseless love. But that love returned to its center, toward truth and eternal beauty. That love, which had for so long run after lies, had become perfect love. This was humble love. This was love that brought itself down to nothing in order to love better.

Augustine no longer loved himself, so much did he love God. He no longer saw anything through his own mind. His great genius—so fertile, so lively, so broad, so lofty, so fearless as to contemplate the highest truths—that genius was cast down.

So, what has become of that man who used to penetrate the greatest difficulties, who was accustomed to reasoning so subtly, whose habit was to speak and make decisions with so much assurance? What is left of him? Well! All I see is the simplicity of a child. He follows without seeing, he believes without understanding. Simple and humble love has become his only guiding light. He no longer seeks to know through his own faculties, but the anointing of love teaches him all truth. He finds the truth contained within disregard for his entire self, and in the love of God, which is the only good. "Who am I?" he cries out. "Only a voice that shouts, 'God is everything, and he is all there is.'"

What a profound doctrine! The most precious light is that everlasting light that brings all human enlightenment down to nothing. It is that state of darkness and obscurity where, without seeing anything in mortals, perfect love sees everything in a divine way. This is the intimate, personal taste and thirst for truth that no longer sets truth before eyes of flesh and blood, but causes it to live in the deepest recesses of ourselves.

Who will give me that dear knowledge of Jesus, in comparison with which everything is only nothing? Who will give me to it?

Teach me to love, Lord, and I will have knowledge of all your Scriptures. All their pages will teach me that the soul that loves knows all that you desire for us to know.

Love, teach me through the heart, and not the mind. Disabuse me of my vain intellect, of my blind ability to govern and discipline myself by the use of reason, of all desires that are unworthy of a soul who loves you. Let me die, like Augustine, to everything that is not you.

⌒ 20
ALL SAINTS' DAY
(NOVEMBER 1)

On All Saints' Day, the church honors those who have entered heaven.[126]
The book of Revelation describes the saints in heaven as they worship the
Lamb:

> *They sing a new song:*
> *"You are worthy to take the scroll*
>   *and to open its seals,*
> *for you were slaughtered and by your blood you ransomed for God*
>   *saints from every tribe and language and people and nation;*
> *you have made them to be a kingdom and priests serving our God,*
>   *and they will reign on earth."* [127]

In this meditation, Fénelon tells of his love of the saints, and of his desire to
be among them. "I hear the voice of the Savior saying that God knows how
to change even stones into children of Abraham," he writes. "Jesus, word of
the Father, yet word of everlasting truth! Bring that word into completion
within me."

The church's intention is to honor today all the saints taken together.
I love them, I petition them for help and support,[128] I unite myself to
them, I join my voice with theirs to praise the One who made them
saints. May I gladly cry out with that heavenly church, "Holy, holy,
holy!"[129] "To God alone be the glory!"[130] Let everything be humbled
and brought low before him!

I see the saints of every age, of every temperament, of every condition.
Therefore, there is no age, or temperament, or condition that excludes
a person from sainthood. Outwardly, they faced the same obstacles,
the same battles as we do. Inwardly, they had the same contradictions
and inconsistencies, the same susceptibilities, the same temptations,
the same moments of rebellion of corrupt nature. They had tyrannical

habits to destroy, backslidings and relapses to repair, illusions to fear, diversions into laxity of zeal to reject, plausible pretexts to overcome, close friendships to fear, enemies to love, pride to be undermined at its very foundation, tempers to repress, and a love of self to pursue relentlessly as far as the very deepest recesses of the heart.

How I love to see the saints! They are weak just as I am, always needing to come to grips with themselves, never having a single moment of certainty of success. I see some of them shrinking, delivered up to the cruelest temptations. I see some of them in the most formidable states of prosperousness and in the foulest commerce with the things of this age. The grace of the Savior bursts forth everywhere, in order to show its power all the better, and in order to take away any excuse from those who resist it! There is no deep-rooted habit, no violent or fragile temper, no overwhelming affliction, no poisoning prosperity that can excuse us, if we do not put the Gospel into practice. This throng of examples sets the course:[131] grace takes all the most diverse forms, according to the various needs. It makes kings humble as easily as it turns solitaries into repentant contemplatives. Everything is easy when we do not resist its drawing.

I hear the voice of the Savior saying that God knows how to change even stones into children of Abraham.[132] Jesus, word of the Father, yet word of everlasting truth! Bring that word into completion within me: I who am a hard and unfeeling rock, I who can be chiseled only under redoubled blows of the hammer, I who am rebellious, unteachable, and incapable of anything good.

Lord, take this rock. Glorify yourself. Soften my heart.[133] Bring it to life by your Spirit. Make it receptive to your eternal truths. Form within me a child of Abraham who treads upon the smallest traces of Abraham's faith.[134]

Will I say with this foolish world, "I am willing to be saved, but I do not aspire to be a saint"? Well! Who can hope for salvation without becoming holy—without becoming a saint?[135] Nothing impure will enter the kingdom of heaven. No spot can enter it: as slight as it may be, it has to be eliminated, and everything has to be purified to the core by the avenging fire of divine justice, either in this world or the next. Everything that does not consist of complete self-denial and pure love that ascribes everything to God without turning back, is still tainted.

How holy is my God, in whose eyes the very stars are not pure enough! Righteous and just God, who will judge all our imperfect righteousness,[136] put your righteousness into my deepest inner parts[137] in order to make me new. Do not leave anything of myself in me.

⁓ 21
ALL SOULS' DAY
(NOVEMBER 2)

On All Souls' Day, the church remembers all of the faithful departed, those members of the Church Expectant who are awaiting entrance into heaven.

In this meditation, Fénelon ponders two kinds of death. To be sure, physical death will come to us all. But his emphasis in this meditation is on the death that he longs for while still in this life: death to self. "Make me die to everything before I die," he asks of God. "Then I will be dead, and you yourself will live in me." These words echo those of Saint Paul, who wrote, "I have been crucified with Christ; and it is no longer I who live, but it is Christ who lives in me."[138]

Dear God, I look with comfort at this ceremony of your church, which places death before our eyes. What a deep pity! Must we need to be reminded of it? Everything is only death here below. Humankind is falling into ruin on every side before our very eyes. A new world has been raised up on the ruins of the one that saw our birth.[139] And this new world, which has already grown old, is about to disappear—each of us dies every day without knowing it.[140] People are like grass, which flowers in the morning: in the evening it fades, dries up, withers, and is trodden under foot.[141] The past is only a dream. The present escapes us in the blink of an eye where we want to see it. The future does not belong to us. Perhaps it will never happen, and if it does, what are we to think about it? It is coming, it is drawing close, there it is! It is already gone. It has fallen into that bottomless chasm of the past into which everything is swallowed up and lost from sight, and is brought to nothing.

Dear God, you are all there is. You alone are the true Being. Everything else is only an illusion, an image of being, a shadow that flees away. Truth! My all! I take delight in the fact that I am nothing. To you alone it belongs to be forever. Blind mortals, you think you are living, and all you are doing is dying!

But death, which makes all nature shudder—will I be afraid of it like a coward? No! For the children of God, it is the passage to life. All it robs us of is vanity and corruption. It is death that must endow us with everlasting gifts. Death, good death! When will death desire to reunite me with the only thing I love? When will it give me the kiss of the bridegroom? [142] When will the bonds of my slavery be broken?[143] Eternal love! Truth that will cause to shine a day that will have no end! Peace of the kingdom of God, where God himself will be completely in everyone! Heavenly homeland! Beloved Zion, where my impassioned heart will lose itself in God! If my heart does not desire you, what will it desire?

But, dear God, my love, it is your glory and not my happiness that I long for. I love your will better than my bliss. Therefore, I consent, for love of you, to dwell still far from you in this place of exile, in this valley of tears,[144] as long as it is your will. You know that it is not out of attachment to the earth or to this body of clay, this wretched body of sin, but out of a sacrifice of my whole self to your good pleasure that I consent to keep on languishing here below. But make me die to everything before I die. Snuff out in me every desire. Uproot every movement of my will. Tear away every ounce of self-interest. Then I will be dead, and you yourself will live in me. Then I will no longer be myself.[145]

Precious death that must come before the death of the body! Death, which is divine life, transformed into Jesus Christ, in such a way that our life is hidden with him in the bosom of his heavenly Father! Death, after which we are ready to die or live without it making any difference! Death that begins the kingdom of heaven on earth! Seed out of which comes the new being!

Then, dear God, I will be in the world as if I were not there. I will seem as one of the dead who will rise from the tomb,[146] those you will raise up on the last day.[147]

ACKNOWLEDGMENTS

The task of rendering the late seventeenth-century French of the beloved author Fénelon into modern English must be undertaken with a grasp not only of the French language as it was used in that period, but of the author's life and thought and the times that shaped them.

The search for the best rendering of French words was greatly aided by consulting Harrap's *New Standard French and English Dictionary* (London and Paris: Harrap, 1981) and Merriam-Webster's Online Dictionary, www.merriam-webster.com. Passages from the New Revised Standard Version of the Bible were made more readily accessible by the *oremus Bible Browser* at www.devotions.net/bible/00bible.htm.

Special thanks are owed to LaVonne Neff, whose editing skills, command of French, and love of Fénelon's writings combined to produce insightful suggestions for improvement in the presentation and content of Part Three.

Finally, heartfelt thanks are owed to the staff of Paraclete Press, whose patience through this book's revisions is gratefully acknowledged.

NOTES
INTRODUCTION

1   *Brother Lawrence   The Practice of the Presence of God* is available as a volume of the Paraclete Living Library. (Brewster, MA: Paraclete Press, 1985)

2   *Bossuet was a court preacher*   "Reflections on the Character and Genius of Fenelon" (the introduction by Thomas Merton) from *Fenelon: Letters of Love and Counsel*, published by Harvill Press, 1964. Reprinted by permission of The Random House Group Ltd. This excerpt is taken from pages 11–12.

3   *Fénelon's statements were not always as safe as Bossuet's*   Merton, "Reflections on the Character and Genius of Fenelon," 12–13.

4   *Perhaps, after all, this gives us a clue*   Merton, "Reflections on the Character and Genius of Fenelon," 26.

NOTES FOR PART ONE
The Royal Way of the Cross

1   *God chose the foolish things of the world to shame the wise*   1 Corinthians 1:27.

2   *Nothing can happen in the world but by God's permissive will*   The word *permissive* has been added to avoid any temptation to call God the author of evil.

3   *bondage to decay . . . glorious freedom*   Romans 8:21.

4   *Learn from me*   Matthew 11:29.

5   *Knowledge puffs up . . . love builds up*   1 Corinthians 8:1.

6   *we have none of Martha's trouble*   Luke 10:41–42, "Martha, Martha," the Lord answered, "you are worried and upset about many things, but only one thing is needed. Mary has chosen what is better, and it will not be taken away from her."

7   *those "lukewarm"*   Revelation 3:16, "So, because you are lukewarm—neither hot nor cold—I am about to spit you out of my mouth."

8   *the Father of compassion*   2 Corinthians 1:3.

9   *Taste and see that the LORD is good*   Psalm 34:8.

10 *If anyone would come after me*   Matthew 16:24.

11 *I would rather feel it than know how to define it . . .*   *The Imitation of Christ,*
    Book I, Chapter I, 3.

12 *wisdom of the world . . . is foolishness with God*   1 Corinthians 3:19.

13 *think . . . with sober judgment*   Romans 12:3.

14 *I care very little*   1 Corinthians 4:3.

15 *all men are liars*   Psalm 116:11.

16 *the costly pearl*   Matthew 13:45–46.

17 *Those who make them will be like them*   Psalm 115:8.

18 *And the peace of God*   Philippians 4:7.

19 *In all things God works for good*   Romans 8:28.

20 *We are fools for Christ*   1 Corinthians 4:10.

21 *by their fruit you will recognize them*   Matthew 7:16.

22 *Delight yourself in the* LORD   Psalm 37:4.

23 *It is good for us to be here*   Matthew 17:4.

24 *like Mount Zion*   Psalm 125:1.

25 *Though he slay me*   Job 13:15.

26 *only one thing is needed*   Luke 10:41–42.

27 *Yet I hold this against you*   Revelation 2:4–5.

28 *man of God*   1 Timothy 6:11.

29 *forsaken his first love*   This is a reference to the words spoken to
    the church at Ephesus recorded in Revelation 2:1–7. "Yet I hold
    this against you: You have forsaken your first love" (Rev. 2:4).

30 *remember the height from which you have fallen*   Revelation 2:5a.

31 *I will set out and go back to my father*   Luke 11:18–19.

32 *remove your lampstand from its place*   Revelation 2:5b.

33 *Do not be afraid of those who kill the body*   Matthew 10:28.

34 *Walk before me, and be blameless*   Genesis 17:1.

35 *the real kingdom of God within you*   Luke 17:21, "The kingdom of
    God is within you."

36 *A word from the Lord stilled the raging of the sea*   Mark 6:47–52.

37 *I have set the* LORD *always before me*   Psalm 16:8.

38 *Whom have I in heaven but you?*   Psalm 73:25–26.

39 *God works for the good of those who love him*   Romans 8:28.

40 *pottery for noble purposes*   Romans 9:21.

41 *The kingdom of God is within you*   Luke 17:21.

42 *If any man would come after me*   Matthew 16:24.

43 *You are not your own*   1 Corinthians 6:19.

44 *You, my brothers, were called to be free*   Galatians 5:13.

45 *That law is not made for the righteous*   1 Timothy 1:9.

46 *For our light and momentary troubles*   2 Corinthians 4:17.

47 *Happy are those who weep*   Psalm 126:5, "Those who sow in tears will reap with songs of joy."

48 *I have been crucified with Christ*   Galatians 2:20.

NOTES FOR PART TWO
Talking with God

1 *Our God comes . . . Hear, O my people*   Psalm 50:3, 7 (RSV).

2 *The Spirit intercedes . . . We do not know what we ought to pray for*   Romans 8:27, 26 (NIV).

3 *I slept but my heart was awake*   Song of Solomon 5:2 (NIV).

4 *Blessed are those servants*   Luke 12:37 (RSV).

5 *our Father knows what we need before we ask him*   Matthew 6:8.

6 *with sighs too deep for words*   Romans 8:26 (NRSV).

7 *We can judge the life of the root only by the fruit it bears*   Matthew 7:15–20.

8 *hold the truth in unrighteousness*   Romans 1:18 (KJV).

9 *Praise be to God who has not rejected my prayer*   Psalm 66:20 (NIV).

10 *Whoever walks with the wise becomes wise*   Proverbs 13:20 (NRSV).

11 *Turn away my eyes from beholding vanity*   Psalm 119:37 (KJV).

12 *He is a compassionate High Priest*   Hebrews 4:15.

13 *I can do everything through him who gives me strength*   Philippians 4:13 (NIV).

14 *May the one who began a good work among you*   From Philippians 1:6 (NRSV).

15 *The LORD hath made all things for himself*   Proverbs 16:4 (KJV).

16 *Whoever of you does not renounce all that he has*   Luke 14:33 (RSV).

17 *For the form of this world is passing away*   1 Corinthians 7:31 (RSV).

18 *with the affection of Christ Jesus*   Philippians 1:8 (NIV).

19 *that we become one spirit*   1 Corinthians 6:17, "But he who unites himself with the Lord is one with him in spirit."

20 *For the letter kills*   2 Corinthians 3:6 (NRSV).

21 *You have the words of eternal life*   John 6:68 (RSV).

22 *God is continually speaking to us*   *The Imitation of Christ*, III, 2a: "I taught the prophets from the beginning, saith the Lord, and cease not, even to this day, to speak to all; but many are hardened and deaf to my voice."

23 *two-edged sword . . . piercing even to the dividing asunder of soul and spirit* Hebrews 4:12 (KJV).

24 *His secret is with the simple*   Proverbs 3:32 (VULGATE). His meaning is, "His secret dwelling place is with the simple."

25 *will come to him, and make our home with him*   John 14:23 (NIV).

26 *Show me your face*   Song of Solomon 2:14 (NIV).

27 *Who has resisted him and come out unscathed?*   Job 9:4 (NIV).

28 *do not let this liberty be for you an occasion or a pretext for doing evil* This is a paraphrase of Galatians 5:13.

29 *the law is not made for the righteous*   See 1 Timothy 1:9.

30 *to what lies ahead*   Philippians 3:13 (NIV).

31 *I will become even more undignified than this*   2 Samuel 6:22 (NIV).

32 *No one living is righteous before you*   Psalm 143:2 (NIV).

33 *When I am weak, then I am strong*   2 Corinthians 12:10 (NIV).

34 *My power is made perfect in weakness*   2 Corinthians 12:9 (NIV).

35 *Where the Spirit of the Lord is*   2 Corinthians 3:17 (NIV).

36 *Blessed are the poor in spirit*   Matthew 5:3 (NIV).

37 *ate the loaves and had their fill*   John 6:26.

38 *Rabbi, it is good for us to be here*   Mark 9:5 (NIV).

39 *the just shall live by faith*   Hebrews 10:38 (KJV).

40 *the most excellent way*   1 Corinthians 12:31 (NIV).

41 *not self-seeking*   1 Corinthians 13:5 (NIV).

42 *put behind us childish things*   1 Corinthians 13:11.

43 *we will never be shaken*   Psalm 30:6 (NIV).

44 *Can a mother forget the baby*   Isaiah 49:15 (NIV).

45 *The wind blows wherever it pleases*   John 3:8 (NIV).

46 *When I am weak, then I am strong*   2 Corinthians 12:10 (NIV).

47 *I can do everything through him*   Philippians 4:13 (NIV).

48 *Each day has enough trouble of its own*   Matthew 6:34 (NIV).

49 *You shall know them by their fruits* Matthew 7:16 (KJV, slightly modified).

50 *Lord, what wilt thou have me to do?*   Acts 9:6 (KJV).

51   *Teach me to do your will*   Psalm 143:10 (NIV).

52   *carry each other's burdens*   Galatians 6:2 (NIV).

53   *Where the Spirit of the Lord is*   2 Corinthians 3:17 (NIV).

54   *The kingdom of heaven belongs to such as these*   Matthew 19:14 (NIV).

55   *No one living is righteous before you*   Psalm 143:2 (NIV).

56   *the heavens are not pure in the eyes of our Judge*   Job 15:15.

57   *we all stumble in many ways*   James 3:2 (NIV).

58   *Surely God is good to Israel*   Psalm 73:1 (NIV).

59   *Tomorrow will worry about itself*   Matthew 6:34 (NIV).

60   *Those who seek the* LORD *lack no good thing*   Psalm 34:10 (NIV).

NOTES FOR PART THREE
Meditations on the Heart of God

1   *where he finds the vessels empty*   *The Imitation of Christ*, Book IV, chapter 15.

2   *there is no evil that God has not allowed to befall a city*   Amos 3:6 (NRSV), "Is a trumpet blown in a city, and the people are not afraid? Does disaster befall a city, unless the LORD has done it?"

3   *As St. Cyprian said*   The reference is to St. Cyprian's treatise on the Lord's Prayer.

4   *let us consider whether he will grant us*   The conclusion is clear: certainly he will.

5   *he should pray to obtain comfort*   James 5:13–14 (NRSV), "Are any among you suffering? They should pray. Are any cheerful? They should sing songs of praise. Are any among you sick? They should call for the elders of the church and have them pray over them, anointing them with oil in the name of the Lord."

6   *that sacred source*   The French word *source* also means *spring* or *fountain*. This passage invites us to study the Gospels.

7   *he asks God to teach him to do it*   Psalm 143:10 (NRSV), "Teach me to do your will, for you are my God. Let your good spirit lead me on a level path."

8   *For this slight momentary affliction*   2 Corinthians 4:17 (NRSV).

9 *the kingdom of heaven is taken by violent attacks*   Matthew 11:12 (NRSV), "From the days of John the Baptist until now the kingdom of heaven has suffered violence, and the violent take it by force."

10 *happy are those who weep now*   Matthew 5:4 (NRSV), "Blessed are those who mourn, for they will be comforted."

11 *how terrible it will be for those who laugh now*   Luke 6:25 (NRSV), "Woe to you who are full now, for you will be hungry. Woe to you who are laughing now, for you will mourn and weep."

12 *God himself will wipe away all tears*   Revelation 21:3–4 (NRSV), "See, the home of God is among mortals. He will dwell with them; they will be his peoples, and God himself will be with them; he will wipe every tear from their eyes."

13 *earthly, unspiritual, and devilish*   James 3:15 (NRSV).

14 *I am beginning to be able to do everything in you who strengthen me*   Philippians 4:13.

15 *the Father of mercies and the God of all consolation*   2 Corinthians 1:3 (NRSV).

16 *Lord, where is your steadfast love of old?*   Psalm 89:49 (NRSV).

17 *for whom he does not pray even as he is about to die*   John 17:9 (NRSV), "I am not asking on behalf of the world, but on behalf of those whom you gave me, because they are yours."

18 *Keep me far away from the tents of wickedness*   Psalm 84:10 (NRSV), "For a day in your courts is better than a thousand elsewhere. I would rather be a doorkeeper in the house of my God than live in the tents of wickedness."

19 *If you love me, feed my sheep*   John 21:17 (NRSV), "[Jesus] said to [Peter] the third time, 'Simon son of John, do you love me?' Peter felt hurt because he said to him the third time, 'Do you love me?' And he said to him, 'Lord, you know everything; you know that I love you.' Jesus said to him, 'Feed my sheep.'"

20 *always had the nature of God*   Philippians 2:6–7 (TEV).

21 *Like a lamb about to be slaughtered*   Isaiah 53:7 (TEV).

22 *the flesh is of no avail*   John 6:63 (NRSV), "It is the spirit that gives life; the flesh is useless. The words that I have spoken to you are spirit and life."

23 *the Word became flesh*   John 1:14.

24   *Let anyone be accursed who has no love for the Lord*
     1 Corinthians 16:22 (NRSV).
25   *For I am persuaded* Romans 8:38–39 (KJV).
26   *Those who do so are as unshakable as Mount Zion*
     Psalm 125:1 (NRSV), "Those who trust in the LORD are like Mount
     Zion, which cannot be moved, but abides for ever."
27   *how good you are to make me love your peace!*
     Zechariah 8:19 (NRSV), "Therefore love truth and peace."

NOTES FOR PART FOUR
God of My Heart: Meditations on Feasts and Fasts

1   *Yet whatever gains I had*   Philippians 3:7–14.
2   *The church year consists of two types of celebrations, called* feasts   This
    is a simplified view of the church year: those who study liturgy
    will know that there are further divisions into feasts, memorials,
    commemorations, and solemnities. A concise article explaining the
    church year in greater detail than appears here can be found at
    http://en.wikipedia.org/wiki/Liturgical_year.
3   *Their intention was not to be comprehensive*   Those who would like
    to read in detail about the church year may want to consult Dom
    Prosper Guéranger's fifteen-volume *The Liturgical Year*, written in
    the nineteenth century. This work can be found in English transla-
    tion in libraries and on the Internet.
4   *Shower, O heavens, from above*   Isaiah 45:8a.
5   *the Desire of all nations*   Haggai 2:7 (KJV).
6   *the world did not know him*   John 1:10.
7   *The light shines in the darkness*   John 1:5.
8   *judge those who do not see*   John 9:39, "Jesus said, 'I came into this
    world for judgment so that those who do not see may see, and
    those who do see may become blind.'"
9   *your kingdom come*   Matthew 6:10.
10 *He gave you all authority in heaven and on earth*   Matthew 28:18.
11 *Let the light of your face shine on us*   Psalm 4:6.

12 *The stars will fall from heaven; their light will be extinguished* This paragraph contains a number of references to Mark 13, especially verses 24–25: "But in those days, after that suffering, the sun will be darkened, and the moon will not give its light, and the stars will be falling from heaven, and the powers in the heavens will be shaken."

13 *Heaven and earth will pass away . . . only your word will endure* Matthew 24:35, "Heaven and earth will pass away, but my words will not pass away."

14 *why do you allow the world to be bewitched?* Compare this to Galatians 3:1, "You foolish Galatians! Who has bewitched you?"

15 *I lift up my eyes* Psalm 123:1–2, "To you I lift up my eyes, O you who are enthroned in the heavens! As the eyes of servants look to the hand of their master, as the eyes of a maid to the hand of her mistress, so our eyes look to the LORD our God, until he has mercy upon us."

16 *I will come toward you, as the chief of your apostles taught me* See the story of the apostle Peter walking on the water toward Jesus, in Matthew 10:29.

17 *John recounts the story of Thomas' demand to feel Jesus' wounds* John 20:24–29.

18 *I will boast all the more gladly of my weaknesses* 2 Corinthians 12:9–10.

19 *who lived in darkness and the shadow dark as death* Luke 1:78–79, "By the tender mercy of our God, the dawn from on high will break upon us, to give light to those who sit in darkness and in the shadow of death, to guide our feet into the way of peace."

20 *did not even have eyes to see the light* Romans 11:8, "As it is written, 'God gave them a sluggish spirit, eyes that would not see and ears that would not hear, down to this very day.'"

21 *You have hidden your word from the great and the learned* Matthew 11:25–26, "At that time Jesus said, 'I thank you, Father, Lord of heaven and earth, because you have hidden these things from the wise and the intelligent and have revealed them to infants; yes, Father, for such was your gracious will.'"

22 *blessed are those who have not seen and yet have come to believe* John 20:29.

23 *So that everyone who believes in him may not perish*   John 3:16.

24 *Let the little children come to me*   Matthew 19:14.

25 *blessed are the poor in spirit*   Matthew 5:3.

26 *Jesus Christ will be our life, our righteousness, and our wisdom*
1 Corinthians 1:30–31, "He is the source of your life in Christ
Jesus, who became for us wisdom from God, and righteousness
and sanctification and redemption, in order that, as it is written,
'Let the one who boasts, boast in the Lord.'"

27 *the disciple whom Jesus loved*   John 21:7, among others.

28 *God is love*   1 John 4:16b.

29 *placing his head on Jesus' breast*   John 13:23, 25 in traditional
translations such as KJV and the ones that Fénelon used. Modern
translations such as NRSV render this passage as "reclining next to
Jesus."

30 *unless you change and become like children*   Matthew 18:3.

31 *lean with John on your breast*   John 13:23, 25 (KJV).

32 *his anointing teaches you about all things*   1 John 2:27.

33 *fools in the eyes of the world*   Compare this to 1 Corinthians 1:27, 4:10.

34 *It is a consuming fire*   Hebrews 12:29, "for indeed our God is a
consuming fire."

35 *the perfect sacrifice*   See Hebrews 9.

36 *The Feast of the Circumcision of Our Lord*   Since the Second Vatican
Council (1962–65), most Roman Catholics celebrate January 1 as
the Solemnity of Mary, Mother of God. January 1 nonetheless still
incorporates elements of the Feast of The Circumcision of Our
Lord, and is also the Octave (eighth day) of Christmas.

37 *Do not think that I have come to abolish the law*   Matthew 5:17.

38 *I am taking up my cross to follow you*   Luke 9:23, "Then [Jesus] said
to them all, 'If any want to become my followers, let them deny
themselves and take up their cross daily and follow me.'"

39 *the rubbish of the world*   1 Corinthians 4:13, "We have become like
the rubbish of the world, the dregs of all things, to this very day."

40 *Epiphany commemorates the arrival of the wise men*   Epiphany (Greek
for *appearance* or *revelation*) also celebrates Jesus' baptism in the
Jordan river by John the Baptist, and the miracle of Jesus' changing
water into wine at the wedding at Cana.

41 *Where is the child who has been born king of the Jews?*   Matthew 2:2.

42 *My eyes have seen your salvation*   Luke 2:30–32.

43 *Woe to the world*   Matthew 18:7.

44 *We are fools for the sake of Christ*   1 Corinthians 4:10.

45 *Lord, what do you want me to do?*   This is a modern rendering of Saul's response to Jesus in Acts 9:6 as shown in KJV and the older versions of the Bible that Fénelon used. Although modern versions such as NRSV omit these words, the question certainly expresses Saul's attitude.

46 *It is hard for you to kick against the goads*   This is a modern rendering of Jesus' words to Saul in Acts 9:5 as shown in KJV and the older versions of the Bible that Fénelon used. Although modern versions such as NRSV omit these words, they represent a tender expression of Jesus' merciful treatment of Saul, despite Saul's having persecuted Jesus' followers.

47 *Who has resisted him, and succeeded?*   Job 9:4, "He is wise in heart, and mighty in strength—who has resisted him, and succeeded?"

48 *I will not take the Lord's yoke upon me*   In Matthew 11:29, Jesus said, "Take my yoke upon you, and learn from me; for I am gentle and humble in heart, and you will find rest for your souls."

49 *chosen instrument*   Acts 9:15—The disciple Ananias was afraid to help Saul, who was coming to him blind and helpless after the Damascus Road vision. "But the Lord said to [Ananias], 'Go, for he is an instrument whom I have chosen to bring my name before Gentiles and kings and before the people of Israel.'"

50 *clay jar*   2 Corinthians 4:7, "But we have this treasure in clay jars, so that it may be made clear that this extraordinary power belongs to God and does not come from us."

51 *today, today*   2 Corinthians 6:2, "See, now is the acceptable time: see, now is the day of salvation!"

52 *Love, and do what you will*   This is famous saying by Saint Augustine: "Once and for all, a short rule is laid down for you: Love, and do what you will. If you keep silence, do it out of love. If you cry out, do it out of love. If you refrain from punishing, do it out of love. Let the root of love be within. From such a root nothing but good can come." From John E. Rotelle, OSA, *Augustine Day by Day: Minute Meditations for Every Day Taken from the Writings of Saint Augustine*. New York: Catholic Book Publishing Co., 1986.

Quoted at http://www.artsci.villanova.edu/dsteelman/augustine/days/0524.html

53   *you of little faith*   Matthew 14:31—These are Jesus' words to Peter when Peter got out of a boat and began walking on the water toward Jesus, but then became afraid and began to sink.

54   *I can do all things through him who strengthens me*   Philippians 4:13.

55   *breathing threats and murder*   Acts 9:1.

56   *God's angel struck down the firstborn of the Egyptians*   Exodus 12:29.

57   *God then told Moses to consecrate all the firstborn to him*   Exodus 13:2.

58   *they could bring two doves or two pigeons*   Leviticus 5:7.

59   *Mary and Joseph brought two doves*   Luke 2:22–24.

60   *not even have a place to lay your head*   Luke 9:58: "And Jesus said . . . , 'Foxes have holes, and birds of the air have nests; but the Son of Man has nowhere to lay his head.'"

61   *Jesus' fasting for forty days in the wilderness*   Matthew 4:1–2, "Then Jesus was led up by the Spirit into the wilderness to be tempted by the devil. He fasted for forty days and forty nights, and afterwards he was famished."

62   *My soul longs, indeed it faints*   Psalm 84:2.

63   *that soberness that your apostle spoke of*   See Romans 12:3, "For by the grace given to me I say to everyone among you not to think of yourself more highly than you ought to think, but to think with sober judgment, each according to the measure of faith that God has assigned." See also 1 Peter 5:8—in KJV this was rendered "Be sober, be vigilant"; in NRSV the more modern rendering is "Discipline yourselves; keep alert."

64   *soberness that consists not only of the sparing use of food and drink, but also the cultivation of an earnestly thoughtful character*   This definition of soberness, taken from http://www.merriam-webster.com/dictionary/sober, differentiates Fénelon's use of the word from the ordinary understanding of it as meaning "not being intoxicated by an alcoholic beverage."

65   *the bread that is the true manna*   John 6:57–58, "[Jesus said:] Just as the living Father sent me, and I live because of the Father, so whoever eats me will live because of me. This is the bread that came down from heaven, not like that which your ancestors ate, and they died. But the one who eats this bread will live for ever."

66 *not a spirit of fear and servitude*   2 Timothy 1:7, "[F]or God did not give us a spirit of cowardice [KJV: fear], but rather a spirit of power and of love and of self-discipline."

67 *a jealous God*   Exodus 20:5, "I the LORD your God am a jealous God."

68 *leaving the soul only fainting and ready to expire with love*   These are references to the bride's love for the bridegroom in the Song of Solomon, such as in 5:8, "I adjure you, O daughters of Jerusalem, if you find my beloved, tell him this: I am faint with love."

69 *worship you in spirit and truth*   John 4:24, "God is spirit, and those who worship him must worship in spirit and truth."

70 *Your will be done*   Matthew 6:10, "Your will be done, on earth as it is in heaven."

71 *Jesus' new commandment that the disciples love one another*   John 13:34, "I give you a new commandment, that you love one another. Just as I have loved you, you also should love one another."

72 *Do this in remembrance of me*   Luke 22:19.

73 *Where then is the deep wisdom that formed the universe?*   Job 28:12–13, "But where shall wisdom be found? And where is the place of understanding? Mortals do not know the way to it, and it is not found in the land of the living."

74 *worshiping in spirit and truth*   John 4:24, "God is spirit, and those who worship him must worship in spirit and truth."

75 *Let my soul die the death of the upright*   Numbers 23:10, "Let me die the death of the upright, and let my end be like his!"

76 *that inner death that divides the soul from itself*   Hebrews 4:12, "Indeed, the word of God is living and active, sharper than any two-edged sword, piercing until it divides soul from spirit, joints from marrow; it is able to judge the thoughts and intentions of the heart."

77 *a stumbling-block to Jews and foolishness to Gentiles*   1 Corinthians 1:23.

78 *we have gone out of our minds, like Jesus*   Mark 3:21, "When [Jesus'] family heard it, they went out to restrain him, for people were saying, 'He has gone out of his mind.'"

79 *man of suffering*   Isaiah 53:3, "He was despised and rejected by others; a man of suffering and acquainted with infirmity; and as

one from whom others hide their faces he was despised, and we held him of no account."

80 *Like Saint Peter, we boast*   Mark 14:31, "But [Peter] said vehemently [to Jesus], 'Even though I must die with you, I will not deny you.' And all of them said the same."

81 *one question from a servant*   Mark 13:66–68, "While Peter was below in the courtyard, one of the servant-girls of the high priest came by. When she saw Peter warming himself, she stared at him and said, 'You also were with Jesus, the man from Nazareth.' But he denied it, saying, 'I do not know or understand what you are talking about.'"

82 *Remove this cup, yet . . . not my will but yours be done*   Luke 22:42.

83 *the comforting moments of the Transfiguration*   Matthew 17:1–9, Mark 9:2–8, and Luke 9:28–36 tell the story of Jesus' taking three disciples up on a mountain to pray. There, his appearance changed and his clothes became dazzling white, and he was seen in his glory talking with Moses and Elijah. Then a voice came from a cloud, saying, "This is my Son, my Chosen; listen to him!"   (Luke 9:35).

84 *deeply grieved, even to death*   Matthew 26:38—As Jesus prayed in the garden of Gethsemane as he was about to be betrayed, he said to his disciples, 'I am deeply grieved, even to death.'"

85 *hidden with Christ in God*   Colossians 3:2–3, "Set your minds on things that are above, not on things that are on earth, for you have died, and your life is hidden with Christ in God."

86 *Therefore we have been buried with him by baptism into death*   Romans 6:4.

87 *a filthy cloth*   Isaiah 64:6, "We have become like one who is unclean, and all our righteous deeds are like a filthy cloth."

88 *I have not died with Christ*   Romans 6:8, "But if we have died with Christ, we believe that we will also live with him."

89 *the old self . . . the new self*   Ephesians 4:22–24, "You were taught to put away your former way of life, your old self, corrupt and deluded by its lusts, and to be renewed in the spirit of your minds, and to clothe yourselves with the new self, created according to the likeness of God in true righteousness and holiness."

90 *Everything will be given back to us a hundred times over*   Mark 10:29–30, "Jesus said, 'Truly I tell you, there is no one who has

left house or brothers or sisters or mother or father or children or fields, for my sake and for the sake of the good news, who will not receive a hundredfold now in this age—houses, brothers and sisters, mothers and children, and fields, with persecutions—and in the age to come eternal life."

91   *refined of the dross they contain*   Zechariah 13:9, "And I will put [them] into the fire, refine them as one refines silver, and test them as gold is tested. They will call on my name, and I will answer them. I will say, 'They are my people'; and they will say, 'The LORD is our God.'"

92   *the same Spirit who groans and prays in us*   Romans 8:26 (KJV), "We know not what we should pray for as we ought: but the Spirit itself maketh intercession for us with groanings which cannot be uttered." In NRSV this passage is rendered, "We do not know how to pray as we ought, but that very Spirit intercedes with sighs too deep for words."

93   *he withdrew from them and was carried up to heaven*   Luke 24:50–52.

94   *present your bodies as a living sacrifice*   Romans 12:1.

95   *I am with you always*   Matthew 28:20.

96   *the bread that has come down from heaven*   John 6:57–58, [Jesus said:] "Just as the living Father sent me, and I live because of the Father, so whoever eats me will live because of me. This is the bread that came down from heaven, not like that which your ancestors ate, and they died. But the one who eats this bread will live for ever."

97   *valley of tears*   This term refers to Earth and the sorrows we face in life. It is taken from the *Salve Regina* prayer: "To thee do we send up our sighs, mourning and weeping in this valley of tears."

98   *How many glorious things are spoken of Zion!*   Psalm 87:3, "Glorious things are spoken of you, O city of God." "Zion" is used here as a symbol of heaven.

99   *to you alone, Lord, be glory*   Jude 1:25, "To the only God our Savior, through Jesus Christ our Lord, be glory, majesty, power, and authority, before all time and now and for ever. Amen."

100   *the hymn of the conquering Lamb*   Revelation 5:11–12, "Then I looked, and I heard the voice of many angels surrounding the throne and the living creatures and the elders; they numbered myriads of myriads and thousands of thousands, singing with full voice,

'Worthy is the Lamb that was slaughtered to receive power and wealth and wisdom and might and honor and glory and blessing!'"

101 *comfortless . . . orphaned*   John 14:18, "I will not leave you comfortless" (KJV); "I will not leave you orphaned" (NRSV).

102 *the Advocate . . . will teach you everything*   John 14:25, "But the Advocate, the Holy Spirit, whom the Father will send in my name, will teach you everything, and remind you of all that I have said to you." The Advocate is called "the Comforter" in older translations such as KJV.

103 *suddenly from heaven there came a sound*   Acts 2:2–4.

104 *a new heart like yours*   After he had sinned grievously, King David asked God to give him a "clean heart," "a new and right spirit" (Psalm 51:10). As a result, says St. Paul, "[God] testified concerning him: 'I have found David son of Jesse a man after my own heart; he will do everything I want him to do'" (Acts 13:22).

105 *peace . . . that flows like a river*   Isaiah 66:12 (NIV), "For this is what the LORD says: 'I will extend peace to her like a river, and the wealth of nations like a flooding stream; you will nurse and be carried on her arm and dandled on her knees.'"

106 *spring of life*   Revelation 21:6, "To the thirsty I will give water as a gift from the spring of the water of life."

107 *the Spirit, who blows where he will*   John 3:8—Jesus said to Nicodemus, "The wind* blows where it chooses, and you hear the sound of it, but you do not know where it comes from or where it goes. So it is with everyone who is born of the Spirit." [*The same Greek word means both *wind* and *spirit*.]

108 *the true God of glory*   The martyr Stephen described God this way in Acts 7:2.

109 *immortal and impassible . . . undivided and unchanged*   Here, Fénelon uses technical theological terms to explain the presence of Christ in the Eucharist. This doctrine was spelled out by the eleventh-century bishop Guitmond in his three-volume *De veritate corporis et sanguinis Jesus Christi in Eucharistia* (*On the True Body and Blood of Jesus Christ in the Eucharist*). An in-depth explanation of the doctrine can be found in French in *Dictionnaire de Patrologie* (Paris: Migne, 1852), pages 1638–1640. Referring to Jesus in the Eucharist, Guitmond said, *qu'étant immortel et impassible, il ne peut*

être ni blessé ni mis en pièces, et qu'encore que son corps paraisse divisé lorsqu'on le distribue aux fidèles, il y en a autant dans la plus petite partie que dans l'hostie tout entière. . . .

In English translation, the complete passage reads as follows: "Being immortal and impassible, he [Jesus] can neither be harmed nor divided into pieces. Although his body seems to be divided when it is distributed to the faithful, there is as much in the smallest part as in the host [the communion bread] when it is whole. So therefore, each separate particle is the body of Jesus Christ, and three separate particles are not three bodies, but one single body of Jesus Christ. He gives himself entirely to each one of the faithful, and all receive him in equal measure, even though a thousand masses might be celebrated at the same time. It is one single, indivisible body of Jesus Christ, and although the host seems to be divided into several parts, the flesh of Jesus Christ is nonetheless not divided. What those particles are before the dividing of the host, they are after their separation."

110 *It will form his new creature*   2 Corinthians 5:17, "So if anyone is in Christ, there is a new creation: everything old has passed away; see, everything has become new!"

111 *He is . . . all truth*   John 16:13–14, "[Jesus said:] When the Spirit of truth comes, he will guide you into all the truth; for he will not speak on his own, but will speak whatever he hears, and he will declare to you the things that are to come. He will glorify me, because he will take what is mine and declare it to you."

112 *who is truth itself*   John 14:6, "Jesus said to [Thomas], 'I am the way, and the truth, and the life. No one comes to the Father except through me.'"

113 *the true worship that you are looking for*   John 4:24, "[Jesus said:] God is spirit, and those who worship him must worship in spirit and truth."

114 *But Mary stood weeping outside the tomb*   John 20:11–18.

115 *from whom you cast out seven demons*   Luke 8:1–2, "Soon afterwards [Jesus] went on through cities and villages, proclaiming and bringing the good news of the kingdom of God. The twelve were with him, as well as some women who had been cured of evil spirits and infirmities: Mary, called Magdalene, from whom seven demons had gone out. . . ."

116 *all of your disciples ran away*   Luke 26:56, "Then all the disciples deserted him and fled."

117 *the fragrance of your perfumes*   Song of Solomon 1:2–3, "For your love is better than wine, your anointing oils are fragrant, your name is perfume poured out."

118 *Where is he?*   Song of Solomon 3:1–3, "I sought him whom my soul loves; I sought him, but found him not; I called him, but he gave no answer. 'I will rise now and go about the city, in the streets and in the squares; I will seek him whom my soul loves.' I sought him, but found him not. The sentinels found me, as they went about in the city. 'Have you seen him whom my soul loves?'"

119 *we can do all things through you*   Philippians 4:12–13, "I know what it is to have little, and I know what it is to have plenty. In any and all circumstances I have learned the secret of being well-fed and of going hungry, of having plenty and of being in need. I can do all things through him who strengthens me."

120 *constantly devoting themselves to prayer*   Acts 1:14, "[The disciples] were constantly devoting themselves to prayer, together with certain women, including Mary the mother of Jesus, as well as his brothers."

121 *worshiping in spirit and truth*   John 4:23–24, "But the hour is coming, and is now here, when the true worshipers will worship the Father in spirit and truth, for the Father seeks such as these to worship him. God is spirit, and those who worship him must worship in spirit and truth."

122 *They want to lean . . . on an arm of flesh*   2 Chronicles 32:7–8, [King Hezekiah spoke to the people as they were about to be attacked:] "Be strong and of good courage. Do not be afraid or dismayed before the king of Assyria and all the horde that is with him; for there is one greater with us than with him. With him is an arm of flesh; but with us is the LORD our God, to help us and to fight our battles."

123 *To set out like Abraham*   Hebrews 11:8, "By faith Abraham obeyed when he was called to set out for a place that he was to receive as an inheritance; and he set out, not knowing where he was going."

124 *what had been far off from you*   Ephesians 2:13, "But now in
Christ Jesus you who once were far off have been brought near
by the blood of Christ."

125 *fountain of mercies*   This term is from a prayer of Saint Ambrose,
who strongly influenced Augustine. Here is a portion of that
prayer: "Gracious God of majesty and awe, I seek your protec-
tion, I look for your healing. Poor troubled sinner that I am,
I appeal to you, the fountain of all mercy. I cannot bear your
judgment, but I trust your salvation. Lord, I show my wounds to
you and uncover my shame before you. I know my sins are many
and great, and they fill me with fear, but I hope in your mercies,
for they cannot be numbered." (The complete Prayer of Saint
Ambrose can be found at http://www.christusrex.org/www1/
mcitl/prayers.html)

126 *On All Saints' Day, the church honors those who have entered heaven*
Fénelon believed firmly in the Communion of Saints: the universal church consists of the Church Triumphant—those who
are in heaven, the Church Militant—Christians who are alive on
earth, and the Church Expectant—the departed faithful who are
awaiting entrance into heaven. All Christians are united in the
Communion of Saints and support each other in prayer.

127 *They sing a new song*   Revelation 5:9–10.

128 *I petition them for help and support*   This is a rendering of *je les
invoque*, meaning "I invoke them." Fénelon called on the saints in
heaven to intercede before God for him, their fellow Christian
who remained on earth. Revelation 5:8 speaks of these prayers:
"When he had taken the scroll, the four living creatures and the
twenty-four elders fell before the Lamb, each holding a harp and
golden bowls full of incense, which are the prayers of the saints."

129 *Holy, holy, holy!*   Revelation 4:8, "Day and night without ceasing
they sing, 'Holy, holy, holy, the Lord God the Almighty, who was
and is and is to come.'"

130 *To God alone be the glory*   1 Timothy 1:17, "To the King of the
ages, immortal, invisible, the only God, be honor and glory for
ever and ever. Amen."

131 *This throng of examples sets the course*   Hebrews 12:1–2, "Therefore,
since we are surrounded by so great a cloud of witnesses, let us

also lay aside every weight and the sin that clings so closely, and let us run with perseverance the race that is set before us, looking to Jesus the pioneer and perfecter of our faith, who for the sake of the joy that was set before him endured the cross, disregarding its shame, and has taken his seat at the right hand of the throne of God."

132 *God knows how to change even stones into children of Abraham* Matthew 3:8–9, "Bear fruit worthy of repentance. Do not presume to say to yourselves, 'We have Abraham as our ancestor'; for I tell you, God is able from these stones to raise up children to Abraham."

133 *Soften my heart* Ezekiel 36:26, "A new heart I will give you, and a new spirit I will put within you; and I will remove from your body the heart of stone and give you a heart of flesh."

134 *who treads upon the slightest traces of Abraham's faith* Romans 4:3, "For what does the scripture say? 'Abraham believed God, and it was reckoned to him as righteousness.'"

135 *Who can hope for salvation without becoming holy, without becoming a saint?* In French this reads, *Qui peut espérer son salut sans la sainteté?* The word *sainteté* means both "holiness" and "sainthood."

136 *who will judge all our imperfect righteousness* Isaiah 64:6, "We have all become like one who is unclean, and all our righteous deeds are like a filthy cloth."

137 *put your righteousness into my deepest inner parts* Psalm 51:5–6, "Indeed, I was born guilty, a sinner when my mother conceived me. You desire truth in the inward being; therefore teach me wisdom in my secret heart."

138 *I have been crucified with Christ* Galatians 2:19–20.

139 *A new world has been raised up on the ruins of the one that saw our birth* In this passage, Fénelon echoes the words of Ecclesiastes 1:2–4, "Vanity of vanities, says the Teacher, vanity of vanities! All is vanity. What do people gain from all the toil at which they toil under the sun? A generation goes, and a generation comes, but the earth remains for ever."

140 *each of us dies every day without knowing it* 1 Corinthians 15:31, "I die every day! That is as certain, brothers and sisters, as my boasting of you—a boast that I make in Christ Jesus our Lord."

141 *People are like grass*   Isaiah 40:6–8, "A voice says, 'Cry out!' And I said, 'What shall I cry?' All people are grass, their constancy is like the flower of the field. The grass withers, the flower fades, when the breath of the LORD blows upon it; surely the people are grass. The grass withers, the flower fades; but the word of our God will stand for ever."

142 *When will it give me the kiss of the bridegroom?*   Song of Solomon 1:2–3, "Let him kiss me with the kisses of his mouth! For your love is better than wine, your anointing oils are fragrant, your name is perfume poured out; therefore the maidens love you."

143 *When will the bonds of my slavery be broken?*   Romans 6:6–7, "We know that our old self was crucified with him so that the body of sin might be destroyed, and we might no longer be enslaved to sin. For whoever has died is freed from sin."

144 *in this place of exile, in this valley of tears*   This term refers to Earth and the sorrows we face in life. It is taken from the *Salve Regina* prayer: "To thee do we send up our sighs, mourning and weeping in this valley of tears. Turn then, most gracious advocate, thine eyes of mercy toward us; and after this our exile, show unto us the blessed fruit of thy womb, Jesus."

145 *Then I will no longer be myself*   Galatians 2:19–20, "I have been crucified with Christ; and it is no longer I who live, but it is Christ who lives in me. And the life I now live in the flesh I live by faith in the Son of God, who loved me and gave himself for me."

146 *the dead who rise from the tomb*   1 Thessalonians 5:16, "For the Lord himself, with a cry of command, with the archangel's call and with the sound of God's trumpet, will descend from heaven, and the dead in Christ will rise first."

147 *those you will raise up on the last day*   John 6:54, "[Jesus said:] Those who eat my flesh and drink my blood have eternal life, and I will raise them up on the last day."

FOR FURTHER READING

WORKS IN ENGLISH

Chadwick, Harold J. *The Best of Fenelon*. Gainesville, FL: Bridge-Logos Publishers, 2002. This 303-page volume in the Pure Gold Classic series contains three of Fénelon's most famous works, *Maxims of the Saints*, *Spiritual Letters*, and *Christian Counsel*.

Collier, Winn. *Let God: The Transforming Wisdom of François Fénelon*. Brewster, MA: Paraclete Press, 2007. In this 140-page, easily accessible volume by a young pastor, forty-two of Fénelon's letters are presented in the form of conversations with this wise mentor.

Fénelon, François. *Fénelon: Meditations on the Heart of God*, translated by Robert J. Edmonson. Brewster, MA: Paraclete Press, 1997. In a departure from presenting only letters, this 192-page volume gives eighty-five of Fénelon's meditations on themes from Scripture, with a comprehensive introduction to Fénelon's life and his influence.

———. *Fenelon: Selected Writings*, edited by Chad Helms. Mahwah, NY: Paulist Press, 2006. Available in hardcover and paperback, this 400-page volume in the Classics of Western Spirituality series gives Fénelon's major spiritual writings, including *Maxims of the Saints* and other seminal works of fiction and spiritual direction, such as his *Letter to Louis XIV*.

———. *Let Go*. Amberson, PA: Scroll Publishing Co., 2007. This inexpensive, 72-page volume presents forty of Fénelon's letters translated in a formal style.

———. *Let Go*. New Kensington, PA: Whitaker House, 1973. This inexpensive, little 96-page volume has become a classic. It gives forty of Fénelon's letters translated in an easy-to-read style.

———. *The Royal Way of the Cross*, edited by Hal M. Helms. Brewster, MA: Paraclete Press, 1982. This 158-page volume presents fifty-two of Fénelon's wise letters, with an introduction by a seasoned pastor.

———. *The Seeking Heart*. Beaumont, TX: The SeedSowers, Christian Books Publishing House, 1992. This 206-page Volume 4 of The Library of Spiritual Classics includes a short biography and a number of Fénelon's letters.

———. *Talking with God*, edited by Hal M. Helms. Brewster, MA: Paraclete Press, 1997. This 150-page volume presents fifty-one of Fénelon's letters of spiritual counsel, with an introduction by a seasoned pastor.

WORKS IN FRENCH

Devillairs, Laurence, *Fénelon, une philosophie de l'infini*. Paris, Le Cerf, 2007. In this 258-page book, Devillaires shows how Fénelon proves that the rationalism introduced by Descartes can become one of the best ways to reach out to God and his love.

Fénelon, François. *Correspondance de Fénelon*, edited by Jean Orcibal. Volumes I through V of Fénelon's letters with extensive notes. Paris: Klincksieck, 1972–1976. This publisher provides the first five volumes of the complete correspondence of one of the most prolific letter writers of the late seventeenth and early eighteenth centuries, along with extensive notes.

———. *Correspondance de Fénelon*, edited by Jean Orcibal, Jacques Le Brun, Bruno Neveu, and Irénée Noye. Volumes VI through XVIII of Fénelon's letters with extensive notes. Geneva, Switzerland: Librairie Droz, S.A., 1987–2007. This publisher provides the remaining thirteen volumes of the complete correspondence of this prolific letter writer, along with extensive notes.

———. *Fénelon: Œuvres*, Volume I, 1696 pages; Volume II, 1856 pages. Edited by Jacques Le Brun. Number 307 (Volume I) and Number 437 (Volume II) of the authoritative collection in French *Bibliothèque de la Pléiade*. Paris: Éditions Gallimard, 1983 (Volume I), 1997 (Volume II). These two volumes give a comprehensive overview of Fénelon's works, with excellent notes by Jacques Le Brun.

Fénelon, Jacques, and Roger Parisot. *Fénelon*. A volume of the *Expérience de Dieu* (Experience of God) collection. Montréal, Canada: Fides, 2003. This 139-page work gives an overview of Fénelon's works, with particular emphasis on his spiritual journey.

Melchior-Bonnet, Sabine. *Fénelon*. Paris: Éditions Perrin, 2008. This 468-page volume by a French historian paints an in-depth picture of Fénelon. In a review in *Madame Figaro* (21 March 2008), Évelyne Lever calls this work "an admirable portrait of this prophet of the Enlightenment, the inventor of a modern Catholicism. . . ." [Editor's translation].

ABOUT PARACLETE PRESS

WHO WE ARE

Paraclete Press is a publisher of books, recordings, and DVDs on Christian spirituality. Our publishing represents a full expression of Christian belief and practice—from Catholic to Evangelical, from Protestant to Orthodox.

We are the publishing arm of the Community of Jesus, an ecumenical monastic community in the Benedictine tradition. As such, we are uniquely positioned in the marketplace without connection to a large corporation and with informal relationships to many branches and denominations of faith.

WHAT WE ARE DOING

Books

Paraclete publishes books that show the richness and depth of what it means to be Christian. Although Benedictine spirituality is at the heart of all that we do, we publish books that reflect the Christian experience across many cultures, time periods, and houses of worship. We publish books that nourish the vibrant life of the church and its people—books about spiritual practice, formation, history, ideas, and customs.

We have several different series, including the best-selling Paraclete Essentials and Paraclete Giants series of classic texts in contemporary English; A Voice from the Monastery—men and women monastics writing about living a spiritual life today; award-winning poetry; best-selling gift books for children on the occasions of baptism and first communion; and the Active Prayer Series that brings creativity and liveliness to any life of prayer.

Recordings

From Gregorian chant to contemporary American choral works, our music recordings celebrate sacred choral music through the centuries. Paraclete distributes the recordings of the internationally acclaimed choir Gloriæ Dei Cantores, praised for their "rapt and fathomless spiritual intensity" by *American Record Guide*, and the Gloriæ Dei Cantores Schola, which specializes in the study and performance of Gregorian chant. Paraclete is also the exclusive North American distributor of the recordings of the Monastic Choir of St. Peter's Abbey in Solesmes, France, long considered to be a leading authority on Gregorian chant.

Videos

Our videos offer spiritual help, healing, and biblical guidance for life issues: grief and loss, marriage, forgiveness, anger management, facing death, and spiritual formation.

Learn more about us at our website: www.paracletepress.com, or call us toll-free at 1-800-451-5006.

SCAN
TO
READ
MORE

If you enjoy the PARACLETE GIANTS,
you will also enjoy these PARACLETE ESSENTIALS

The Joy of Full Surrender
by Jean-Pierre de Caussade
Introduction by Michael Casey, OCSO

ISBN: 978-1-55725-609-6
$15.99, 206 pages

"I count myself blessed that, at an important juncture in my life, a wise elder introduced me to the writings of Caussade. From them I gained not only the guidance I needed to traverse a difficult terrain, but also a permanent element in my outlook on life: an appreciation of the operation of God's providence and my need to be receptive of that providence despite the lack of full understanding and the pressure of contrary desires."

—Michael Casey, OCSO, from the Introduction

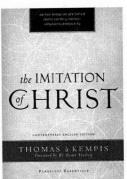

The Imitation of Christ
by Thomas à Kempis
Introduction by Br. Benet Tvedten

ISBN: 978-1-55725-608-9
$15.99, 260 pages

"When I graduated from high school, my pastor gave me a book. Intending to major in English when I went off to college, I would have preferred receiving a novel by Steinbeck or Hemingway. But he no doubt thought I was a pious boy or should become one. The book I received as a gift was *The Imitation of Christ*. He inscribed the title page: 'You will have a happy life by adhering to the wisdom in this book.'"

—Br. Benet Tvedten, from the Introduction

Visit us online to see our other Classic series:
The Paraclete Giants and the *Living Library Series.*

Available from most booksellers or through Paraclete Press:
www.paracletepress.com; 1-800-451-5006. Try your local bookstore first.